W9-CSU-638

STARTING OUT in STAINED GLASS

STARTING OUT in STAINED GLASS

The Mt. Tom Stained Glass Artisans

PRENTICE HALL PRESS
New York London Toronto Sydney Tokyo

Copyright © 1983 by Mt. Tom Stained Glass Artisans
All rights reserved, including the right of reproduction
in whole or in part in any form.

Published in 1987 by Prentice Hall Press
A Division of Simon & Schuster, Inc.
Gulf + Western Building
One Gulf + Western Plaza
New York, NY 10023

Originally published by Arco Publishing, Inc.
Photographs by Gordon Himmelman and Michael Monahan.
Pattern designs and illustrations by Rudy Swol.

PRENTICE HALL PRESS is a trademark of Simon & Schuster,
Inc.

Library of Congress Cataloging-in-Publication Data

Main entry under title:
Starting out in stained glass.

Includes index.
1. Glass craft. I. Mt. Tom Stained Glass Artisans.
II. Title: Stained glass.
TT298.S72 1983 748.5′028 82-18438
ISBN 0-668-05984-2 (Reference text)
ISBN 0-668-05577-4 (Paper edition)

Manufactured in the United States of America

10 9 8 7 6 5

Contents

Acknowledgments

There are some special people we'd like to thank who have contributed a great deal to our book and to our lives with their friendship:

Rudy Swol, our gifted artist, designer, and for three of us, our mentor. It is not mere flattery or hyperbole when we say that we could not have written this book without Rudy's talent, encouragement, and professional assistance.

Lisa Wenzel, Anita's daughter and our efficient secretary and model. Lisa relieved us of many of the tedious but most important details connected with our work. Her cheerful willingness to do anything we asked made our time that much more productive.

Duane Cokely, our colleague at Mt. Tom Studio, for his encouragement, advice, loyalty, and solo coverage of many of our classes which freed up much needed time for our project work and writing.

Lorraine Himmelman and June Monahan, Bo's and Mike's wives, respectively, whose loving patience and personal sacrifices allowed us to devote needed time and energy to our books. We owe them both much more than we can repay.

And, our hundreds of stained glass students, who were the inspiration, in one sense, for our writing this book. We hope that it reflects the many things that you taught us over the years.

Introduction

It may sound arrogant, but we believe that *Starting Out in Stained Glass* and its companion book, *Challenging Projects in Stained Glass*, are the best and most up-to-date books on stained glass techniques that are available today. A comparison with other books on the subject will prove that our statement is not an empty boast.

In the pages that follow we write about and illustrate our stained glass system, which has been taught to more than two thousand students. We reveal our "secret" methods—which aren't really that secret at all—and try to take the mystery out of this thousand-year-old craft.

In doing this we debunk some myths about stained glass and criticize, disagree with, and label as wrong many of the techniques that other manuals describe but that really don't work very well.

We present our integrated system for approaching each individual process in the creation of a stained glass project, we describe and evaluate materials and tools, and we present developmental exercises and challenging projects for each stage of your development. And most important, we not only tell you *what* to do but *why* you're doing it.

There's no doubt in our minds that if you want to learn how to work with stained glass, and if you follow our suggestions, you will become a good stained glass craftsperson. And if you're already an accomplished artisan, you'll become a better one. With this art, there's always room for improvement.

The results we describe won't happen magically or overnight; you'll need time, patience, perseverance, and practice. But we're convinced that we can make your involvement with stained glass more interesting, much easier, and more fun.

Inez M. Adamowicz, Gordon D. Himmelman,
Michael Monahan, and Anita M. Wenzel

THE MT. TOM STAINED GLASS ARTISANS

STARTING OUT in STAINED GLASS

1

Patterned Glass Cutting

We will start by saying that glass cutting is the most important step in the construction of a stained glass project. Some people may argue that design is the most vital consideration in stained glass work, but we believe that glass cutting is the foundation upon which everything else is built.

As you use this book, you'll see why each process and technique necessarily takes a back seat to glass cutting. If the design demands physically impossible cuts, then the design must be modified to accommodate the cuts. If, after initial cutting, there are gaps between pieces which should butt together, then the lead came will not accommodate the glass, or the copper-foiled seams will be of a too variable and inconsistent width. If in this case the gaps are too wide, then your soldering technique will naturally suffer. If there are too many gaps caused by inaccurate or sloppy cutting, then support and stability problems will surface. In short, most problems that crop up with stained glass can be traced back to poor glass cutting techniques.

And conversely, a well-developed and skillful glass cutting technique facilitates the work required and enhances the entire project. It is the meticulous attention you pay to acquiring a good glass cutting technique that will differentiate the quality work from the poor work.

Since, in our opinion, few manuals devote much space or offer any new or progressive ideas on patterned glass cutting, we intend to cover this subject thoroughly and in detail. It might help if you visualize our stained glass system as a pyramid with glass cutting as the fulcrum block that balances and supports the entire structure (*See* Fig. 1). We'll continue building our pyramid analogy as we systematically progress from process to process, constantly referring to the necessary interdependency of each technique upon the success of the project, whether it is a 5-piece sun-catcher or 1,000-piece lampshade.

One mild admonition: Patterned glass cutting technique requires a certain level of personal commitment and determination which no instruction can provide. The cardinal virtues of patience and fortitude are two special prerequisites to a good glass cutting technique, especially for the novice. Don't be discouraged if things aren't going as smoothly or as quickly as you'd like. Practice cutting until you can do our exercises correctly. If you approach patterned glass cutting with this proper mental set, you'll be surprised how things will fall into place. Like the proverbial tortoise, slow and steady will win this particular race.

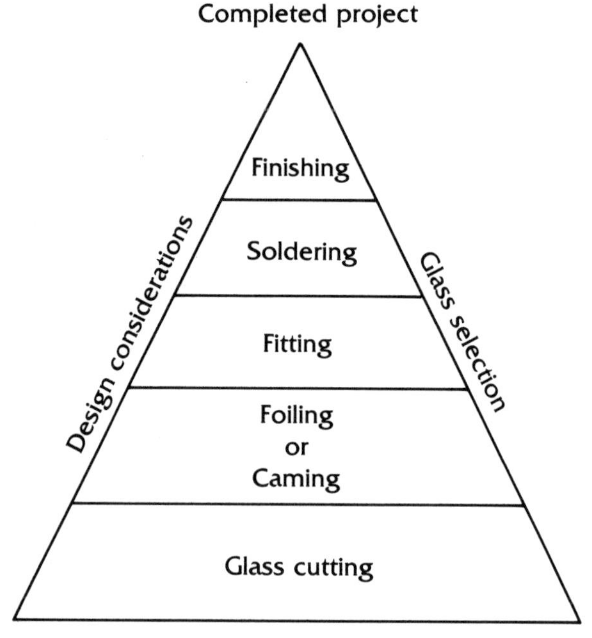

MT. TOM'S PYRAMIDAL STAINED GLASS SYSTEM

Fig. 1

Tools and Materials

We don't necessarily believe that a poor workman blames his tools; on the contrary, we feel that good tools make the craftperson. Besides just listing tools and materials that you'll need (*see* Illustration 1-1), we feel that a discussion of what they do and *why* they're needed will go a long way toward accelerating your glass cutting development.

Small Jar. Get a small baby food jar which will be a repository for all your cutters. Place a small piece of cotton gauze on the bottom and pour into the jar approximately one inch of kerosene which you can buy in small amounts at your local hardware store. The kerosene lubricates the wheel of the cutter and allows you more time to pull your glass apart after you've scored it by preventing the score from annealing. The cotton will clean the cutting wheel and catch minute chips of glass that might have accumulated on the wheel after cutting. If they're not removed, these chips of glass will eventually dull the wheel and make scoring more difficult.

Also, place in the jar a small flux brush which you will use for spreading kerosene over a score line when cutting.

Glass Cutters. You'll need two basic cutters: (1) a Fletcher #07 ball-tipped cutter identified by a blue band around its neck; and (2) a small German-made (Diamantor) wooden-handled cutter. The primary difference and reason for having at least these two

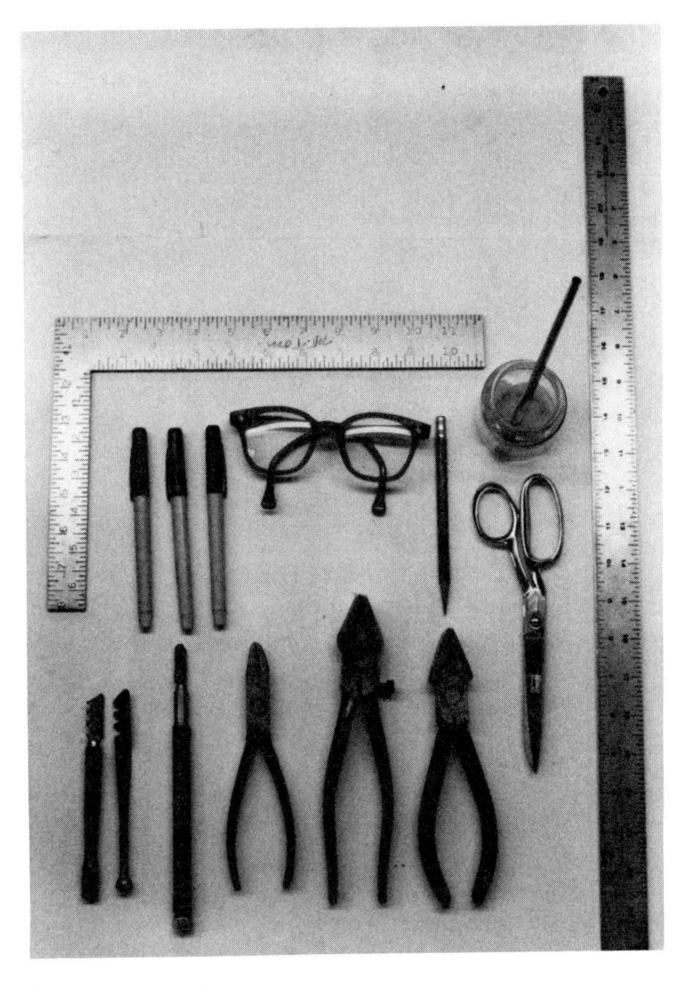

Illustration 1-1

types is the size of the wheels: The Fletcher wheel is large, used for cutting "hard" glass (e.g., opalescent) and making straight cuts; the Diamantor wheel is small, used to cut "soft" (e.g., cathedral, antique) glass and cut out small, more complexly curved patterns.

A third type of cutter, the oil or kerosene-fed with a carbide wheel, is now readily available. We believe this cutter is superior to the other two. However, it costs ten times more than the conventional cutters. But, since we feel this cutter will pay for itself in glass saved, and we use this cutter for practically everything we cut, we recommend that after you master the techniques involved with the other cutters, you turn your attention to mastering this one. The techniques (except where we will indicate) are practically exactly the same as the techniques we'll outline for the standard cutters.

Pliers. Different types of pliers are used for pulling apart pieces of glass after scoring and for grozing (a method of filing excess glass) the edges of glass when excess glass remains after the cut. You'll need three types: (1) the Knipex Art Glass Grozing pliers, which have a curved upper lip and a level, jagged lower section. These pliers are used for filing away tiny pieces of glass from a rough break or edge; (2) running pliers or cut/run pliers.

TOOLS AND MATERIALS

Tool/Material	Brand/Description	Source
Jar	Small baby food	Grocery store
Kerosene	General, 6 oz.	Hardware store
Flux brush	4'' long	Hardware store/art store
Window glass	8'' x 10'', 5 single-pane sheets	Hardware/glass supply
Straightedges	Metal	Art stores
T-Squares	Metal	Art stores
Triangles	Metal	Art stores
Templates	Metal	Art stores
Felt, foam rubber	Backing for the straightedges	Millinery/hardware store
Felt-tip marker	Sharpie® Extra Fine	Stationery
Cutters		
a. Fletcher® #07	Ball-tipped, large wheel	Hardware/stained glass supplier
b. German	Diamantor®, wooden-handled, small wheel	Stained glass supplier
c. Oil-fed	Metal or plastic	Stained glass supplier
Pliers		
a. Breaking	Art glass	Stained glass supplier
b. Cut/run	Metal	Stained glass supplier
c. Grozing	Knipex® Art Glass	Stained glass supplier
Carborundum stone or wet stone		Hardware/stained glass supplier

We prefer the steel pliers to the plastic ones. After scoring, these pliers will start the fracture "running" along the score line no matter what the pattern. We have found these pliers to be an invaluable aid in cutting and separating the pieces of glass, especially with curvilinear patterns; and (3) breaking pliers, which are used to pull apart or break off individual pieces of glass.

Markers. A most necessary tool, usually left unmentioned in other treatments of stained glass materials and techniques, is the glass marker used to trace your pattern on the glass. We suggest the Sharpie® Extra Fine Point felt-tip marker because the ink will not be easily washed off by either kerosene or water. And the fine line outlines your pattern more accurately than the broader mark of other felt-tip pens.

Carborundum Stones and Glass Files. These stones come in handy for filing down and smoothing rough edges of glass. A smooth edge on your pieces of glass facilitates the next step after cutting which is foiling and caming.

Straightedges. The best type of straightedge, T-square, or ruler is a steel or aluminum one. Wooden straightedges will eventually warp amd make a straight cut impossible. To the back of any straightedge you use, attach with tape or glue some type of rubber, cloth, cork, or thin, spongy weatherstripping that will prevent it from slipping or sliding when you're cutting. Make sure, though, that the backing is not so thick as to raise the straightedge above the glass and make it rock back and forth.

These are the basic tools you'll need for cutting glass. (You'll probably acquire others as you become more experienced.) You won't be able to carry out our suggestions or develop a good glass cutting technique unless you have them. It's been our experience that people who don't want to spend the initial money for these tools (and they really don't cost that much) become more easily frustrated with this extremely important activity in stained glass work. After all, if you can't cut the glass, you can't work with stained glass; and these tools will make your introduction much more pleasant and provide incentive for continuing.

Methods

What's important to remember when developing good technique is the necessity of following the same general rules and repeating the same procedures in the same manner until they become almost an instinctive habit. For instance, always make sure that the glass you're cutting is at room temperature (cold glass is brittle). Always cut on the smoother side of the glass. And in regard to methods, always try to cut glass at the same place or on the same cutting surface. A clean, flat workbench or table (if the table is not flat, place a piece of plywood on top of it), exposed to ample light that casts no shadows on the glass, is the ideal glass cutting environment. You should provide a cushion for the glass that will prevent unwanted breakage by laying out an even piece of felt, canvas, burlap, or newspaper of sufficient size to accommodate the glass. If you use newspaper (and we do because of its disposability), make sure the newspaper's crease is as flat as possible and there is an equal amount of newspaper on top and bottom.

By your side you should lay a clean rag to wipe off tiny chips of glass that will fall onto the newspaper after each score or break. These tiny chips, if allowed to remain on the paper underneath the glass you are cutting, may cause the glass to fracture the wrong way. So, you should have a clean, flat, even cutting surface that is at all times free of glass chips.

You should now have your basic tools at the ready and spread out on your table. For beginning or practice exercises, you should use 8″ x 10″ sheets of normal, plain window glass. You should also do all your glass cutting standing up because of greater leverage and a better line of vision.

Draw a freehand, slightly curved line down the center of a 5″ x 3″ sheet of glass. Pick up the German wooden cutter, "teeth" of the cutter facing you, thumb on the top, fingers wrapped completely around the stem, pinkie finger around the groove at the back. (*See* Illustrations 1-2A through 1-2C.) Keep your wrist flexible and avoid a white-knuckled death grip on the cutter. Wiggle the cutter in the air; you should feel comfortable with the grip; if you don't, move the cutter around and regrip it until you can move your wrist with little restriction.

(Before you attempt to cut the glass, read the next six paragraphs to get an overall concept of the entire technique.)

Illustration 1-2A

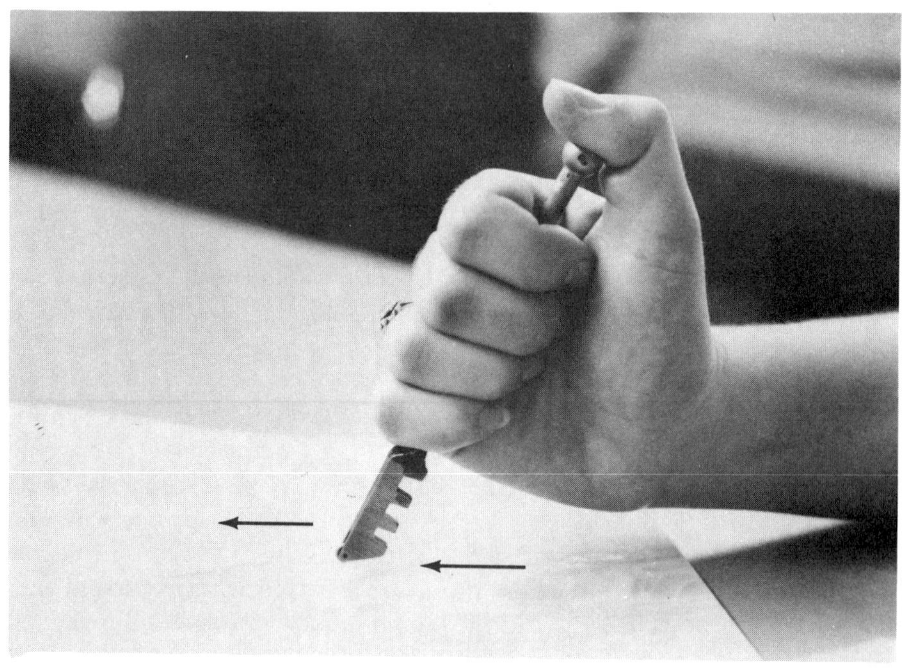

Illustration 1-2B

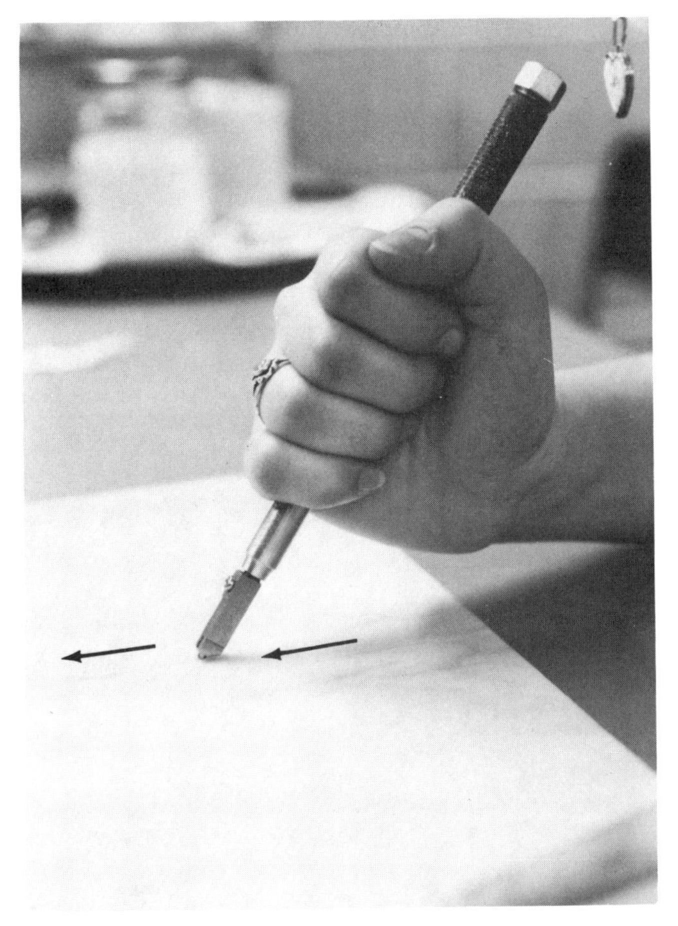

Illustration 1-2C

In pattern glass cutting (*except* for straight cuts) you should always cut away from you; if you're left-handed, you'll cut toward the right; right-handed, toward the left. Place the fingers of your free hand on the glass at the opposite edge and press down. (*See* Illustrations 1-3A and 1-3B.) Your index or middle finger will prevent your cutter from running off the edge thereby crushing the edge of the glass and thumping the wheel into your table and dulling the wheel, which will make the cutting more difficult as you go along. With the sole of the cutter parallel to the surface of the glass (*see* Illustration 1-4), and with a steady and unwavering wrist (avoid rocking or tilting the cutter from side to side as you go along), which will prevent a jagged, uneven score, push the cutter with the thumb of your free hand slowly yet firmly along the surface, applying gentle, even pressure as you go along the line, stopping just short of the edge. (*See* Illustration 1-5.) Watch your wheel at all times by getting down close to it and moving your body, not just your wrist, if necessary.

One note of caution: *Do not apply such severe pressure that you overscore*. Some people, men especially, bear down so hard that they exert too much pressure and shatter the glass before they finish the score. And if one does finish the score, it will be nearly impossible to pull the glass apart.

What you're actually doing when "cutting" glass is grinding out a groove in the glass, thus creating a weakness in it: The term cutting is actually a misnomer. If you make

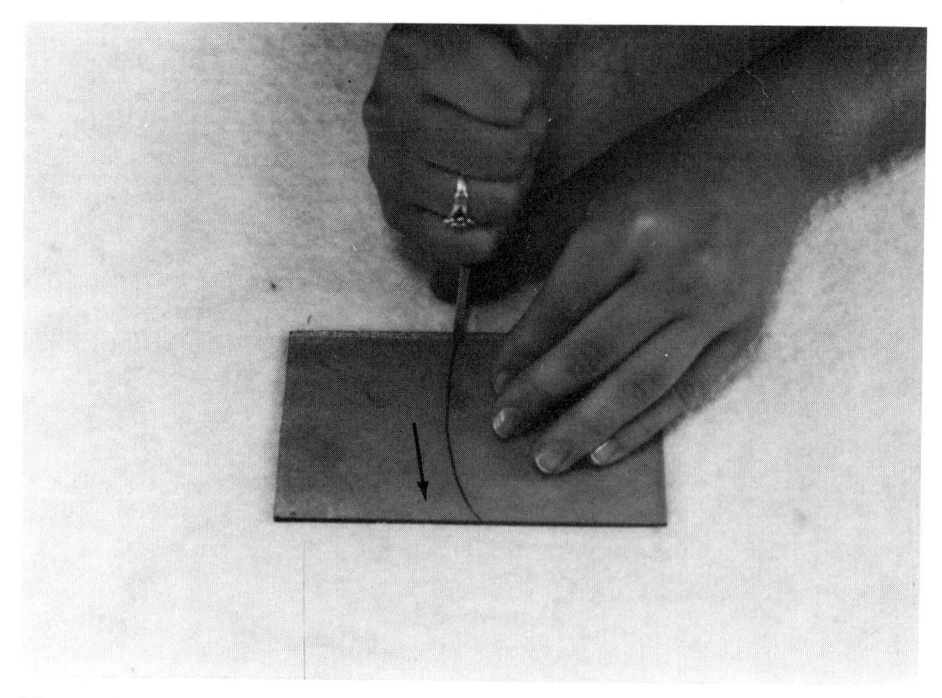

Illustration 1-3A

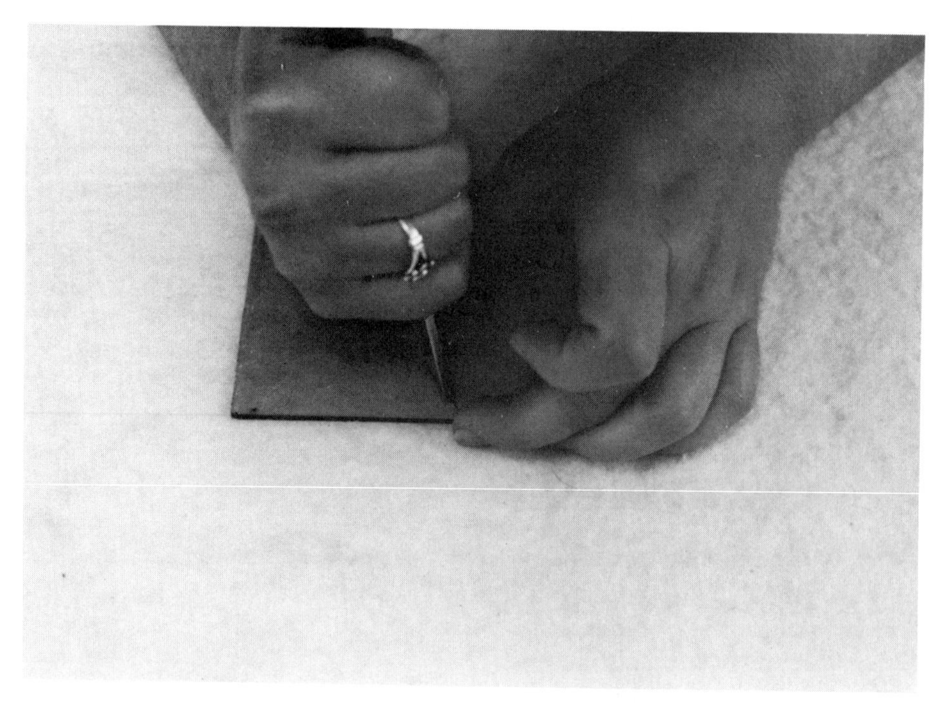

Illustration 1-3B

Illustration 1-4

a good score, you should hear a *slightly soft, crackling sound,* and tiny fragments of glass will jump from the score. This all-important sound is the best indication that you have made a good score, and this sound will become more easily recognizable as an accurate cutting guide as you become more experienced.

When beginning your score, it is very important that you keep your arms close to your body, elbows in, laying your shoulder close to your thumb, moving your entire body and shoulder, *not just your wrist*. (*See* Illustration 1-6.) You right-handers should always place your score line to the left of your body and cut in that general direction, with your elbows proceeding outward from your body as you cut. (Left-handers should reverse our directions.) By cutting to the left you will not restrict the mobility of your shoulder movement. You'll find that if you do try to run your score to the right, your body will inhibit your elbow movement.

This technique will make it easier to exert equal pressure to the score with a minimum of effort. We can't emphasize enough the *importance of providing equal pressure* in one continuous motion throughout the score. This will allow a clean, crisp, even break that is of prime concern when trying to remain faithful to the pattern, and in the later stages of fitting and soldering.

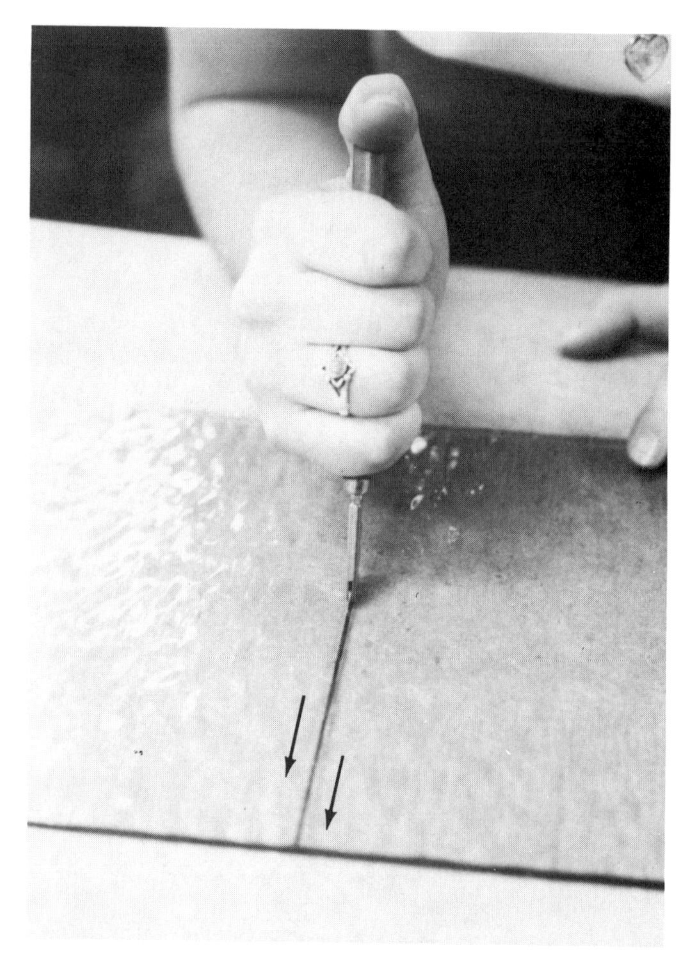

Illustration 1-5

This basic technique will also prevent you and your cutting arm from growing weary, which will become very evident when every other piece you cut breaks incorrectly. If your finger, hand, or wrist begins to hurt, you're doing something wrong. You must develop your technique so it's one fluid motion, generating from the shoulder, through the arm, beyond the hand and glass. Granted, it's easier said than done, and there's no shortcut to mastering this technique except one: practice, practice, and practice.

So, now you've made a score and you probably want to know how you're going to break the glass. Two methods we *don't* recommend (except in rare and very specific cases which we'll mention later) are (1) the tapping method, where you tap with your ball end along the score line; and (2) the "seesaw" break, or fulcrum method, where you place an object under the score and snap off the piece by pushing down. Both of these methods can cause uneven breaks at best and usually cause chips, cracks, or weaknesses in the glass, if it doesn't break incorrectly first.

We believe the best method is the fist-and-knuckle approach where you *pull apart* the two pieces of glass: make two fists, thumbs on top of your index fingers, knuckles of each hand touching each other, with the score between each thumb-index finger pair.

Illustration 1-6

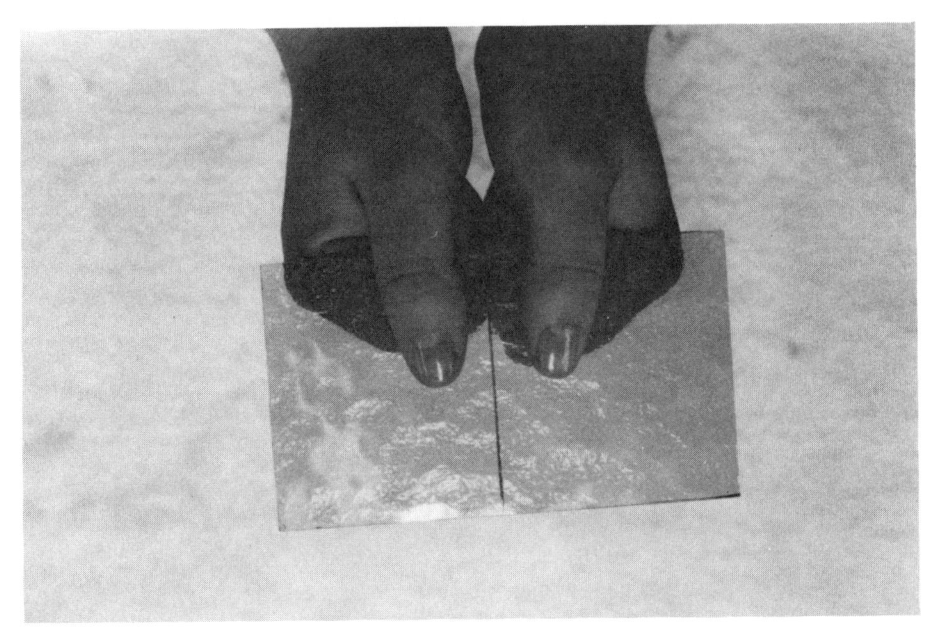

Illustration 1-7

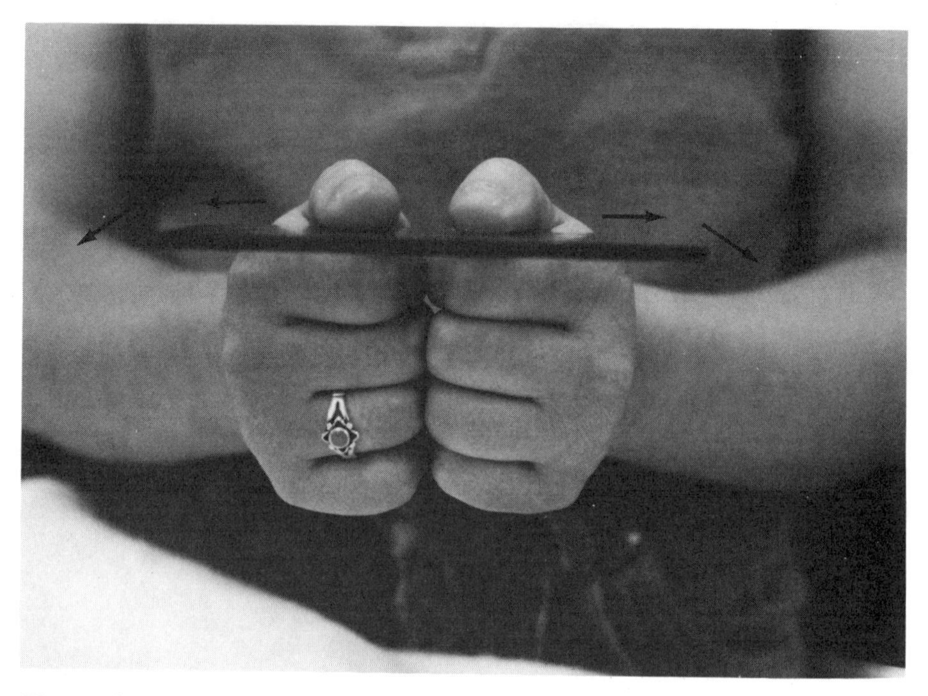

Illustration 1-8

(*See* Illustrations 1-7 and 1-8.) Now, *pull, not break*, the two pieces apart by rolling your knuckles away from each other in a downward manner. (*See* Illustration 1-9.) The reason we are emphasizing that you pull the glass apart is because people have a tendency to try to literally "break" the glass. When doing this, you are actually bending the glass and this will indeed cause the glass to "break" or fracture, but incorrectly so.

Practice pulling apart the glass by halving several pieces of glass. Don't move on to the rest of this chapter (or book, for that matter) until you've built up some skill and confidence so that the glass is pulling apart easily and you're not afraid of its shattering while you're pulling. *Listen for that soft, crackling sound when you score*: that's the indication that your glass will break easily. It is essential at this stage that you can cut across a piece of glass easily and know what a good (and bad) score sounds and looks like. This only comes with repeated cutting. Some people learn to do this quickly, even after only fifteen minutes; for some of you, it might take longer. In any case, don't proceed until you can do these simple score and break exercises.

While you're practicing the cutting, you should also develop an organized pattern for the entire process. For example, always:

1. Lay out your tools in the same relative positions.
2. Take your cutter out of the jar of kerosene.
3. Make your cut.
4. Place your cutter back in the jar.
5. Break your glass.
6. Wipe your cutting surface (newspaper) with your cloth.
7. Place your glass back on the cutting surface.

And also get into the habit of occasionally removing the top layer of your newspaper to eliminate the possibility of hidden chips of glass underneath it. These chips

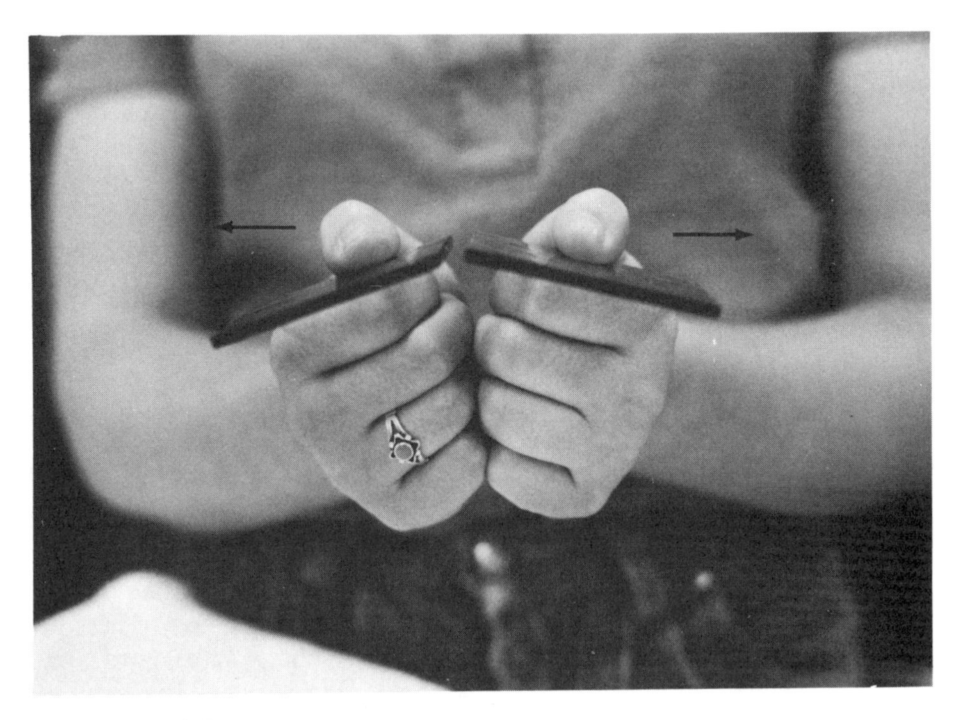

Illustration 1-9

of glass will create an uneven cutting surface and contribute to unwanted shattering.

This systematic by-the-numbers approach will help you cut down your glass breakage and, when repeated to the point where everything you do becomes almost instinctive, will prevent you from making mental errors that will frustrate this extremely important activity.

In many cases, you will need to use tools other than your cutter to either pull the glass apart or shape the glass to the pattern. Grozing pliers are dual-purpose pliers which enable you to file or pull away small pieces of excess glass from an imperfect score or break. When grozing, you move the jaws of the pliers slightly while you work the glass up and down in order to chip away small sections to make the glass conform to the pattern line. Or, when just a small piece needs to be broken off, you can pull it apart in the same manner as the "fist-and-knuckle" method, using the grozing pliers as a stronger hand. (*See* Illustrations 1-10A through 1-10C.)

Also, in many cases, when it is difficult to obtain leverage for hand-breaking large pieces of glass, or you need extremely thin strips of glass, you can use grozing and breaking pliers in conjunction with one another. Make a relatively straight score that will give you a strip about 1'' wide when pulled free. Pick up the grozing pliers with your dominant hand and place at the first ½'' of your score, the jaws parallel to the score, slightly in front of it. (*See* Illustration 1-11.) *Never put them on the score*. Hold the glass firmly with the breaking pliers in your other hand, elbows tucked in at your sides, and *pull* the pieces apart. (*See* Illustrations 1-12 and 1-13.) The equal pressure or even pull that results from placing your elbows close to your body will ensure a nice even break. Remember, even, consistent pressure and smooth movement are key factors in glass

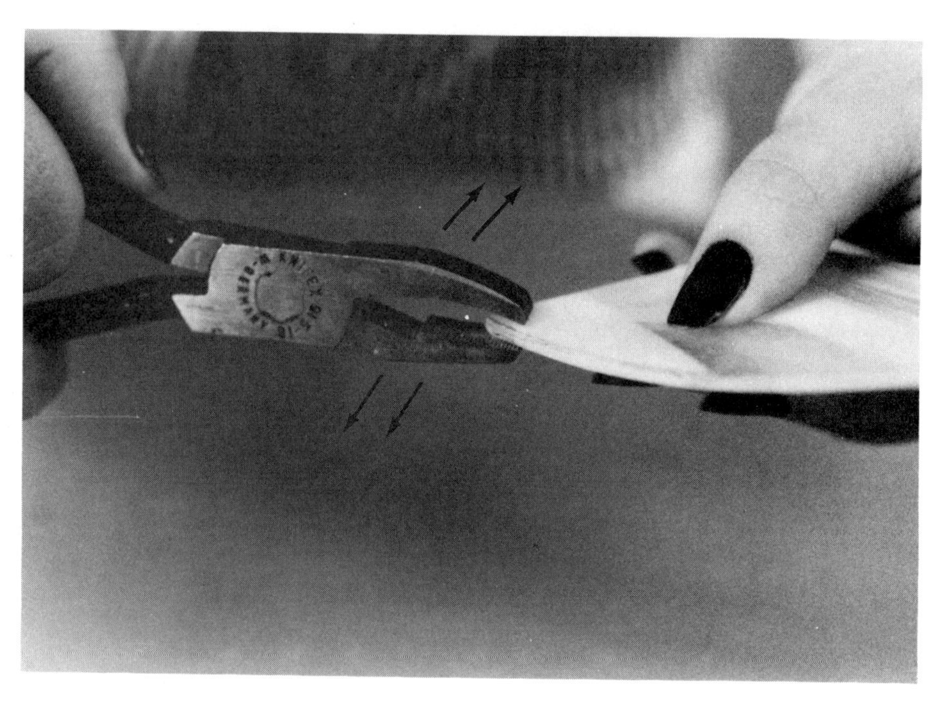

Illustration 1-10A

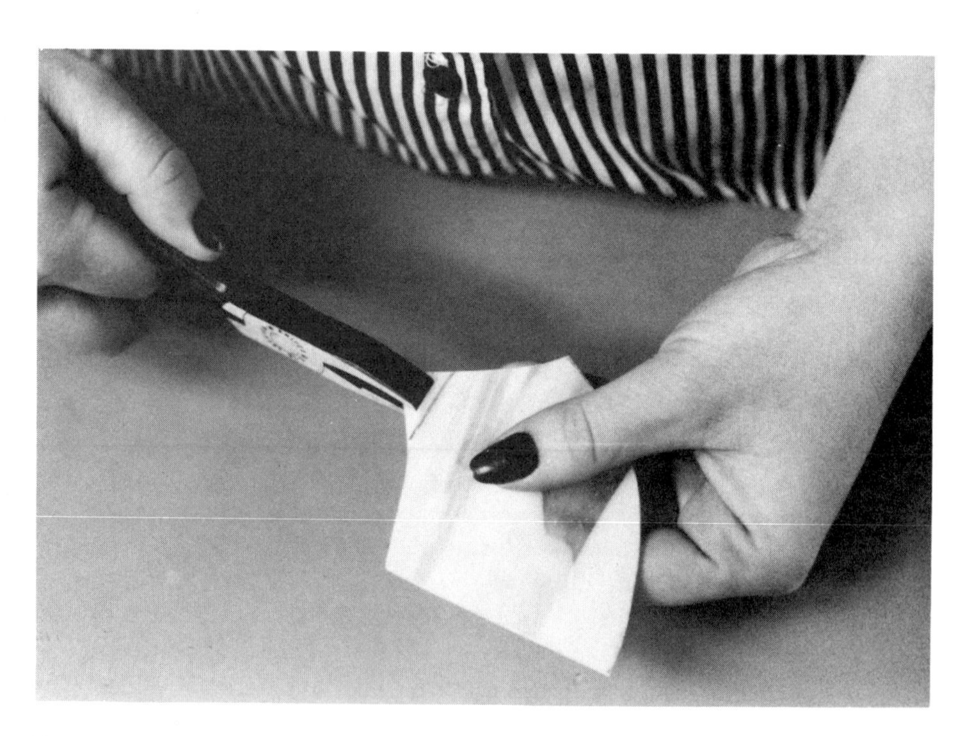

Illustration 1-10B

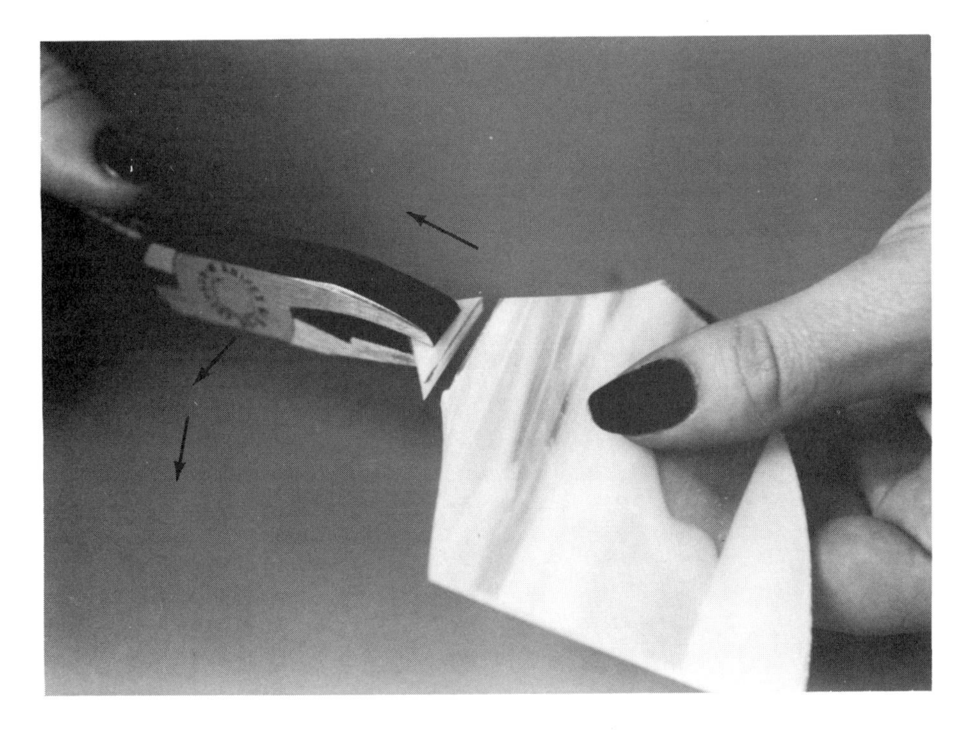

Illustration 1-10C

Illustration 1-11

Illustration 1-12

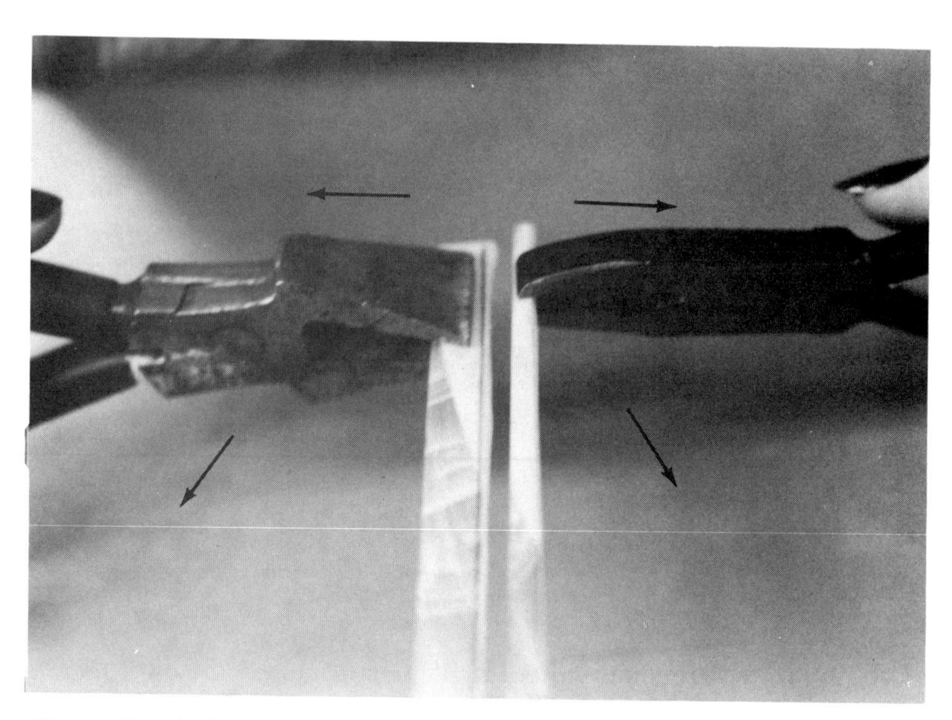

Illustration 1-13

cutting. Try cutting thin strips of glass and breaking other types of cuts with these tools until you feel secure.

Cut/run pliers is an extremely useful tool when you want to assure yourself that you will apply even and equal pressure when trying to break a piece of glass with either a long or complex score line. Cut/run pliers will save you much time and untold frustration (not to mention glass) when dealing with special cuts.

Before you can use the pliers, you need to "set" the pliers for the thickness of the glass. This is done *before* you make the score and in the following manner: (*See* Illustrations 1-14A and 1-14B.)

1. Firmly grip the glass with the jaws of the pliers.
2. Turn the set screw (pointed arrow) clockwise until the jaws of the pliers free themselves from the glass.
3. Reverse the set screw, turning counterclockwise half a turn which will return the jaws to the glass. This will enable the glass to bend slightly.
4. Put your pliers down near your dominant hand.

Now you're ready to make your score. Make a straight score approximately 10″ long and do the following: (*See* Illustrations 1-15 and 1-16.)

1. Set the glass flat on the table. (This prevents the glass from tilting slightly and eliminates the chance of dropping it after it breaks.)
2. Pick up the pliers, set screw on top, two fingers on the outside handle, two fingers on the inside handle, and thumb opposite to them, and lay the notch of the pliers on the score mark approximately ½″ from the edge.
3. *Gently squeeze the pliers' handles, applying steady and equal pressure without attempting to bend the glass*, until you hear a slight "click." The "click" is an indication that your fracture has begun (you can actually see it). The two pieces of glass should fall apart.
4. If the glass doesn't fall apart immediately, turn the glass around and repeat the grasping and squeezing process (steps 2 and 3) to this opposite end.
5. If at this point the glass still does not come apart, use your breaking and grozing pliers to pull the pieces apart (p. 13). (We'll discuss further uses and methods for these pliers on specific problem cuts later on in the book.)

You'll need to practice in order to use this tool effectively, but once mastered, you'll find the cut/run pliers to be of inestimable value in countless glass breaking situations.

In Chapter 5 we'll discuss techniques for difficult cuts. However, you'll need to know how to execute one relatively difficult cut in order to cut some of the pieces of glass in our butterfly and cat projects. For some cuts with an outside curve, small "relief" cuts might be necessary to break down the curve. Practice this cut by drawing the same rough pattern on your glass and proceeding in the following manner:

1. Draw dotted relief lines on your glass. Do this by tracing with your marker a line along the curve line to the point where the curved line begins to turn inward. (*See* Illustration 1-17.)
2. At this point, proceed straight out to the edge of the glass.
3. Continue tracing along the curved edge until you come to another extreme inwardly curved angle and draw another relief line to the edge of the glass.
4. Repeat as needed until you reach the end of the curved line.

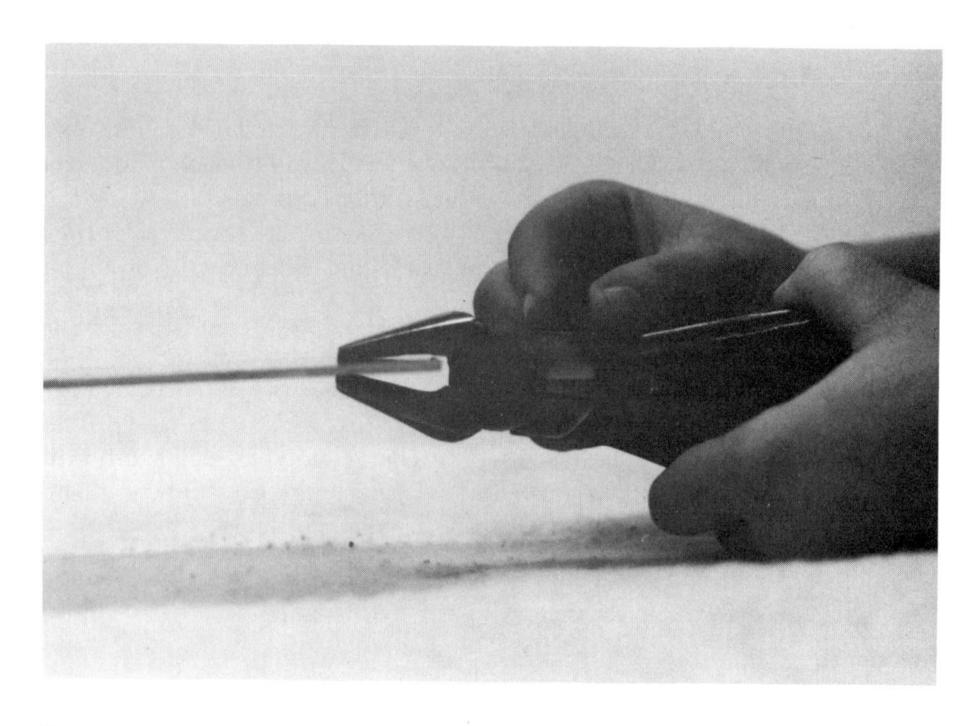

Illustration 1-14A

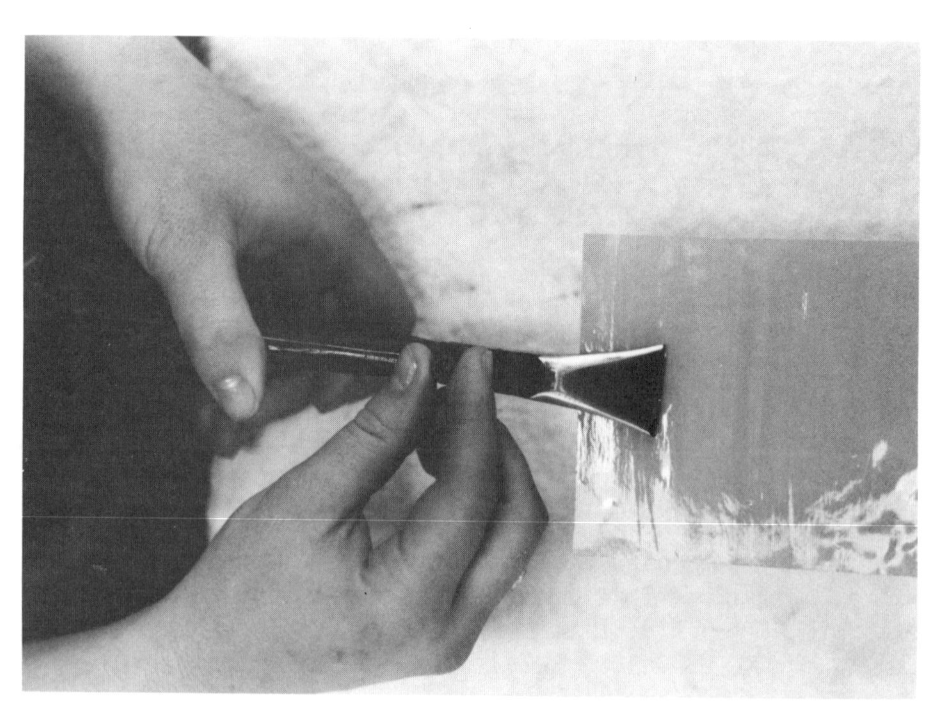

Illustration 1-14B

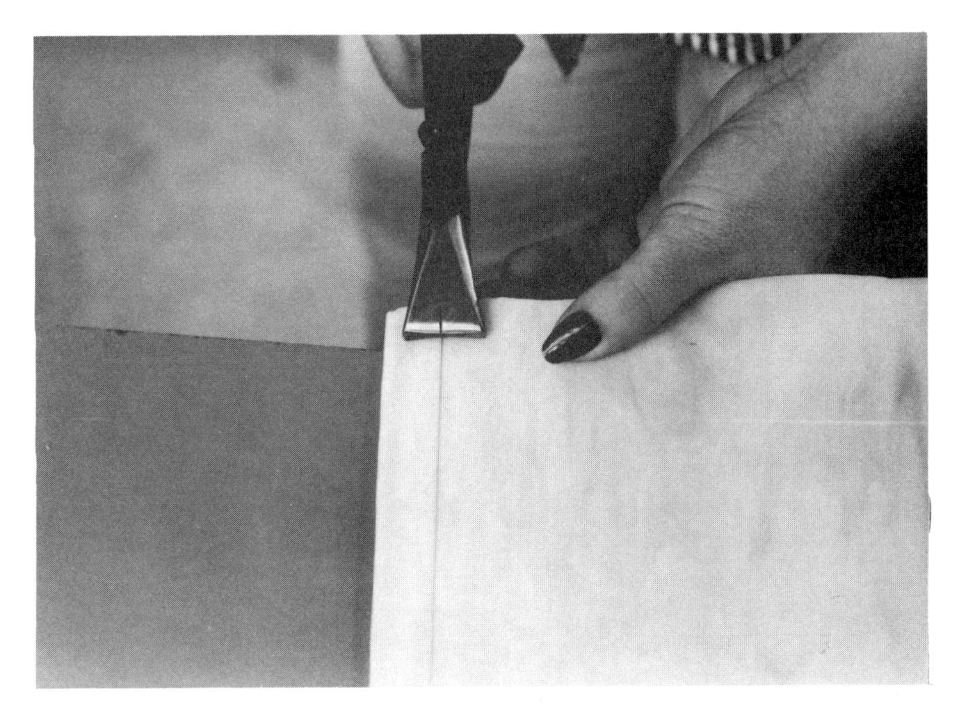

Illustration 1-15

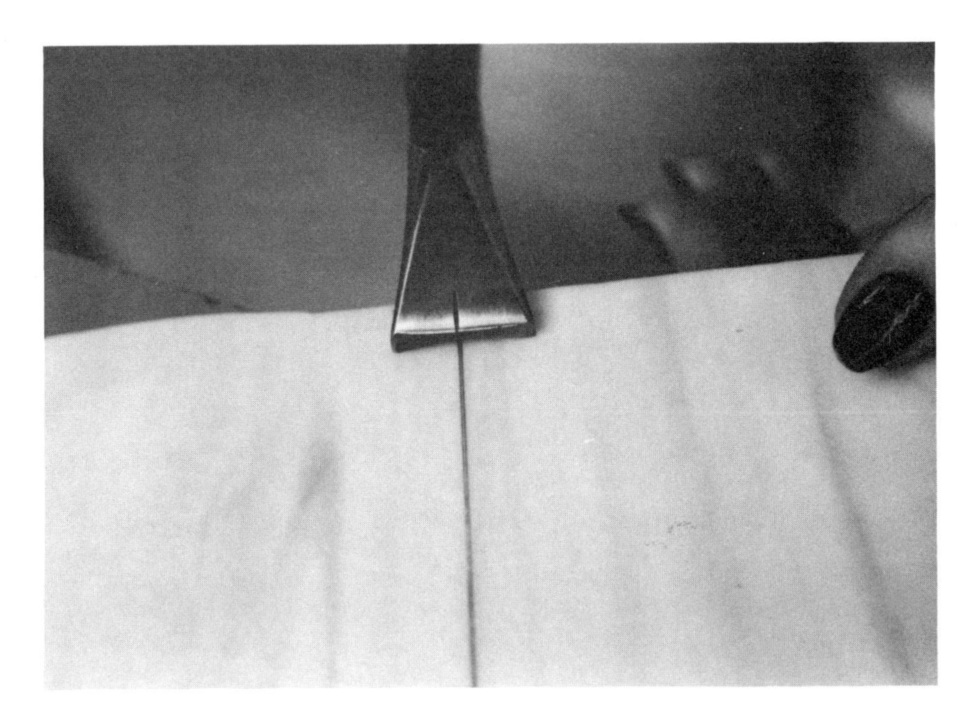

Illustration 1-16

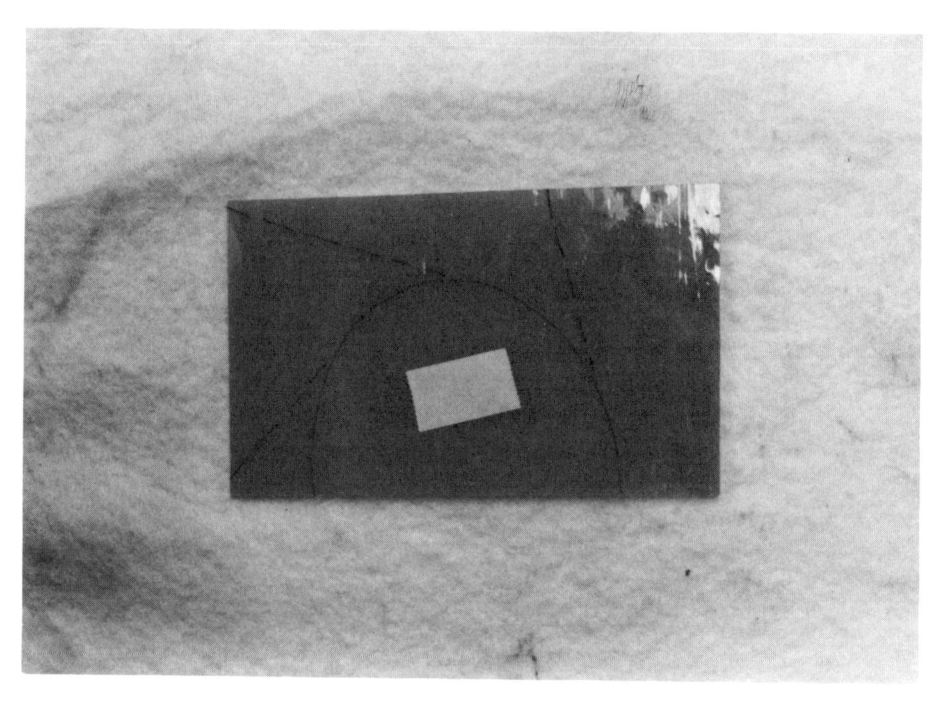

Illustration 1-17

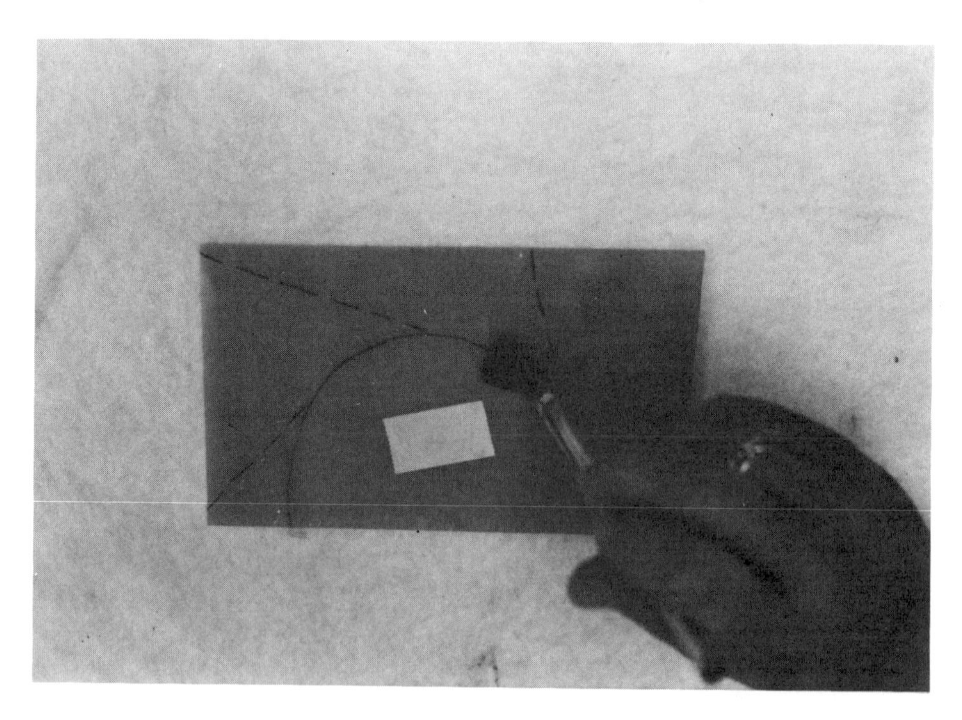

Illustration 1-18

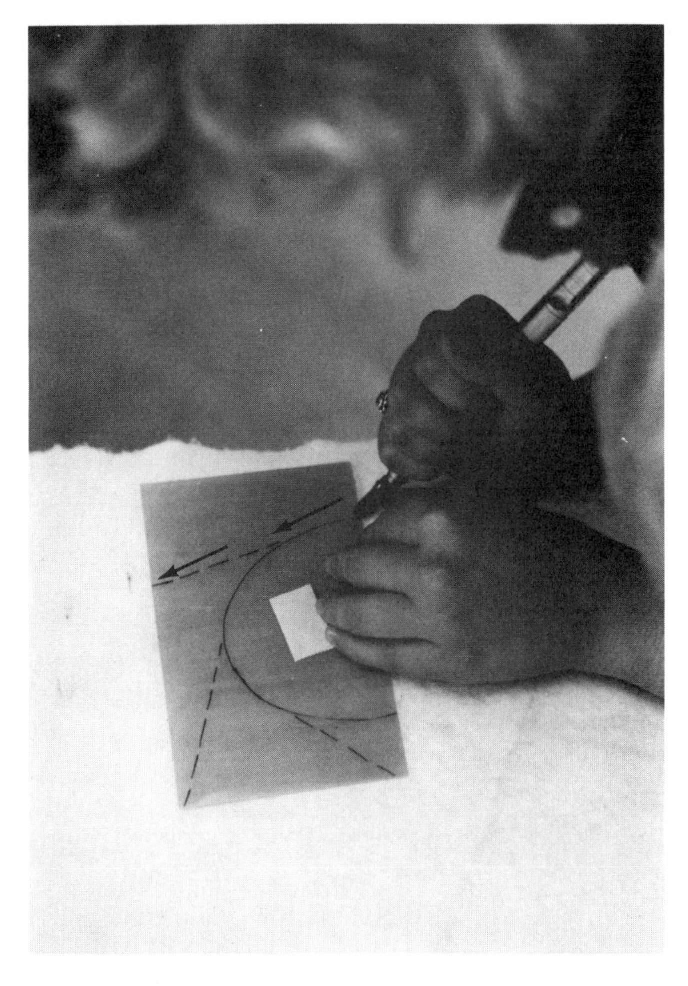

Illustration 1-19A

Each relief line should create a relatively straight line from your original pattern to the edge of the glass. By blocking out the rest of the pattern with your hands you can verify whether the relief line is at the right position along the curve.
(*See* Illustrations 1-18 through 1-23.)

5. Trace your flux brush dipped in kerosene along every line on the glass.
6. Make your score in one fluid motion around the pattern line, moving your entire body, not just your wrist.
7. Make your relief cuts by placing your cutter slightly away from the original score and cut along your first relief line. (The reason for allowing a gap between both scores is to prevent your relief cut from fracturing the piece you want to save.)
8. Fracture with your cut/run pliers and try to pull the glass apart gently.
9. Pull the glass apart by (a) placing your left hand close to the original score, holding the "good" piece firmly; (b) taking your grozing pliers in your dominant hand, placing them parallel to your relief score; and (c) pulling away the excess piece of glass.

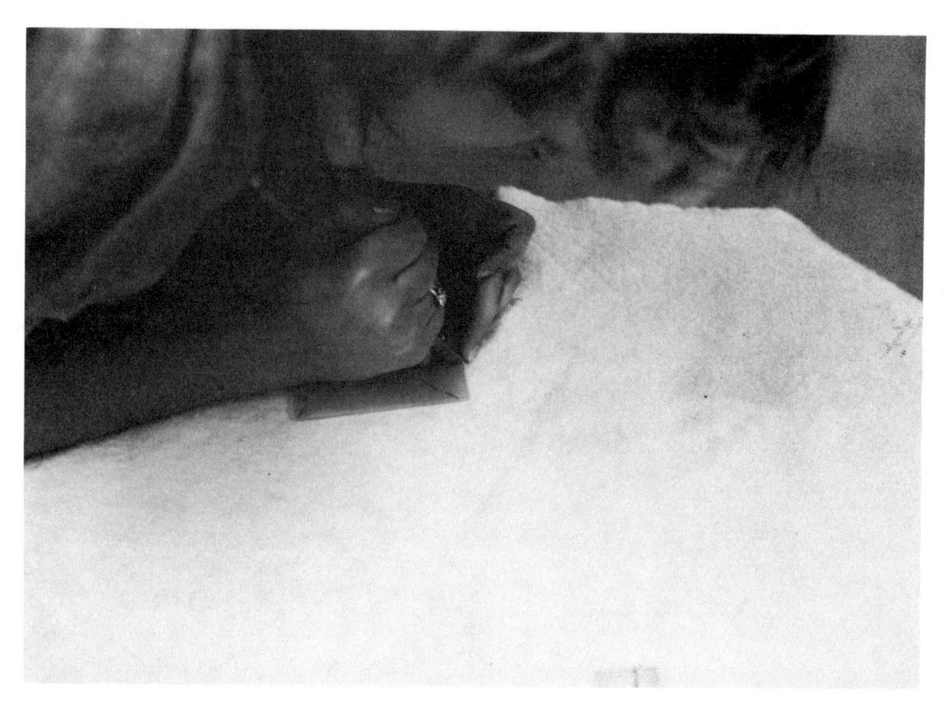

Illustration 1-19B

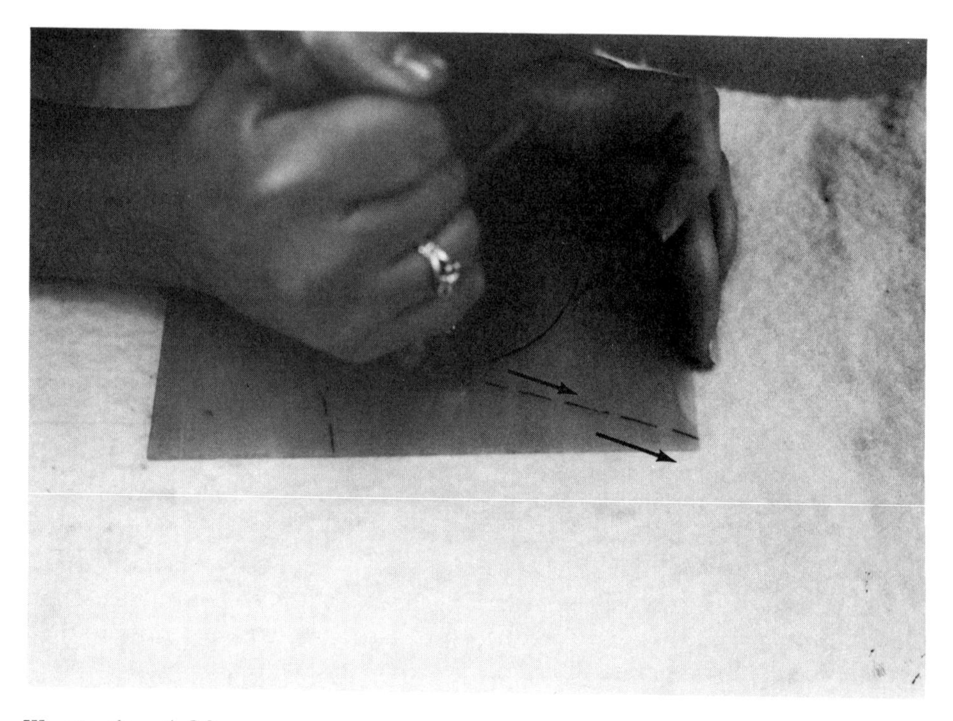

Illustration 1-20

Illustration 1-21A

Illustration 1-21B

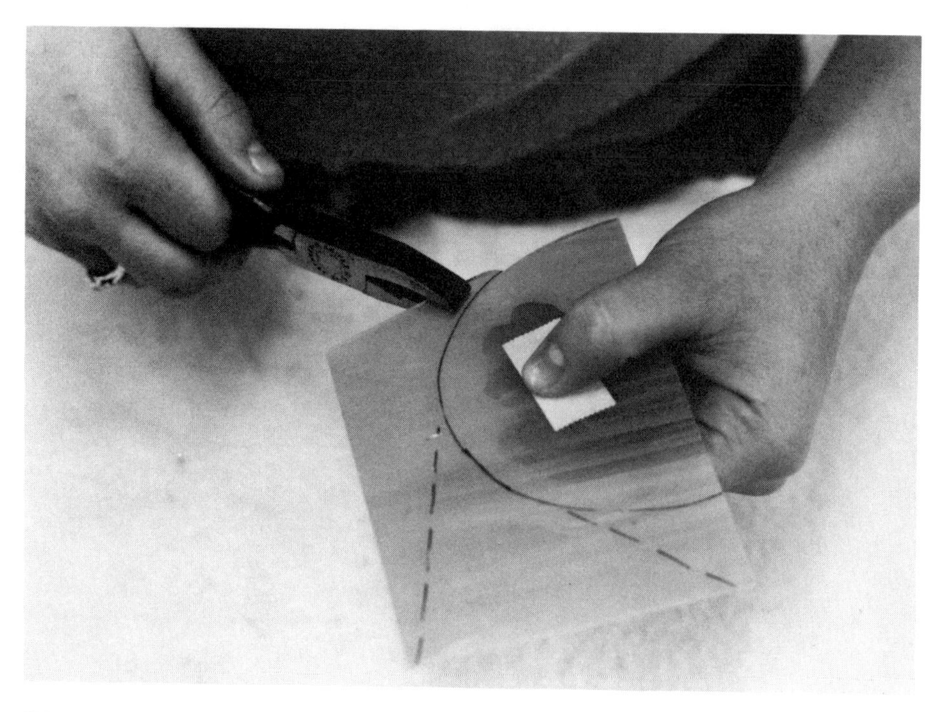

Illustration 1-22

Illustration 1-23

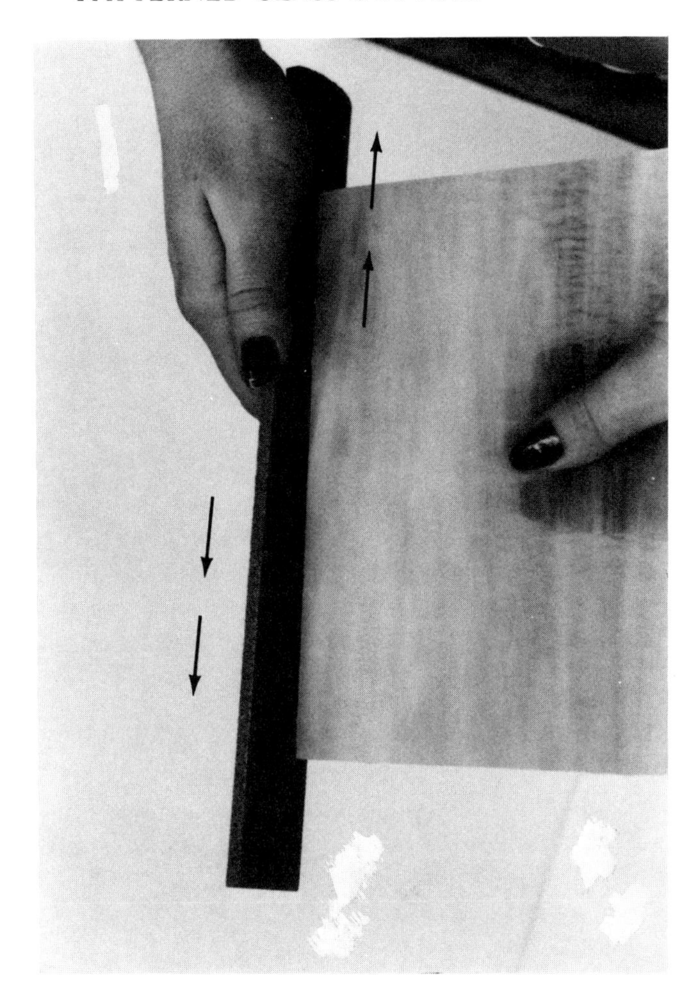

Illustration 1-24

10. Repeat step 9 with every relief cut, *changing hand position* for support with every break, making sure that the grozing pliers are parallel to each relief score line.

After you cut your individual piece of glass into the patterned shape you want by using one or a combination of the tools mentioned, some edges may need to be smoothed out. These rough or sharp edges must be sanded or filed down with a carborundum stone until they are smooth, and then wiped free of glass dust.

This final step in cutting is a very important preparatory procedure for the next major step—foiling or came wrapping (Chapters 2 and 3). You should *always* check all your pieces for uneven, rough, or sharp edges before you move on. The smoother the edge and cleaner the piece of glass, the easier it will be to successfully complete the next building block in the overall stained glass method.

Always keep your carborundum stone soaking in a can of water while you're working. (Take it out when not using it because the water will make it soft to the point of disintegration if left for long periods.) The stone will absorb water which prevents it from chipping the flat surfaces of the glass around the filed edge and will also speed up the taking down of the edge and smoothing it out.

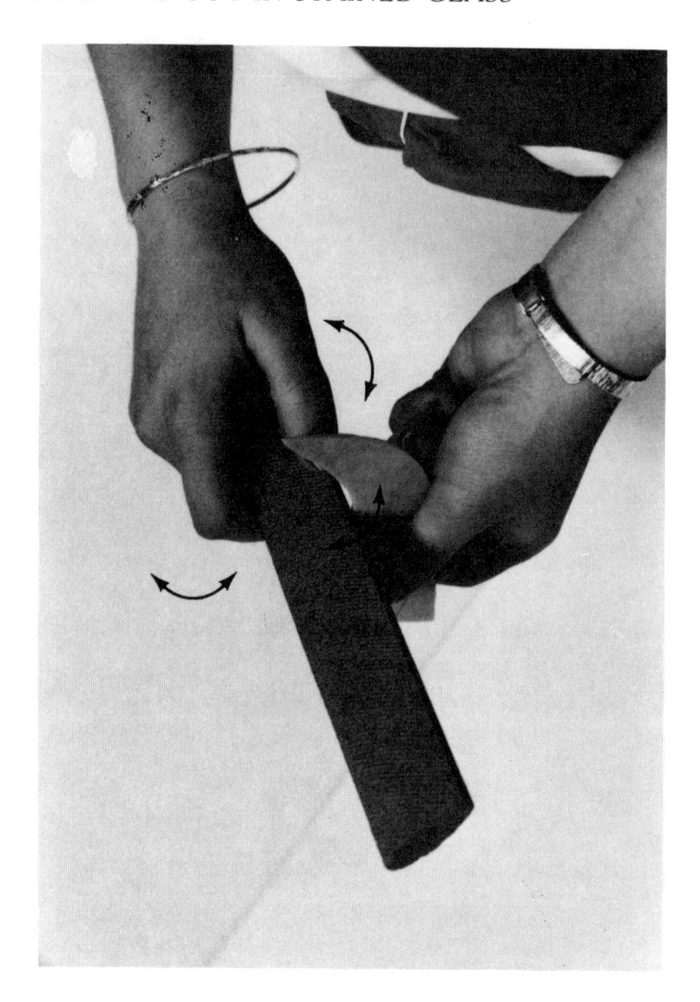

Illustration 1-25

The technique involves the same procedures for both straight edges and curved edges except for one slight difference:
(*See* Illustrations 1-24 and 1-25.)

1. Hold the glass firmly and close to your body.
2. For *straight edges*, hold the stone parallel to and on top of the edge. This will ensure a flat edge. If you tilt the edge of the stone to either side, you will create rounded edges which will cause difficulties when caming and foiling (Chapter 2).
3. File in *one direction* only, always *away* from you. *Never* file back and forth or toward you because either may cause chipping and there is the possibility of glass chips lodging in an eye.
4. For *curved* edges, turn the stone sideways, employing the same filing technique as with straight edges.

Summing Up

Patterned glass cutting involves three things: (1) a basic understanding of what your tools can accomplish; (2) strict adherence to the fundamentals of a good style; and (3) confidence that you can make the cut. Our methods and approach will develop and give you all three elements *provided that you practice what we preach*. Practice with the tools also until they feel comfortable in your hands and you're scoring and breaking glass easily.

You'll become a good and confident glass cutter, salvage a greater amount of glass, and attempt and complete more intricately designed projects as you develop: All you have to do is put in your time and motivate yourself.

We're going to set in place in the next few chapters the rest of the pyramidal stained glass building blocks by walking you through some initial "sun-catcher" projects. Then in Chapters 5 and 6 we'll bring you to the next level of stained glass work. But right now, at this crucial beginning stage, we want to emphasize one point: Do not pass GO, do not collect $200, do not move on to Chapter 2 until you can accomplish the tasks we outline in this chapter. Deluding yourself because of impatience into believing that you can compensate later for your inadequacies in glass cutting will only guarantee frustration and poor workmanship as a final product.

When you do feel ready, move on to Chapter 2, and you can begin your first project.

2

Caming and Soldering

For those of you who have been anxious to get to a stained glass project (we assume that's the reason you've bought this book), here's your chance. We've provided four suncatcher designs for the next two chapters. We recommend that you execute them in the order we suggest and that you carry through with them for the next two chapters. We've chosen these patterns because they combine all the common cuts we've outlined in the previous chapter. All four will give you a good workout for these beginning stages and will be a good introduction to all the individual steps and considerations you'll need to think about when constructing a stained glass project.

We're going to walk you through the two basic techniques of fitting the individual pieces of glass together: the traditional lead came method in this chapter and the copper foil technique in Chapter 3. Since it seems to be more a matter of taste as to which technique is better (although we generally prefer the foil method), you'll have to decide which technique is "better" for you after you've finished some projects. The first two projects, the kite and the butterfly, you'll do in lead came; the third, the water lily, in foil; and for the fourth, the cat, you'll employ a combination. Placing all four finished projects side by side will help you determine more easily which method you'd like to pursue.

We'll tell you right up front that most people find this second step most tedious, and the least enjoyable of all the necessary construction steps. But don't underestimate the importance of this step: If not properly executed, your project will be dubiously held together, weakly supported, and sloppily finished. It may even come apart eventually. You need to remember this as you wrap each individual piece of glass.

Tools and Materials

Glass. It's time to start cutting stained glass instead of plain window glass. *Please* buy and use the quantity and type of glass we recommend on the pattern sheets. You don't necessarily need to know all the characteristics and intricacies of glass and glass selection at this stage. If you don't like our color suggestions, choose your own; but *do not choose* any types of glass other than what we recommend. (We've devoted an entire Chapter 4 to this subject for discussion at a later stage of your development).

TOOLS AND MATERIALS

Tool/Material	Brand/Description	Source
Glass	Plain window or recommended cathedral	Stained glass supplier
Lead hobby came	2 strips, 6′ long, U type 1 strip, 6′ long, H type	Stained glass supplier
Came stretcher		Stained glass supplier
Dyke or wire cutter	Small, spring handled; Snap-On® brand	Hardware store/ electric supply
Small square-tipped hammer	Square head; rubber or leather tipped (explanation in text)	Hardware store
Glue	"527," tube	Hardware store
Soldering iron	100-Watt Esico®	Hardware store/ stained glass supplier
Soldering tips	1 full-wedge 1 semi-wedge	Hardware store/ stained glass supplier
Control box (rheostat)		Hardware store/ stained glass supplier
Solder	60/40, 1 lb. spool	Hardware store/ stained glass supplier
Flux	Kester® paste	Hardware store
Needlenosed pliers	Small	Hardware store
Wet sponge	Large cleaning	
Wire	Copper or ungalvanized	Hardware store
White construction paper	8″ x 10″ sheets	Stationery supply

Lead Came. You can purchase various types, widths, and thicknesses, generally in six-foot lengths. Ask for it straight from the shipping box, not in a rolled-up, prepackaged plastic bag. (The one exception to this rule is hobby came, which is not harmed by packaging.) The rolled-up strips are harder to stretch out and the grooves may be more closed than the strips straight from the shipping box.

For our purposes, you'll require only two strips of U-channel hobby came and one of H-channel hobby came. There are other types and widths but we'll defer discussion and description for when you're at a more advanced level.

Dykes (extra-small wire cutters). For the smaller cames we'll be using for sun-catchers we find that, when cutting the lead, these dykes are much more useful and less damaging to the soft lead than a traditional lead knife. As you progress, and perhaps get more involved in heavier leads and bigger projects, you can decide whether you'll use this tool enough to justify its price.

Small Square-tipped Hammer with a Rubber or Leather Tip. We've tooled these hammers especially for our sun-catcher leading.* Get the smallest, lightest hammer you can find and mount with some glue a rubberized or leather tip. As you strike the lead in order to mold it around the glass, the tip will prevent impressions in the lead.

* If you'd like one of our special hammers, write to us, and we'll send you our descriptive brochure and pricing information.

Soldering Iron. We recommend the Esico 100-watt iron because it consistently provides even heat and we think the workmanship and durability of the iron is superior to others we have used and experimented with. Also, with a control box it is a good general-purpose iron for both caming and foiling.

Control Box (Rheostat). A 100-watt iron is really too hot for most caming work (but it is a perfect wattage for soldering copper foil, as we'll discuss in Chapter 3.) When used in conjunction with your 100-watt iron, a control box allows you to set the wattage at exactly the right level so you won't burn away the lead and to adjust the heat as needed for various other projects. We recommend that you use a control box rather than a rheostat because it is more accurate and precise in selecting temperatures. Without a control box, lead came work is nearly impossible to do, especially for beginners.

Soldering Tips. This Esico iron comes with a full-wedge tip which you will utilize for soldering copper-foiled pieces. However, in addition, you should purchase a semi-wedge tip for soldering came. Neat, delicate solder joints, employing little solder, are the ideal; this smaller wedge will make it easier to achieve these "good" joints. Incidentally, to maintain longer tip life and keep it free from corrosion, we suggest that you remove and clean your tips with a wire brush or steel wool at least once a month.

Solder. Because of its low liquefying or melting point, 60/40 solder (60 percent tin, 40 percent solder) is the most frequently used in stained glass work. Some may substitute 50/50 solder but we feel, because of its finish and slow liquefying property, it is inferior to 60/40.

Because a quality-produced solder has so much impact on your finished project (especially foiled projects) it is imperative that you purchase good solder from a reputable supplier. Impure (recycled), cheap ("B" type as opposed to "A"), or improperly mixed solder (53/37 plus "other ingredients") will not flow properly, will create air bubbles in your bead, and will cool to a wrinkled, dappled finish. Since there is no universal brand name we can recommend, you must rely on your supplier to provide you with good solder. Once you're satisfied with your solder, stick with the same brand and supplier; avoid "sales" if another brand is offered. Pay any fair price you can to work with the same solder. Believe us, the results obtained are worth the price and effort to get a quality solder.

Paste Flux and Acid Brush. Kester flux does the best job for us in that it allows the solder to flow smoothly and with a minimum of odor. The flux and solder work hand in hand to effect good beads and joints; you'll apply the flux with the fifteen-cent acid brush (instead of your fingers!).

A Wet Sponge. There is generally a buildup of residue on your soldering tip that will be transferred to your project and prevent the tip from heating up quickly and to the proper temperature unless it is cleaned. Frequent cleaning of the tip with the sponge will eliminate the residue.

Beginning or Preparatory Procedures

Some people have an initial problem trying to figure out what size sheets of glass to buy and where they should place the patterns on the glass when they begin to cut. In these preparatory stages we'll outline exactly how you should proceed in order to cut the individual pieces and get ready for fitting:

(1) Most stained glass suppliers sell cathedral glass in 8″ x 11″ or square-foot sheets. Don't buy anything larger than these size sheets until you have done a few projects.

We'll begin with the kite below (Fig. 2). Always trace two patterns (putting aside your original copy), one of which you will use as a working copy that you will cut up to

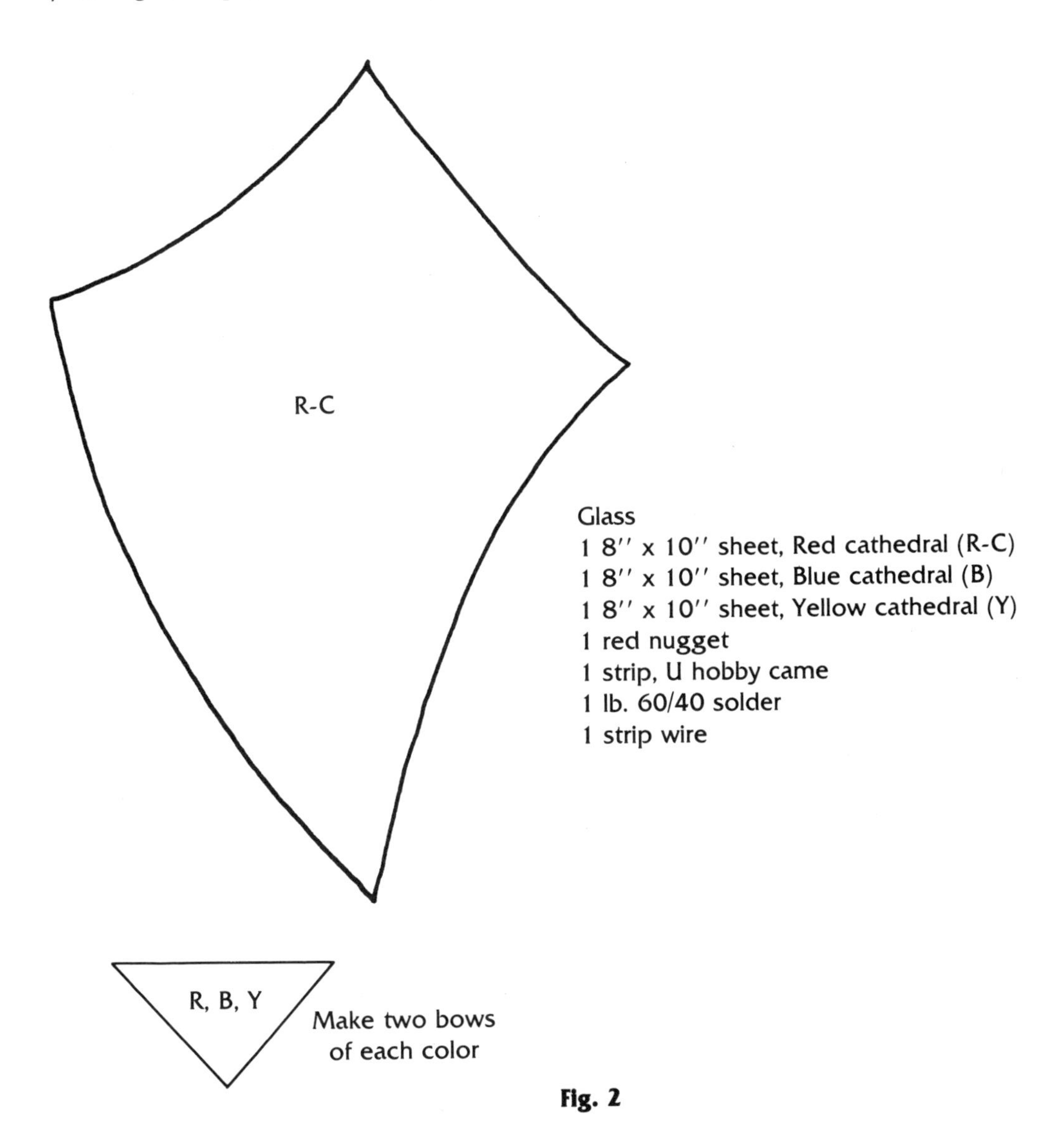

Fig. 2

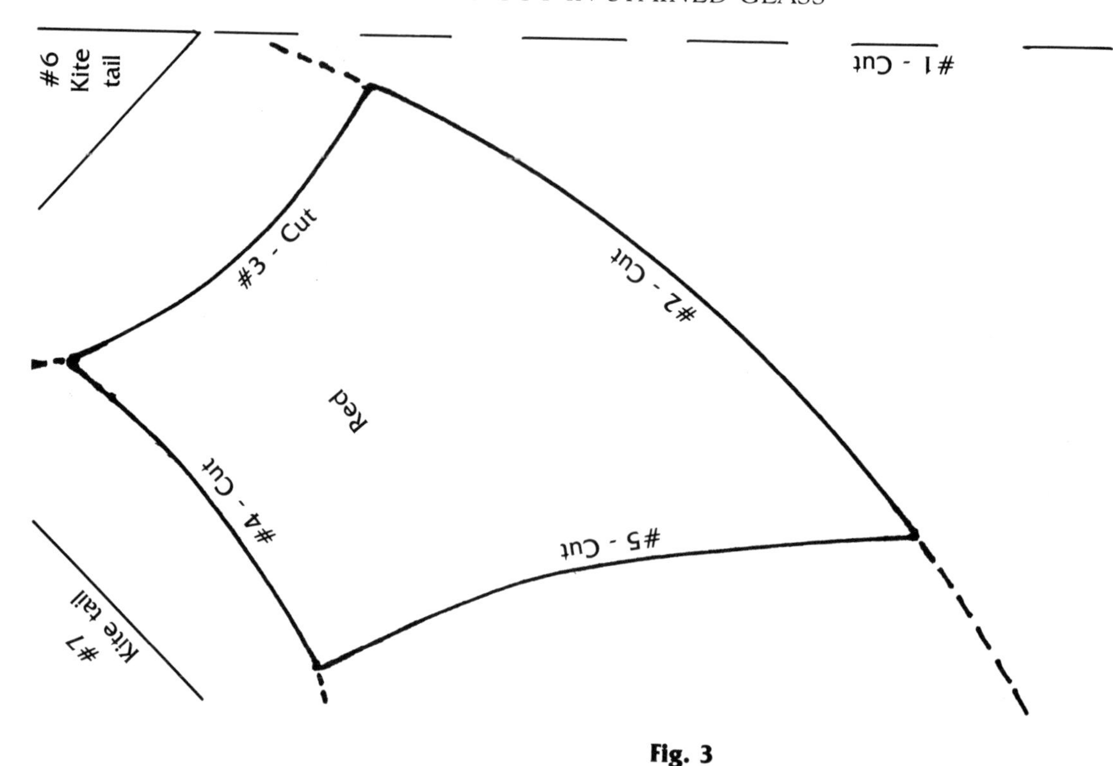

Fig. 3

place on top of your glass; and the other you will use as a master copy for placing your cut pieces on to see how they're coming or butting together. If the pieces do not accurately correlate to the lines on the pattern, and there are large gaps between the pieces, you'll have to recut some pieces so they butt as closely as possible to the ones next to them. (We'll show you how to modify or custom cut a piece of glass in Chapter 3.) But for now, recut any piece that is too far offline. The practice will do you good!

In general, we believe the best way to accurately cut patterns from every type of glass is to place the pattern on top of the glass and with our suggested marker trace the pattern right on the glass. *Following the inside of a line on top of the glass* is a much easier approach than looking through the glass at a pattern underneath. You'll notice that on our pattern sheets, we've indicated exactly where and in what position to place your patterns for all three projects. The numbered dotted lines correspond to your sequence of cuts. You'll notice that the first cut for the kite (*See* Fig. 3) is along one side of the kite. In most cases, you should try to begin your cuts this way. For the tail sections of your kite, smaller sections of your larger sheet and even scrap pieces can be used. If you follow this overall approach for all glass cutting, you'll conserve glass and salvage enough glass to do other projects. And never throw your scraps away. You never can tell when you might utilize them for other projects.

(2) Also, after cutting each piece, make sure the edges of the pieces are smooth and free of nipples or jagged edges. Use your carborundum stone where needed (p. 23). As mentioned previously, this is an extremely important procedure for preparing the edges of the glass to properly receive the lead (and foil), analogous to sizing walls when hanging wallpaper.

(3) Next, remove all your cutting tools. Wipe clean all your pieces of glass. If there is any glass dust or kerosene on them, you'll have a difficult time caming or foiling them. Also, wipe off your work table so that everything will be clean and neat in preparation for fitting.

(4) Lay out all the tools needed for whichever method you choose. Always place them in the same relative position. (If you're left-handed, reverse positions.)

Always follow these first four steps for either method and any sun-catcher you attempt to do. *Remember*: What we're trying to do throughout this book (and all our technique books) is to show you the importance of standardizing your approach, methods, and tool position so you will develop a system that generates automatic and almost instinctive action in regard to stained glass and the individual steps involved with each project. These beginning techniques will lay the groundwork for your entire involvement with stained glass.

We've provided two separate projects for assembly with both the U-came and the H-came. You'll need to know the common and particular methods for approaching projects that would lend themselves to either technique or a combination. When you attempt to do these, *please* try them in the order we present them since our entire approach is a detailed developmental one which should lower your frustration level and accelerate your progress and stained glass output.

Cutting and Wrapping Procedures for U-Came

This may seem an obvious statement, but it's very important that you trace your working patterns accurately and cut them out smoothly. You don't want any inaccurate or jagged-edged paper cutouts caused by poor scissors cutting because this will cause inaccurate glass cutting. Keep in mind that the quality of the finished project depends a great deal on a number of properly executed details and procedures. Just "for the want of a nail" in the proverbial lost-war story, so can artistic failure and collapse of a stained glass project result if one of these details is overlooked.

Although the following instructions may seem elementary, we feel we should include them:

1. Place a plain white sheet of construction paper under the kite pattern and *with a pencil smoothly trace* the pattern. Make three patterns: one "working" that will be cut up; one placement pattern to put the cut pieces onto; and one "good" one to keep as a master.
2. With your scissors open wide, and always taking a full-length "bite" with your blades (not little "staccato" cuts) slowly cut one of the patterns *on the pencil mark*. The thin line of the pencil mark should disappear as you cut.
3. Place the pattern on top of your glass as illustrated in Fig. 3. (If there is a salvage or rolled, bumpy edge, cut that off first so the glass will be flat for pattern tracing and cutting). With your extra-fine Sharpie marker, held

upright to ensure a fine line, slowly and smoothly trace the kite pattern on the glass.

4. Trace the bows as indicated also.

Now you're ready to begin cutting your glass. Have all your cutting tools and materials at the ready. Clear away everything you don't need, and proceed as follows:

1. Cut along dotted line #1 in order to separate the larger excess piece from the smaller "good" piece.
   IMPORTANT: Follow your basic cutting style: relaxed grip, cutter at proper angle, even, continuous pressure, stopping just short of the edge, cutter back in jar, pull glass apart, wipe cutting surface with a rag, replace "good" glass on table, and place excess piece aside.
2. Score dotted line #2. Always place the cutting wheel in the center of the mark and follow it as closely as possible.
3. Turn your glass as you continue to make all the remaining cuts so that it is at a comfortable angle to score.
4. After the piece has been cut out, wipe it with a rag, and place the cutout pattern on top of it to see how closely they match. File down any excess glass or rough edge with your carborundum stone (that should be soaking in a can of water) according to the procedures outlined on p. 23.
5. Cut the indicated corners of your blue glass for the kite tail. Do the same for your green glass and your yellow glass. Once again, make sure you smooth out the edges of your glass with your wet stone, including the points, taking care not to damage them. You just want to dull the point.

All your pieces, cut and laid out, should come together. (*See* Illustration 2-1.)

Clear your worktable of your cutting tools and gather the tools and material needed for caming (p. 29). This process is the traditional method for holding the glass together.

You must first prepare the came by stretching it in a came stretcher. (The main reasons for this are that it gives a stiffer body to the came, straightens out the edges, and most especially, narrows or thins out the channeled grooves so that the glass will fit snugly.) Simply place the came in the stretcher, press the top down, take hold of the "free" end of the came with needlenosed pliers, and pull or stretch it until it "straightens" out. A 6′ piece should be stretched about 5″ longer. (*See* Illustrations 2-2 through 2-4.)

Then carefully, handling the came with respect, lay it down gently on your worktable. (Came marks easily and dents will detract from your finished project.)

Three sets of procedures will be outlined in the next few pages for completing the caming operation and, although seemingly time consuming and involved, it will probably take you less time to do what we outline than read it. Let's start with wrapping the came around the glass:
(*See* Illustrations 2-5 through 2-8.)

1. Starting at the bottom of the kite, wrap the came around the glass by fitting and gently pressing (with your fingers) the glass into the channeled groove. Start with about ½″ excess came protruding past the glass edge, loosely wrap the entire piece, and cut away the remainder of the long came strip to prevent any damage to its shape and/or fragile surface; this will make the came easier to work with. Don't be too concerned with a tight or exact fitting right now because that is step 2.

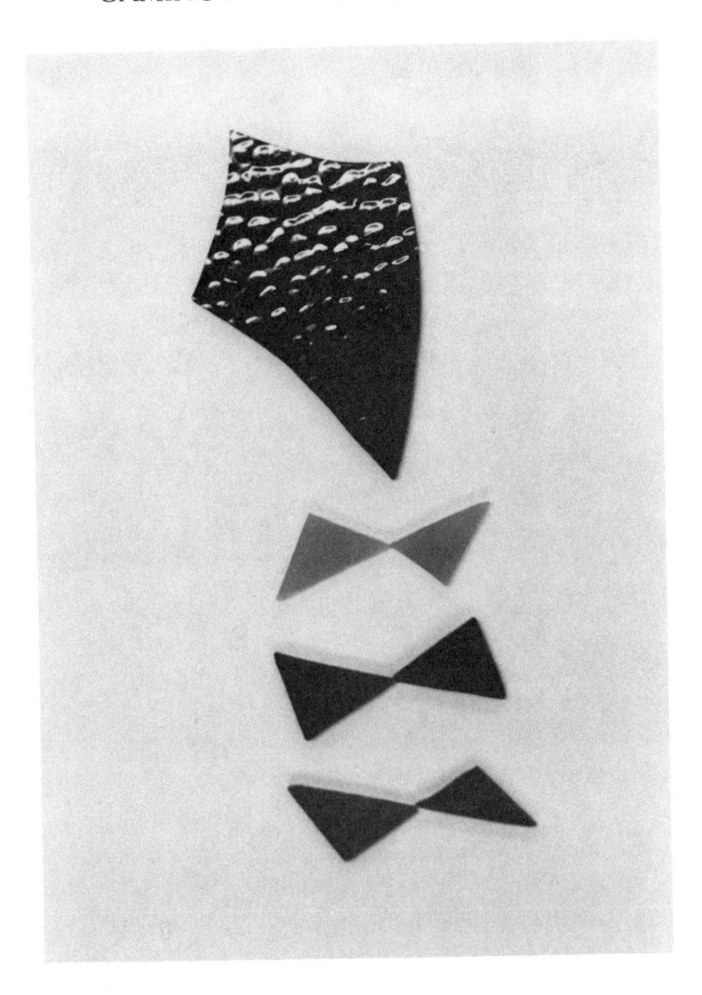

Illustration 2-1

2. Next, with your small rubber-tipped hammer, gently tap the came against the glass. As you go around the glass, lift it to the light, making sure you have tapped out all the air holes.
3. Trim the excess came at the first or beginning point of contact by pushing back one of your sides and, with your small dyke, cut a *straight line* that's even with the glass. (It might be wise to practice cutting straight lines first with scrap or damaged came.) Push the other end against the glass and cut this end flush with your first end-point. (*See* Fig. 4.)
4. Miter the two running edges of each side by cutting a slight 45-degree angle on each runner. Push the two sides back to the glass and make sure the two edges fit together correctly. Retap the came with your hammer to make sure it fits the glass tightly.

Now you're ready for gluing the came to the glass. Gluing will prevent the lead came from separating from the glass later on after it has been hanging by a hook in a window. The procedure is relatively simple:

1. Remove the fitted came from the kite, taking care not to stretch or mark it any more than necessary to free it from the glass. (*See* Illustration 2-9.)

Illustration 2-2

2. At intervals, place a small dot of glue inside the channel all the way round the lead. (*See* Illustration 2-10.)
3. *Immediately* (the glue will harden quite quickly) replace the lead around the glass, tapping the lead with your hammer back into place.

Now you're ready for soldering. As in other procedures, it would be a good idea to practice soldering some scrap came together just before you try your "good" came:

1. Take out your solder, flux, wet sponge, iron, and control box. (*See* Illustration 2-11.) It's time to set your control box. *The ideal setting is one which allows the iron to melt the solder while not burning away the came*. In order to find your ideal setting (since this varies with irons, boxes, and electric outlets), set your control box at 50. With a little bit of scrap came place your iron on the came to see if it dissolves the came. If it does, decrease the setting to 45. Wait one minute (to allow the iron heat to adjust) and try it again. Adjust the setting in increments of 5 until you can place the iron on the came without its melting.

Illustration 2-3

Now place your pound of solder on your table and try melting off the tip of the solder. If it melts easily, you're all set—you've found your custom setting. However, if it does not melt easily, increase your setting in increments of 2 degrees and test again until the solder melts. Once you've programmed your iron and control box to the point where the came will not melt but your solder will, your equipment is ready for use. (It's a good idea to place a piece of tape next to this setting on your box, for future use.)

2. After your iron is sufficiently hot, then clean it on a wet sponge by dipping the tip into the flux paste and wiping on the sponge again. This will prepare the iron for accepting the solder. The flux and solder work hand in hand to accomplish a neat, rounded joint. In essence, the solder depends on the flux to make it flow smoothly (you'll see how important this relationship is in the next chapter on Foiling).
3. Brush some flux onto the kite joint where your two channels of came join together. (As mentioned above, this facilitates the solder transfer and flow.)
4. With your iron, pick up some solder from your roll and transfer it to your fluxed came joint by lightly touching it and lifting the iron at the point of contact

Illustration 2-4

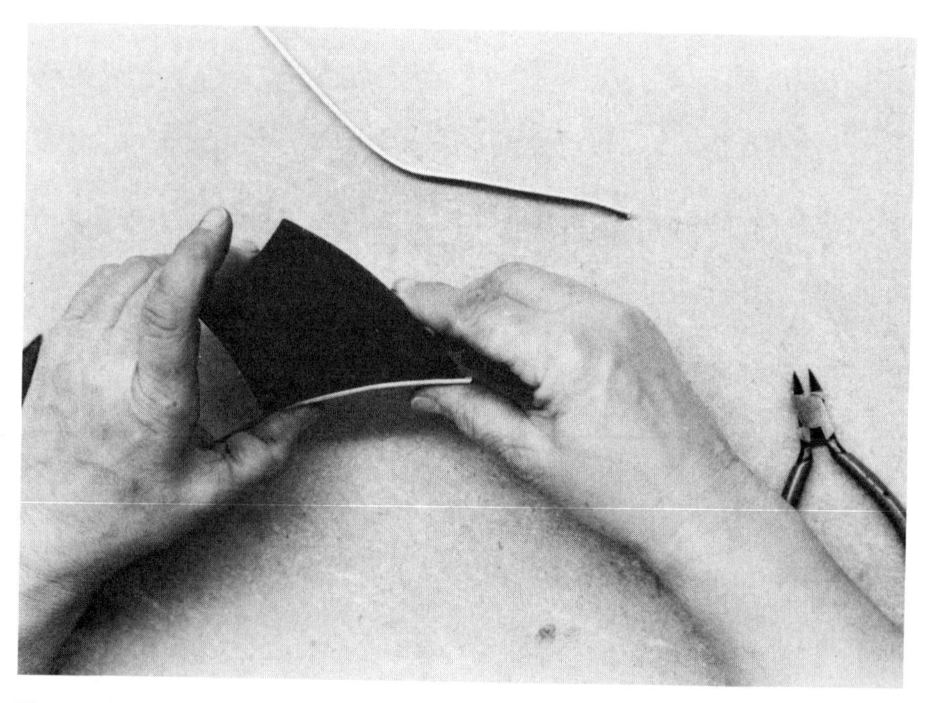

Illustration 2-5

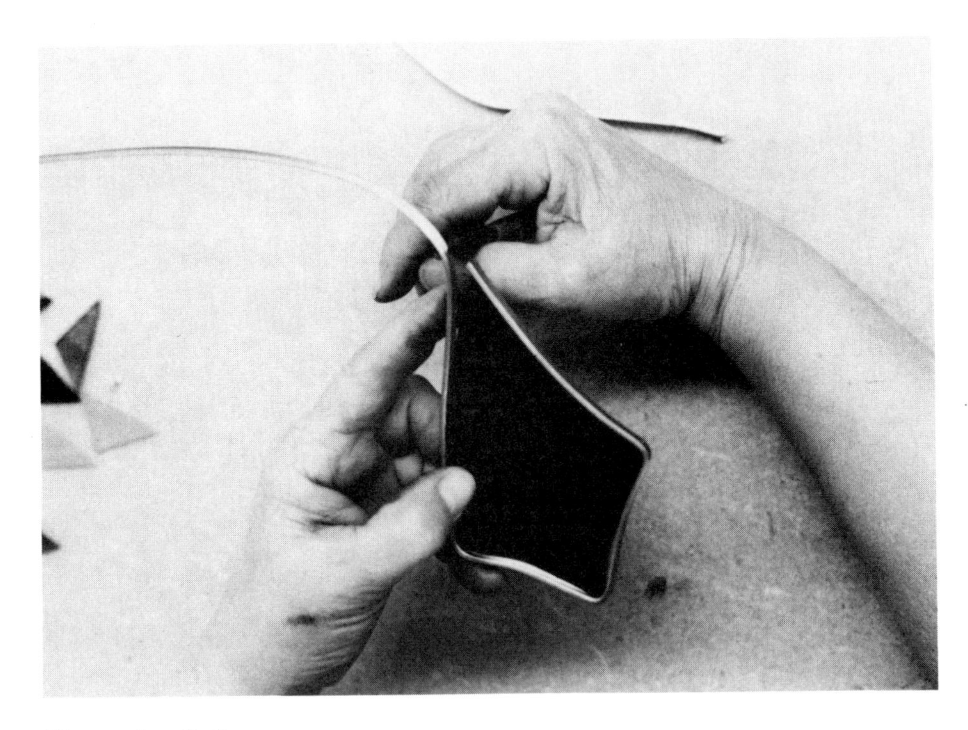

Illustration 2-6

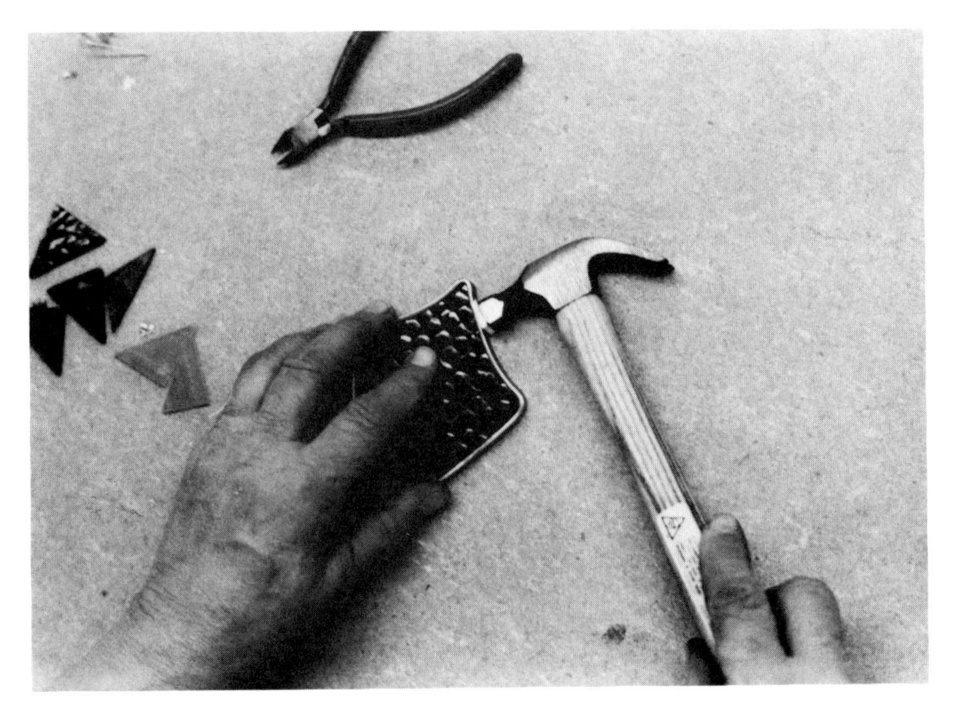

Illustration 2-7

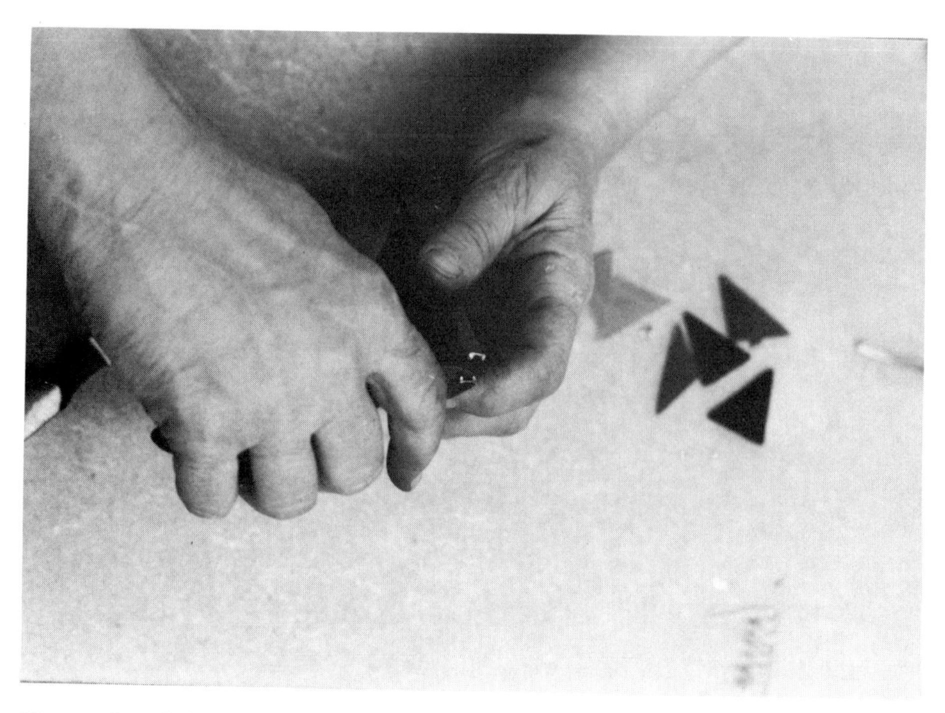

Illustration 2-8

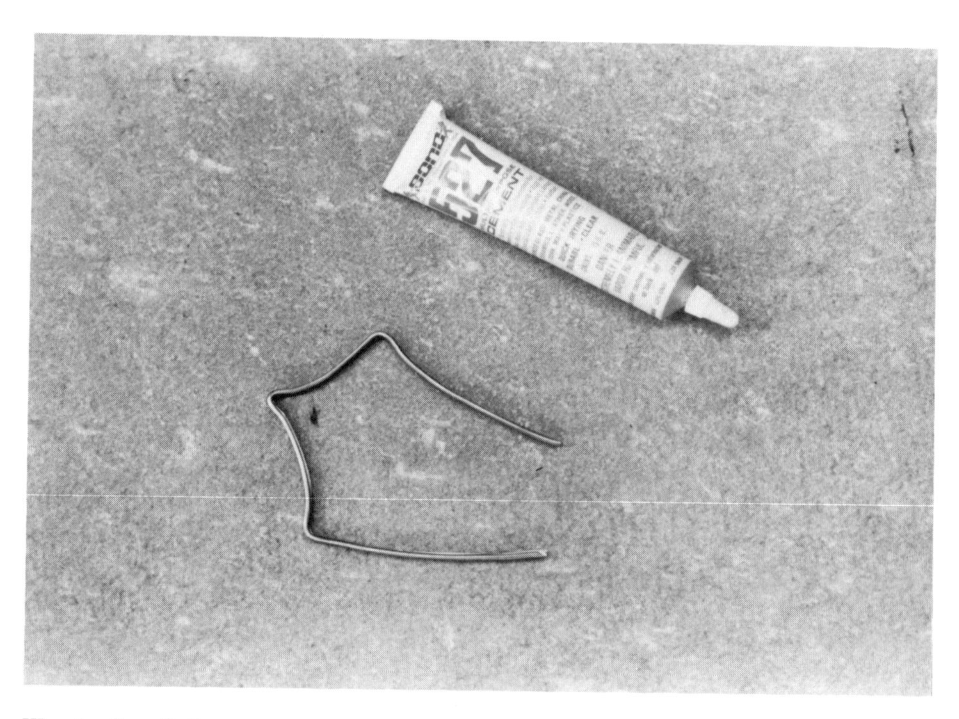

Illustration 2-9

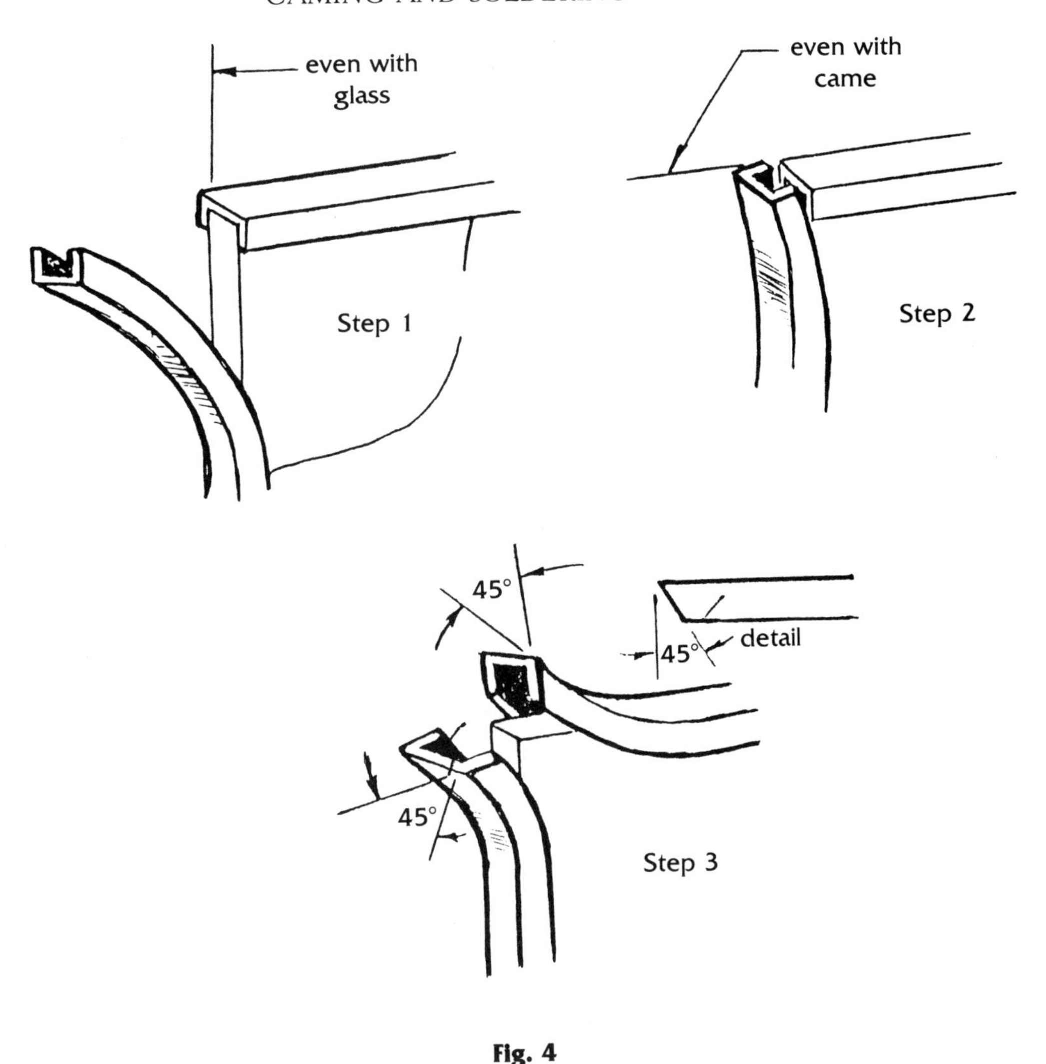

Fig. 4

with the came so that the solder will just roll off your iron onto the came. (*See* Illustrations 2-12 and 2-13.) Smooth out the solder joint with the flat chisel of your tip by gently touching the joint (*See* Illustration 2-14.) *Do not press down on the came and do not simulate with your iron the artist method of short brush strokes*. You'll spread the solder too much and make too large a solder joint. If this happens, you'll have to rewrap your project with new came.

Before wrapping and soldering your kite tails, take a length of silver wire, stretch it out about an arm's length, and come back again so that you have a double piece of uncut wire. Lock the open end into a vise. At the closed end, insert one of the arms of your dyke and twist the wire making a decorative intertwined strip of wire (*See* Illustrations 2-15 and 2-16); sufficiently twist it so that you can cut a piece off and it will not unravel.

To solder the wire to the kite, proceed as follows:

1. Place the wire on *top of the glass, not the came,* butting it tightly against the *inside edge* of the came. (*See* Illustration 2-17.)
2. Solder the top to the came.

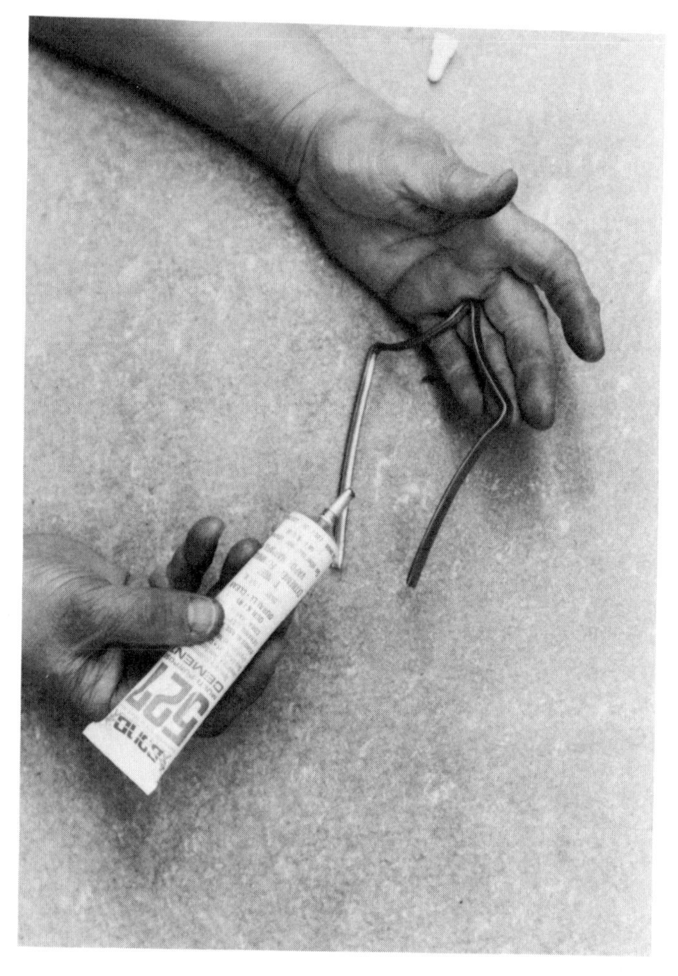

Illustration 2-10

3. Bend or curve the wire to present the illusion of flight.
4. Cut the wire and solder the bottom wire/came joint.
5. Set up, solder, shape, and cut the horizontal piece of wire.
6. Solder the tail section of wire to the bottom of the kite. Make sure this is well secured because it will have to support the weight of the tail section.

Now plan your tail section by evenly spacing and placing the glass tails next to the wire. (*See* Illustration 2-18.) The reason for laying this out is that you will see where you have to begin and end your came wrapping. You want your came joint to butt the wire so that the solder joint will be where the glass tail will join the wire; the end result being only *one* solder joint to accomplish two tasks: the joining of the came and the attaching of the wire.

The methods for wrapping and soldering the tail sections are similar to the methods used for the main kite:
(*See* Illustrations 2-19 through 2-22.)

1. Cut off a small strip of stretched came that is slightly longer than the perimeter of the first kite bow you pick up.

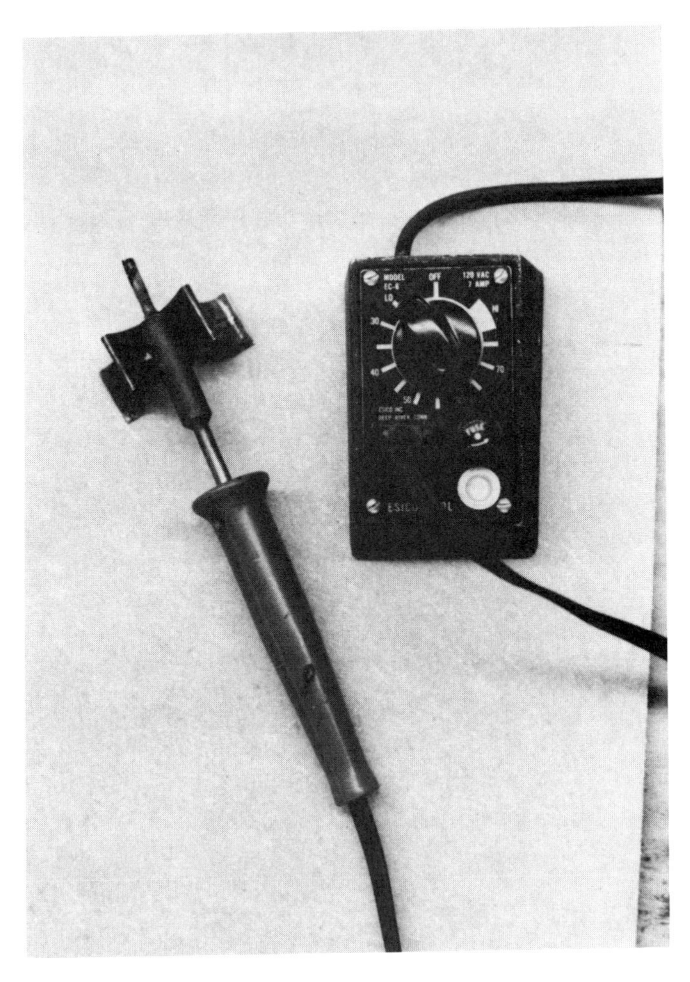

Illustration 2-11

2. Fit and form the came around the bow with your rubber-tipped hammer, beginning and ending at the point where the bow will be soldered to the twisted tail-wire.
3. Cut the came evenly and miter the edges just as you did for the main kite, pp. 34–35.
4. Solder the came (gluing is not necessary because there is no stress on these sections).
5. Wrap, fit, and solder the other five pieces.
6. To attach the bows to the wire, hold one pair down and steady with your fingers, flux the wire and bows, and solder the bows to the wire.
7. Evenly spacing the next two pairs, attach them in the same manner.
8. Turn the tail section over and solder the back and the spaces on top around the tails.
9. Attach the final nugget by wrapping it tightly with came and setting it at the bottom of the twisted wire with the solder joint touching. Flux and solder securely.

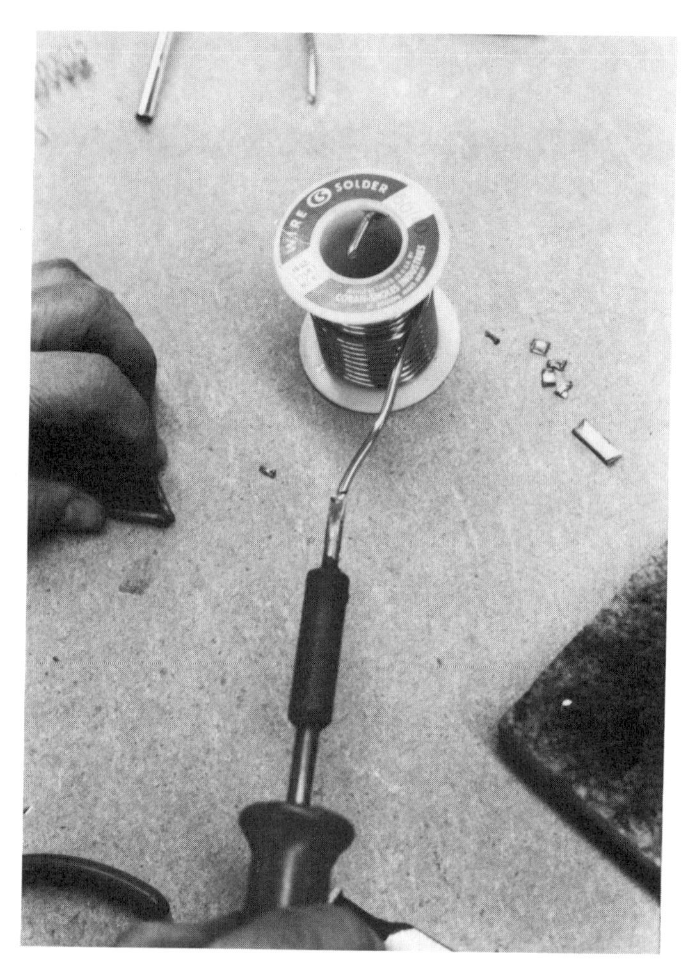

Illustration 2-12

The entire kite should now be completely soldered together. However, all suncatchers require a hook for hanging with fish line or wire on a suction cup. This is why we had you glue the kite's came to the glass so that it won't pull away as a result of the stress placed on it by hanging. Proceed as follows:

1. Balance the kite by picking it up at the top between your index finger and thumb and allowing it to dangle loosely. Balance it in any position you want by moving your fingers until you're satisfied as to how it hangs.
2. Make a slight mark on the came with a pencil where both thumb and finger come together. This is where your hook will be placed.
3. Make a hook by wrapping a piece of wire around a pen or pencil and cutting off the rounded wire. (*See* Illustration 2-23.)
4. Pick up the hook with a pair of needlenosed pliers and place the cut ends on your mark on the came and flux and securely solder the hook to the kite. (*See* Illustration 2-24.)

Illustration 2-13

Finishing Techniques

The final touches you apply to your projects can either detract or enhance the overall aesthetics of your handiwork. After all the hard work and time you've put into crafting a stained glass project, it would be a shame not to exercise the same care and patience at this stage.

CLEANING

You can never be too fussy when cleaning your projects. Ordinary liquid detergent in warm (*not* hot) sudsy water is very good to use to first clean off as much of the residue flux as you can. A soft rag that will leave no lint is the best type of applicator. After you've removed as much flux this way as you can, hold the project (where possible) under running warm water for two or three minutes. This will melt any remaining flux. Go over once again with your rag, making sure you get into every corner and along each seam.

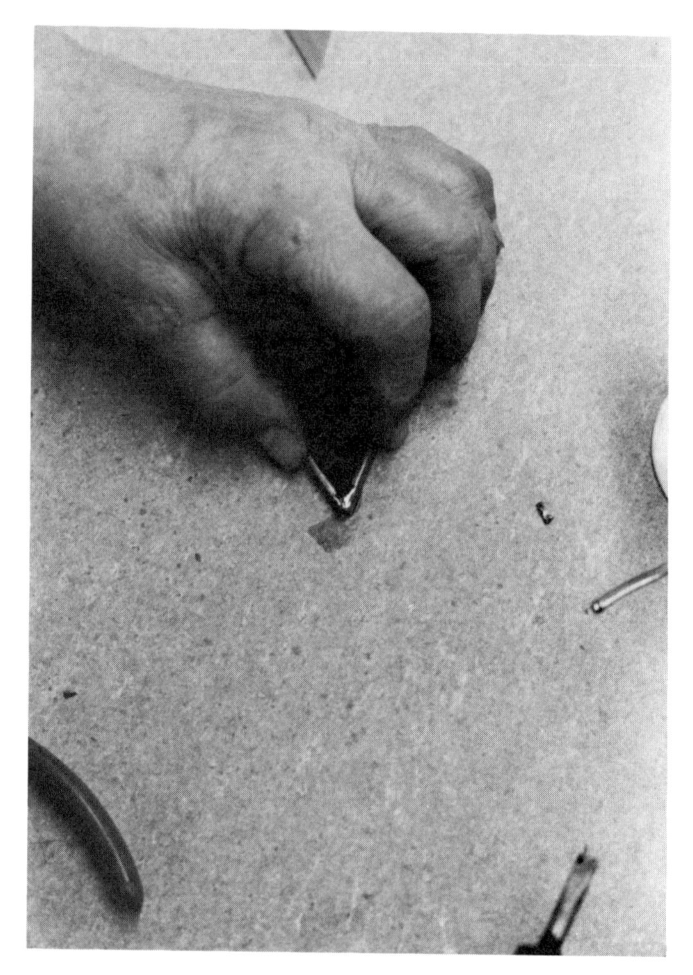

Illustration 2-14

DARKENING AGENTS AND PATINAS

Some people prefer to have their lead came and solder joints darker than the natural gray or silver color. There are various patinas, liquids that form a colored film, that will accomplish this purpose. Different companies provide black, charcoal, and even copper tones that accentuate your lead lines and, in many cases, provide good contrast for your glass.

Should you decide to patina your project, it would be a good idea to try the following technique on some lead scraps before trying it on your project. You can see the darkening effects of the patina as it is applied in various amounts to different strips. You can also practice removing the patina's effect by rubbing the came with fine steel wool to restore it to its original silver shine.

To apply a patina, simply:

1. Make sure your project is clean (free from flux) and dry.
2. With extra-fine steel wool, gently rub all soldered joints (or soldered seams).

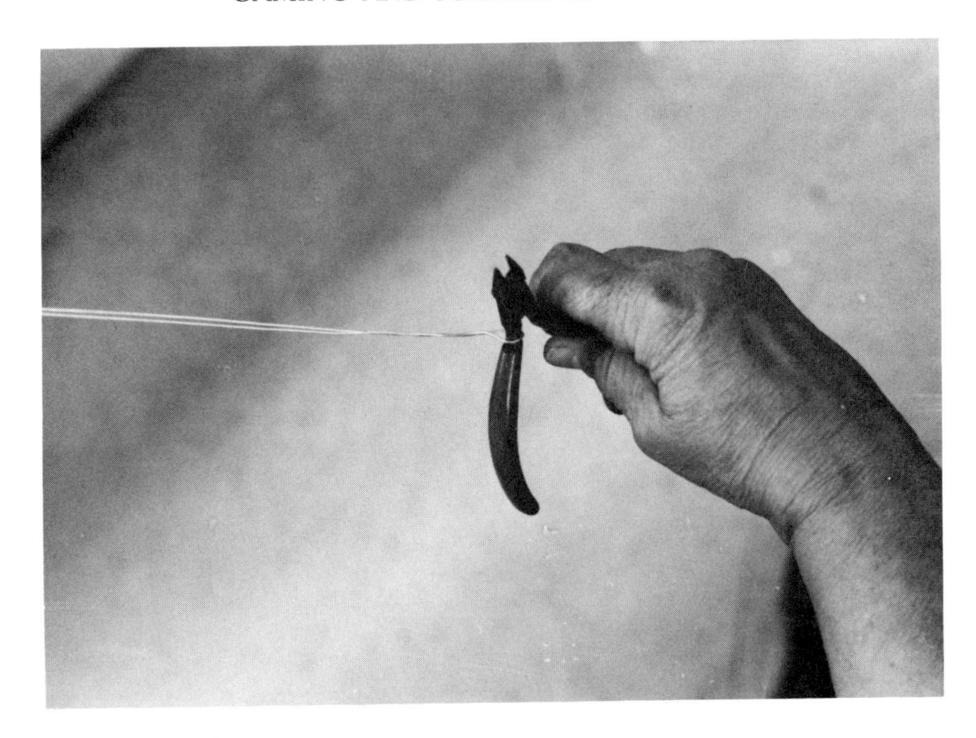

Illustration 2-15

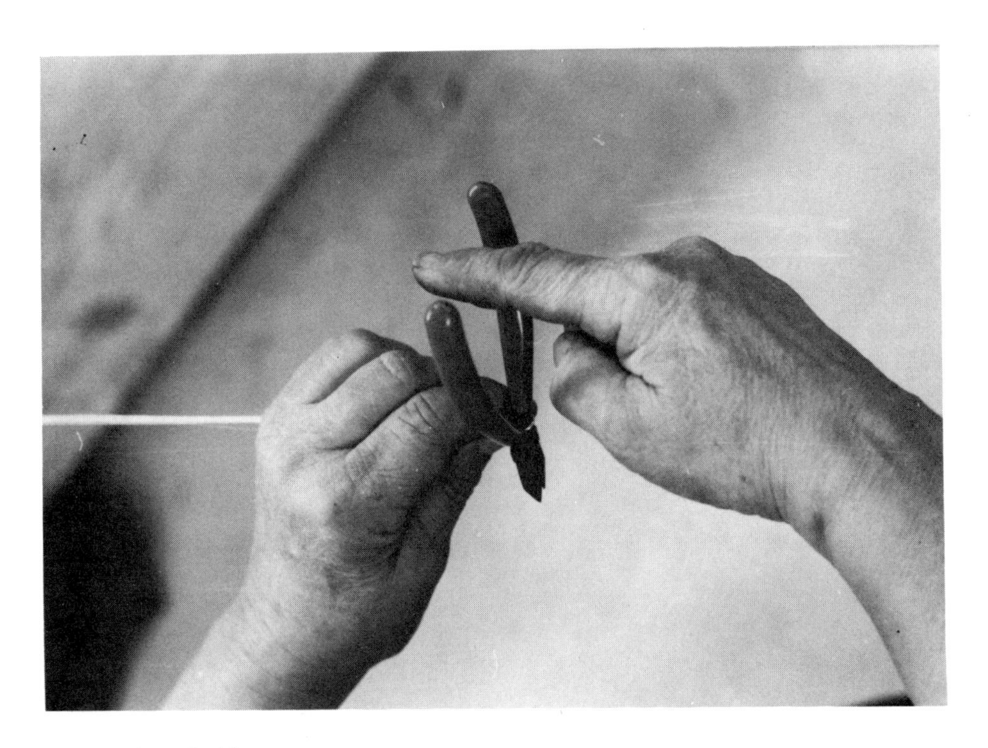

Illustration 2-16

Illustration 2-17

Illustration 2-18

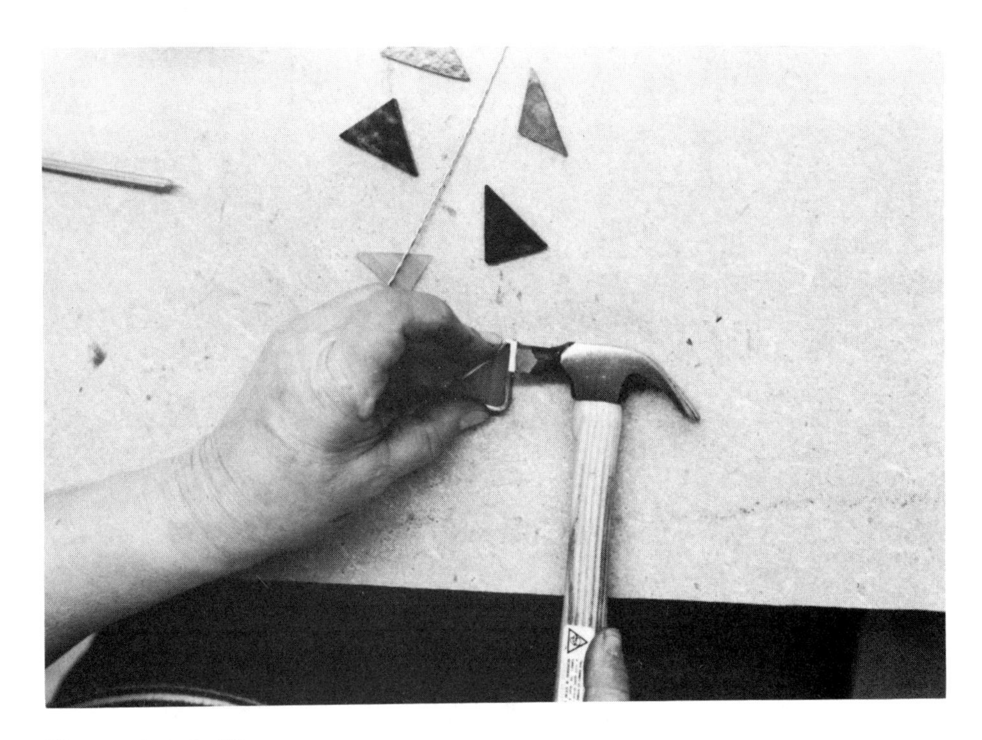

Illustration 2-19

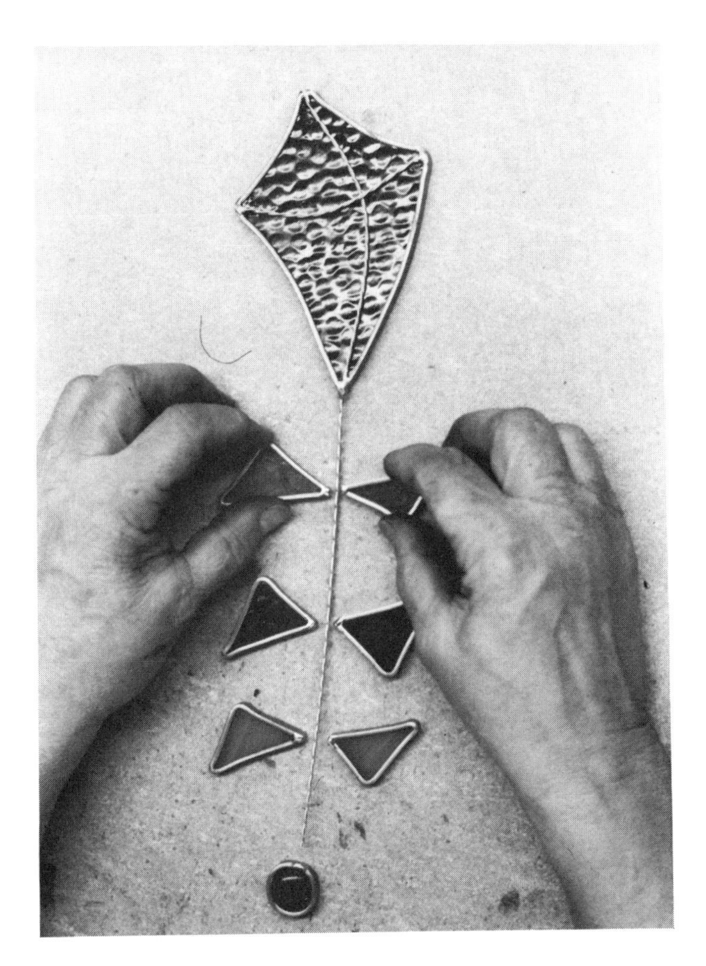

Illustration 2-20

Illustration 2-21

3. Wipe the lead residue off the joints with a dry cloth.
4. Shake the patina well and apply it evenly on your lead and solder with a small, soft cloth or cotton swab.
5. Apply extra coats of patina until the shade or density looks good to you. The more patina you apply, the darker the lead will become.
6. Allow the patina to stand and dry two to three minutes. Don't let the patina stand any longer than this because it will leave a film that is difficult to wash off.
7. Completely wash your project again.

Congratulations! You have just completed your first stained glass project. Give yourself some time to gloat with self-satisfied accomplishment, and then move on to the next project, the slightly more challenging H-camed butterfly (see Fig. 5).

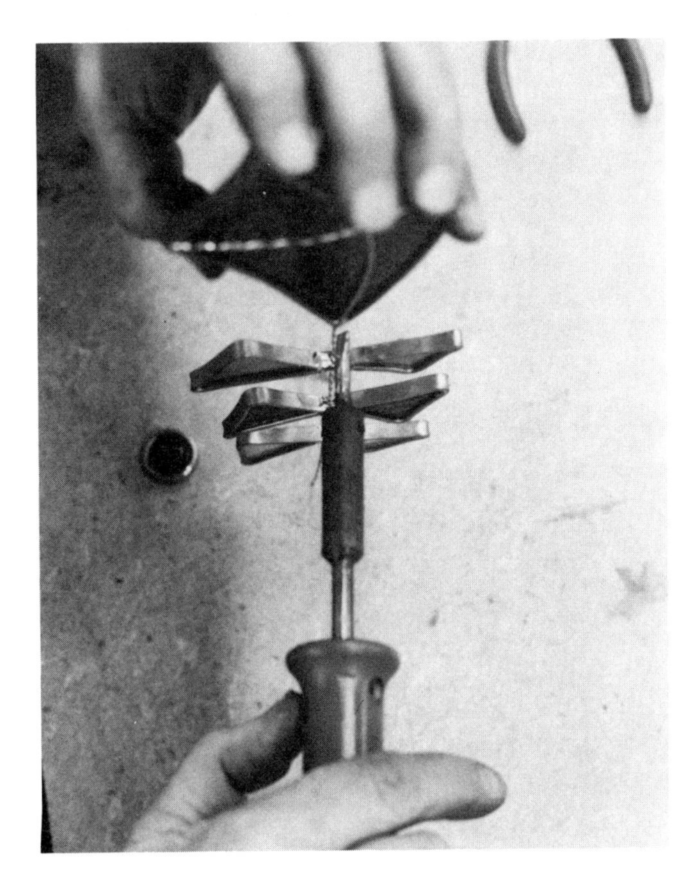

Illustration 2-22

Illustration 2-23

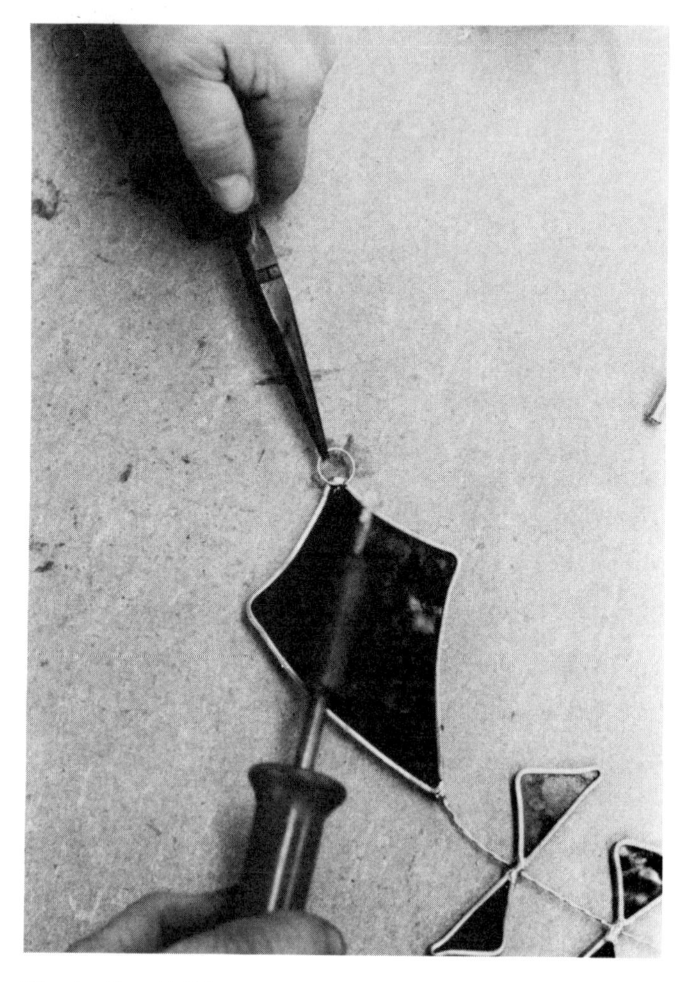

Illustration 2-24

H-Came Method

The reason you will need to use H-came for this side-viewed butterfly is that all the pieces of glass butt each other. H-came is a two-channeled came that accepts one piece of glass on *either* side, not just one side as the U-came does. H-came is generally used internally for all leaded projects and the U is utilized for the exterior edge of projects.

The same tools as those listed on pages 28–30 will be used for this project except for an additional strip of H-came and a roll of masking tape.

So, let's begin.

CUTTING YOUR BUTTERFLY

The important thing to keep in mind when cutting this project is to have the edge of the glass of the lower single wing and the edge of the glass of the upper double wing be

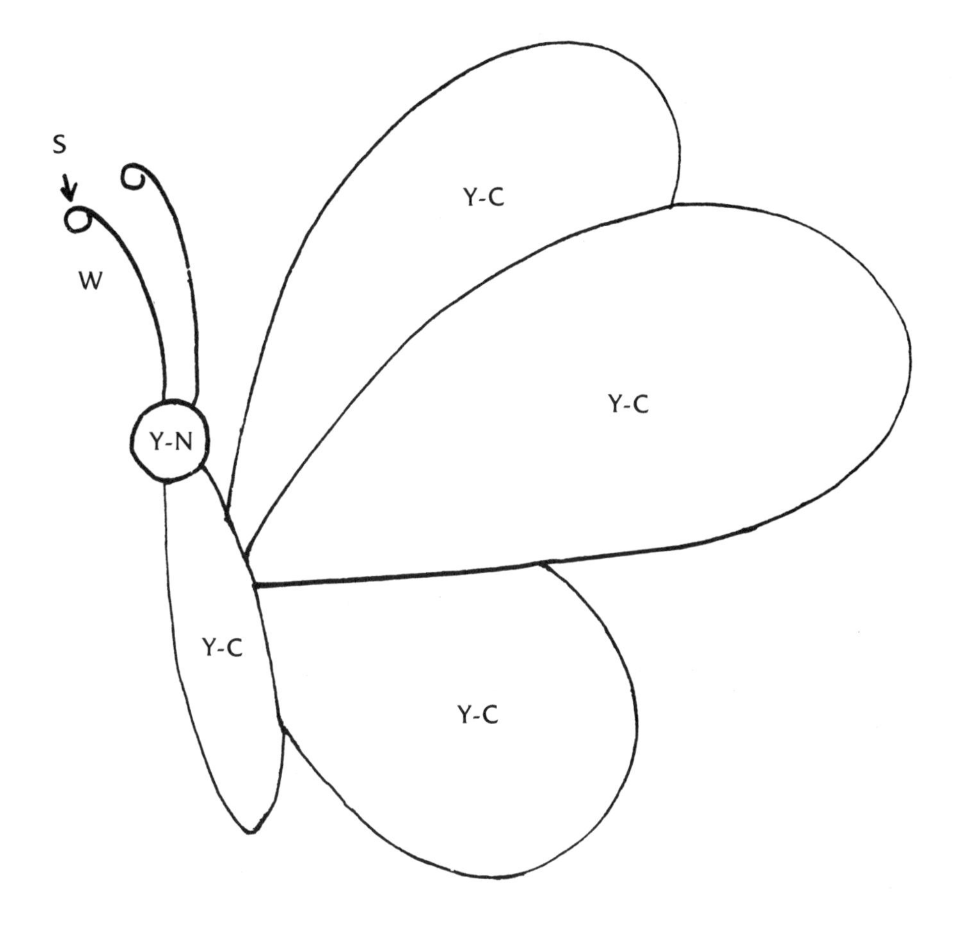

Materials
yellow cathedral (Y-C) glass,
1 8″ x 10″ sheet
1 yellow nugget (Y-N)
1 strip hobby U-came
1 strip hobby H-came
1 lb., 60/40 solder (S)
1 strip wire (W)

Fig. 5

perfectly straight with no visible spaces when they butt. In order to ensure this, trace your pattern on the smooth side of your piece of gold cathedral glass as illustrated (*See* Fig. 6) and proceed as follows:

1. Cut and separate your working glass from the excess glass first (cut #1). (*See* Illustration 2-25.)
2. Separate individual patterns by cutting along dotted lines #2 and #3.
3. Starting with combination pattern #2 and #3, score along the line between 2 and 3. (Also, score your dotted relief line.)
4. Place your cut/run pliers on the glass, ½″ above the X's, and gently squeeze the pliers to run score lines on both ends. Pull glass apart.

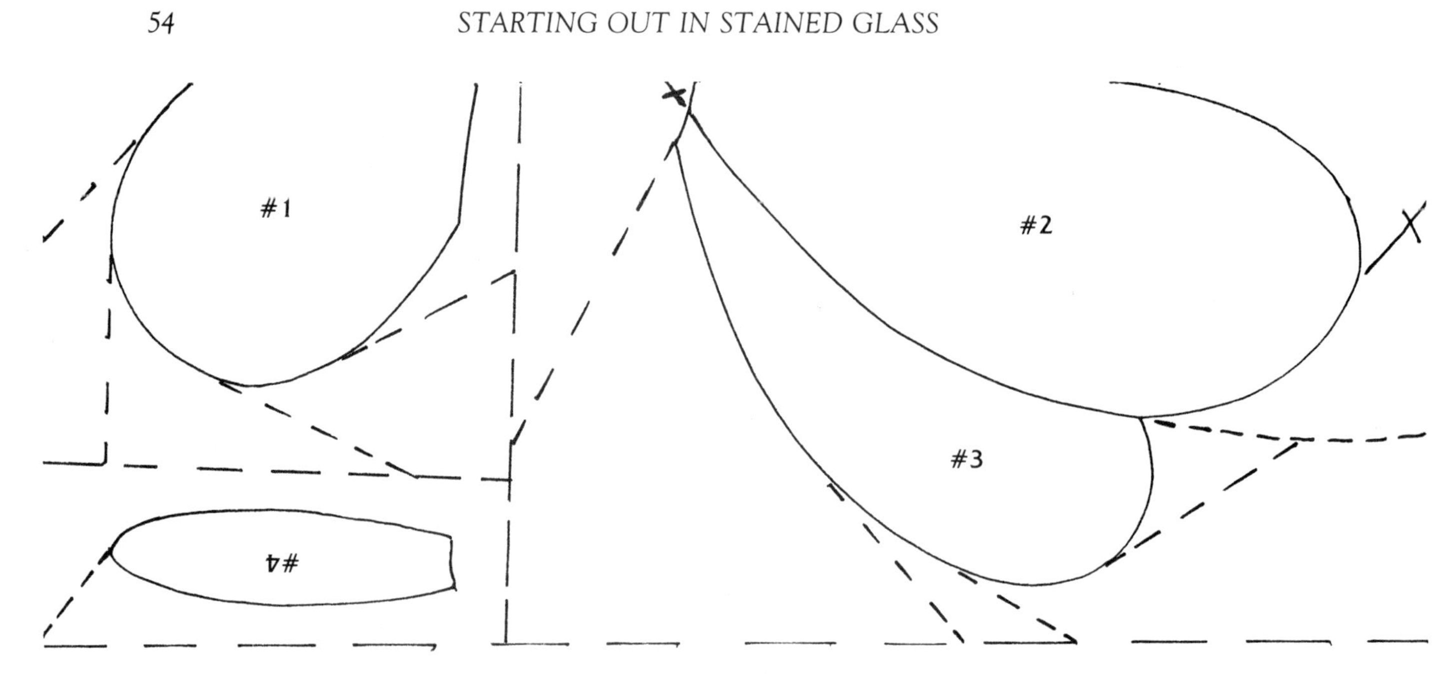

Fig. 6

Illustration 2-25

5. Finish cutting out pattern #2 using your grozing pliers at the smaller end if needed.
6. Place this piece on your master pattern to see if you need to groze away any glass. Do not file or groze the butting edges since they should fit perfectly. *NOTE:* When attempting a project with H-came, your cutting has to be right on the money. Your pieces have to be as exact to the pattern as possible. If you're over the line, mark that point on your glass to aid your filing. If you're under, you'll have to make an adjustment with the butting pieces or recut entirely.
7. When the glass is exact, place it on your master pattern and tape it down as illustrated. (*See* Illustration 2-26.)
8. Cut pattern #3, making relief cuts as necessary. (*See* Illustration 2-27.) (See Chapter 1, p. 21 for a refresher on relief cuts.)
9. Place on master pattern next to #2 to see how it fits. Make adjustments by filing or recutting as necessary and then tape down.
10. For pattern #1, cut the *straight edge first*, continuing right through to the opposite edge of the glass and pull apart. Then score the entire perimeter of the pattern first; then score your dotted relief lines; and using your grozing pliers, separate the "good" piece. Check it with your master pattern, file, and tape it.
11. Cut, file, and tape pattern #1, the body.
12. The butterfly head is merely a glass nugget that requires no cutting. Your pieces, all laid out and taped, should resemble those in Illustration 2-28.

Now, the caming procedure is a little more difficult than with the previous project:

1. Mark your glass pieces at the point where H-came will be placed between two pieces. (*See* Illustration 2-29.) You'll notice that the H-came will only extend to the *outer edge* and *not around it*. U-came will be used on the outer edge to give a more finished look.
2. Stretch your H-came and cut strips to the lengths between two marks.
3. Solder the H-came strips together on both sides (*See* Illustration 2-30) according to the technique outlined on pp. 36–37 using very little solder, carefully avoiding the dripping of solder into the channel. There is only enough room in the groove for the glass; so, if you do drop solder into the channel, you will have to replace that strip.
4. After the H-came is together, take the body (pattern #4) and fit it into the H-came channel.
5. Take a piece of U-came and cut and form a strip around the outer edge of the fitted body and solder one end to the H-came. Hammer the rest of the U-came to fit snugly around the body, even it off, and solder the other end. (*See* Illustration 2-31.)
6. Next *fit* pieces 1, 2, and 3 (the upper wing) into the H-came, butting each other and the body, and squeeze (with your hands) all three pieces tightly together.
7. Cut an approximate length of U-came and solder it to the lower left bottom of the wing (pattern #2). (*See* Illustrations 2-32, -33.)
8. Wrap, fit, hammer U-channel up to the H-came again.
9. Pull back the U-came, glue (since this came will have the hook soldered on and will most likely support the butterfly), replace came, and solder to the H-came. (*See* Illustration 2-34.)

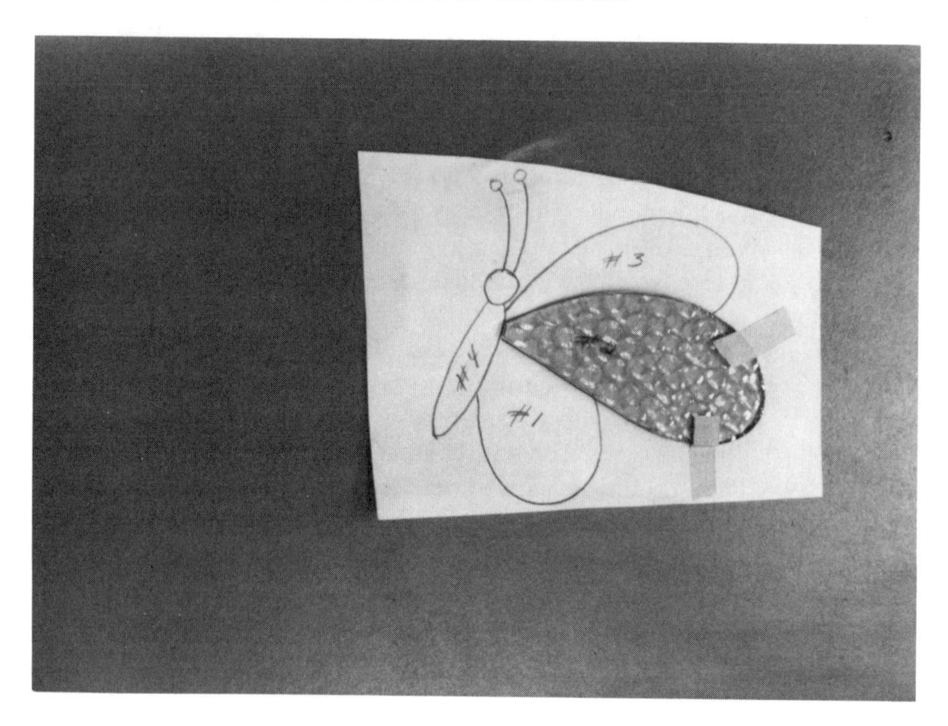

Illustration 2-26

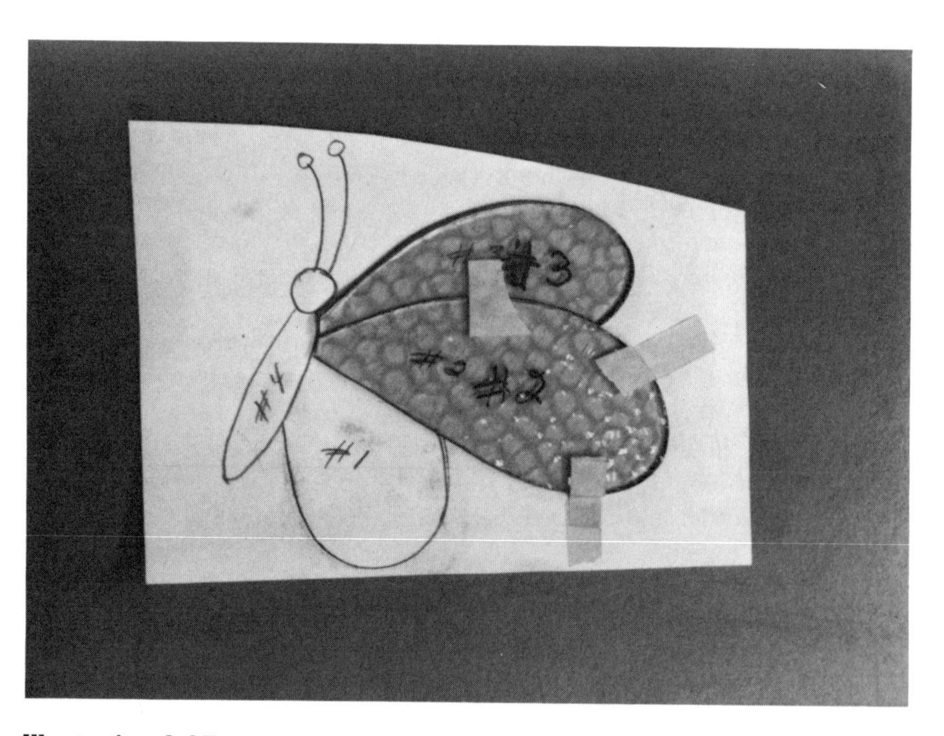

Illustration 2-27

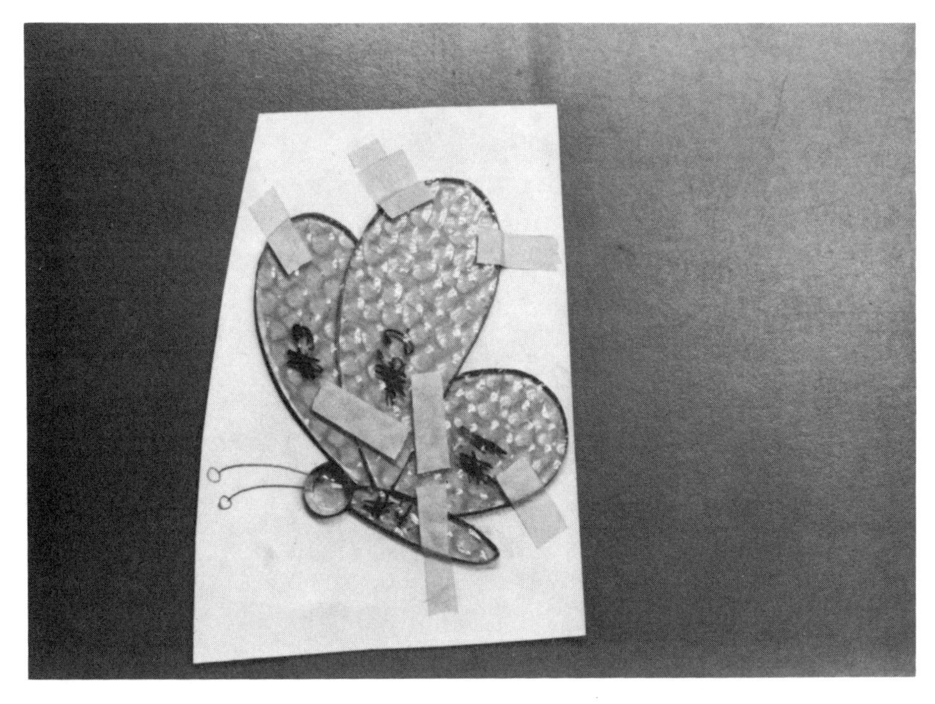

Illustration 2-28

Illustration 2-29

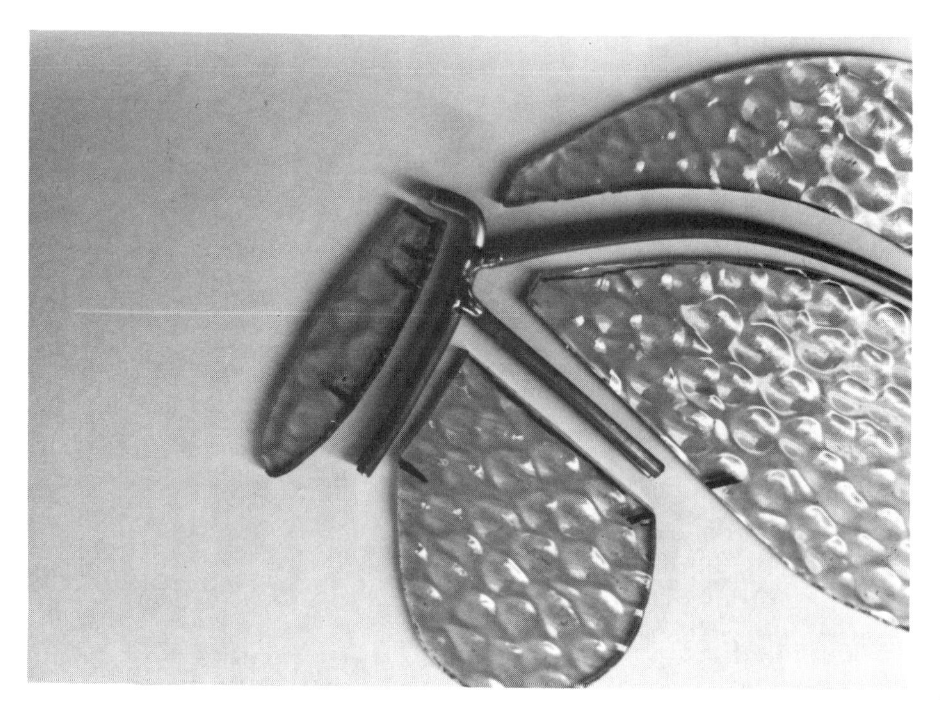

Illustration 2-30

Illustration 2-31

Illustration 2-32

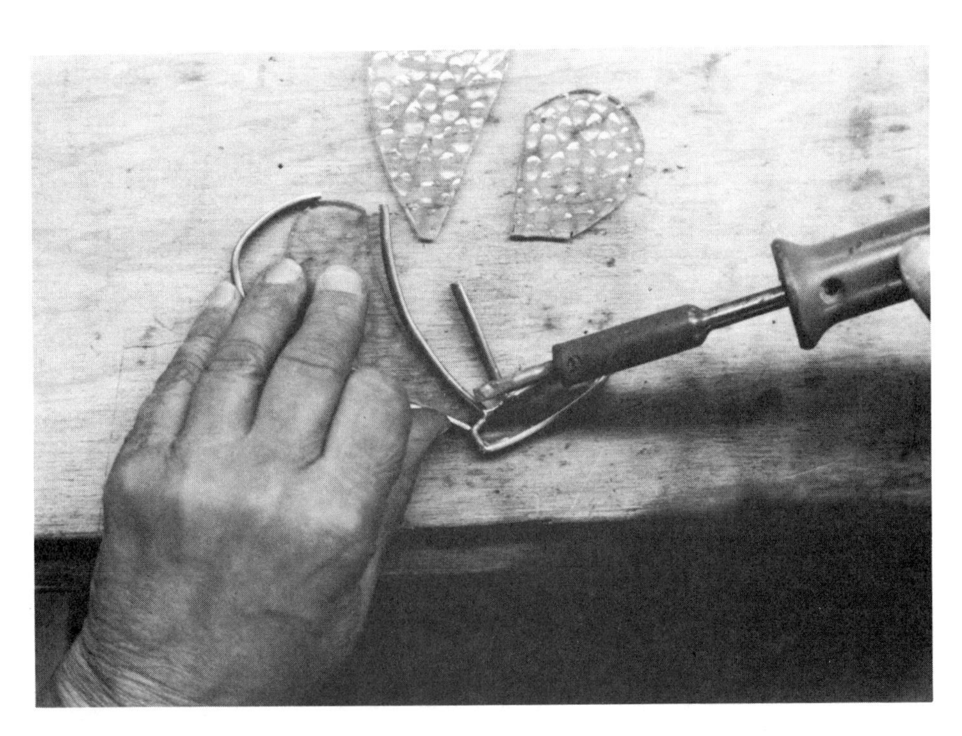

Illustration 2-33

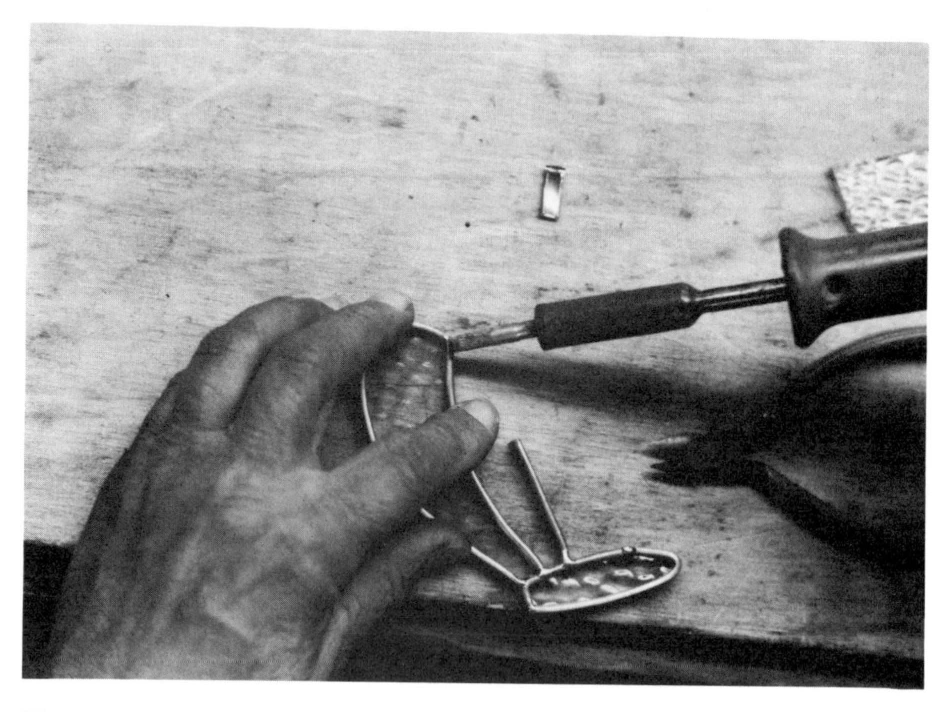

Illustration 2-34

Illustration 2-35

Illustration 2-36

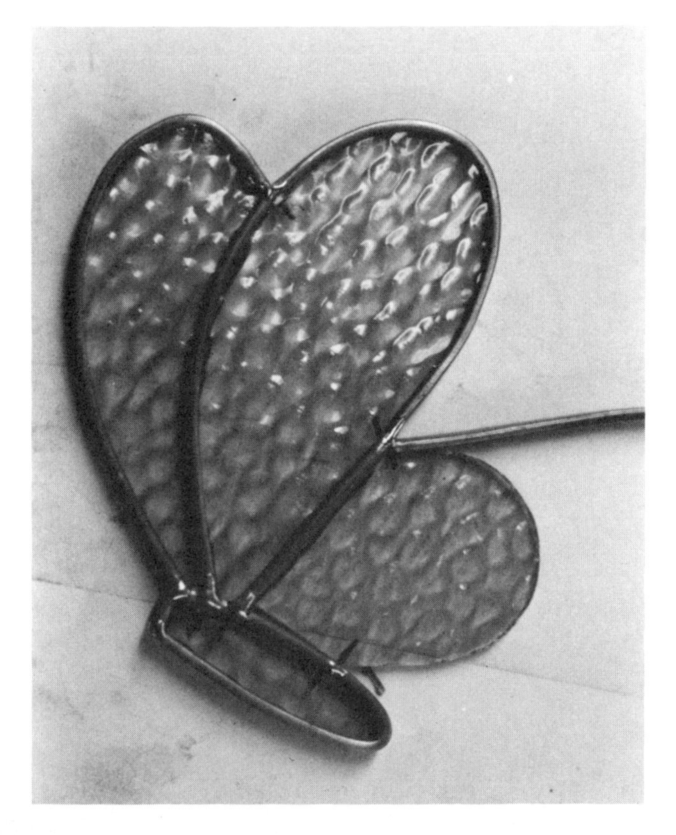

Illustration 2-37

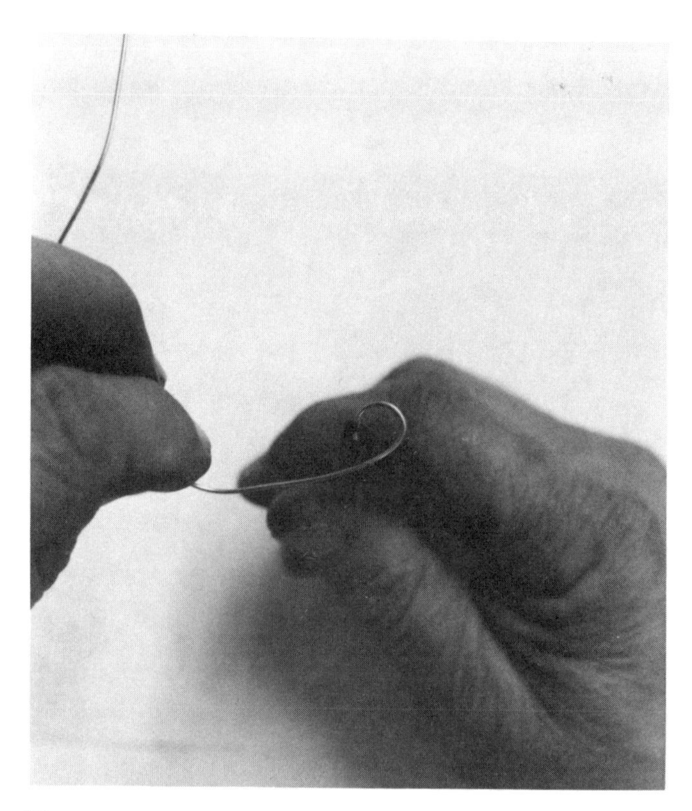

Illustration 2-38

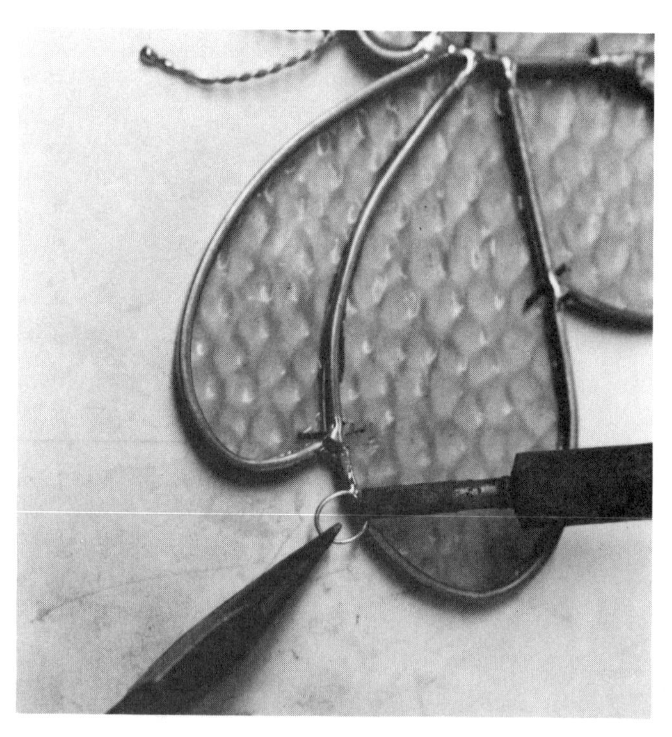

Illustration 2-39

Illustration 2-40

10. Repeat steps 7, 8, and 9 to pattern pieces #3 and #1, soldering first at the top of the previously soldered U/H joint. (*See* Illustrations 2-35 through 2-37.)
11. Wrap your nugget with U-came, but cut out the excess U-came where the body, head, and wings meet. Squeeze the nugget tightly into the body (so that the nugget doesn't rattle) and solder the U- and H-came joints.
12. Finally, twist some wire (as you did for the kite), cut two 1'' strips, drop a bead of solder at each tip, solder each ball-tipped wire to the head for the antennae, and attach a hook as you did for the kite. (*See* Illustrations 2-38 through 2-40.)

Summing Up

These two projects should have given you the fundamentals of the traditional lead came method for assembling stained glass projects. You've probably had a few frustrating moments as you've gone along. Try making one over again now. Much of what we suggest that you do, and the reasons for doing it, will probably make more sense to you this third time around. When you start developing this "stained glass sense" and consciously think about the things you're doing, you'll find that things do indeed get easier.

The next chapter deals with the "newer" copper foil method (developed in the late 1800's) of assembling stained glass projects. Many stained glass artisans find this method more gratifying and more useful for many reasons that we'll mention as we go along. But the method we've introduced in this chapter will have many and varied applications in your stained glass activity for a number of projects, from these basic sun-catchers to large panels and three-dimensional objects.

3

Foiling, Blocking, and Soldering

The second method of fitting and holding pieces of glass together is the copper foil technique. With the development of an adhesive-backed copper foil and wrapping machine, this technique is much less tedious and time consuming today than in LaFarge's and Tiffany's (the originators of the technique) era. It is an extremely supportive and dependable technique for bonding the individual glass pieces together, despite its thin and fragile appearance.

But its great advantage and appeal is in its application for detailed and complexly designed projects involving many small and intricately cut pieces of glass. We generally prefer to use this method for most of our projects because we feel that in most cases it is a superior technique to caming in terms of strength, durability, adaptability to design, and overall finished appearance.

Tools and Materials

You'll need all the tools and materials for foiling as you did for caming (except the came and came stretcher). In addition you'll need the following:

Copper Foil. Copper foil manufactured today has an adhesive backing to it and comes in 36-yard rolls in various strip widths and thicknesses. As a beginner, until your cutting becomes "good", use ¼'' wide, 1½ millimeter thick copper foil. As you become a better and more experienced cutter and craftsperson, you can experiment with 3/16'' or 7/32'' wide foil in order to get a thinner and more delicate bead. However, these copper foil widths leave very little room for cutting errors.

Popsicle stick, pen, or wallpaper seamer. You'll need something to press the copper foil down flat and securely to the glass so it won't pull away from it. We use any of the above; some people use just their fingernails. There are several foil-wrapping machines and a plastic pincher (the "snail" which we use occasionally) which you may decide to purchase and use later. But for now, use any of the above "tools."

Scissors. You'll need these to cut the copper foil off the rolls.

TOOLS AND MATERIALS

Tool/Material	Brand/Description	Source
All the tools listed for soldering on page 19		
Copper foil, 1 roll	¼'' wide, 1½ mil thick	Stained glass supplier
Popsicle stick, wallpaper seamer, or pen		Grocery store/ hardware store
Scissors		
Razor blade	Single edge	
Push pins	One box, ⅝'' leg, steel point, aluminum head	Art store/office supplier
½''-¾'' plywood board	4 square feet	Lumber yard
Foil holder (optional)	Plastic	Stained glass supplier

Razor Blade. Occasionally, you'll need to trim excess foil (especially at the overlap) that will make the solder seam wider and/or uneven. You'll also need it to trim off all the outer-edge foil if you're going to wrap the edge with came, as we shall demonstrate with our cat sun-catcher at the end of this chapter.

One box of Push Pins. For our blocking technique we utilize these push pins to border the foiled pieces of glass to keep them tightly butted and immobile.

½'' Plywood Board. After you've cut and wrapped the pieces of glass, you'll place them on this board and border it with the push pins.

Foil Holder (Optional). Although not really necessary, we find this tool handy for removing the paper backing from the foil and preventing the foil from tangling.

CUTTING OUT THE WATER LILY

Always study the types of cuts that will be necessary for your project *before* you do any actual cutting. Some pieces will need relief cuts, some will require inside or outside curves (we discuss these cutting techniques in Chapter 5), evaluate which cuts can double as a cut for an adjoining piece, and which cuts or pieces should be accomplished first. *Always cut the hardest or most complex first, then proceed to the rest.*

For cutting out the water lily follow the general instructions as outlined in Chapter 2. Always cut out and trace your two working patterns smoothly and accurately, cut the glass, separate it, fit to the master pattern, and tape each piece down to it.

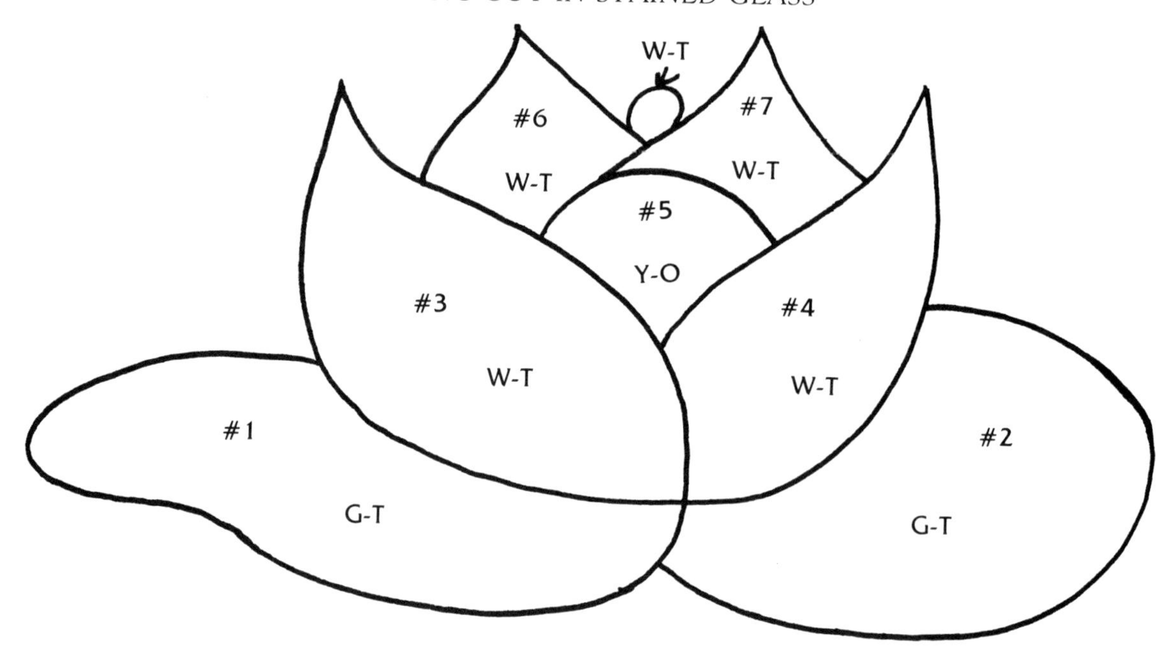

Materials
white translucent opal (W-T) glass
green translucent opal (G-T)glass
yellow opalescent (Y-O) glass
1 roll, ¼″, 1.5-ml copper foil
1 lb. solder, 60/40
1 can flux
1 strip wire (W)

Fig. 7

The two lily pad leaves should be cut first, as indicated (pieces #1 and #2). Follow all your normal cutting techniques (p. 7) and tape to the pattern. (*See* Illustration 3-1.)

Next, the two bottom petals of the white flower (pieces #3 and #4), then the center yellow piece (#5), and last, the top two pointed petals (#6 and #7). (*See* Illustrations 3-2 and 3-3.)

Since this pattern is slightly more difficult to cut and contains more pieces than the previous two patterns, you may have to alter or customize each successive piece in order to fit the pieces together. Of course, the ideal is to cut each piece perfectly and exactly to the pattern. However, except for those who believe their nature to be divine, we are all fallible. If you cut one of the pieces too big you'll have to file down, groze, or make another cut along the pattern line. If you've cut a piece too small, you can adjust the next butting piece by merely placing a white piece of paper *under* the cut piece on your master pattern, retrace a new butting piece, tracing your pencil along the edge that was cut too small, and thereby bringing both pieces back into line to correspond to the master pattern. When you deviate from a pattern in any way, you can always adjust any butting piece using this customizing procedure.

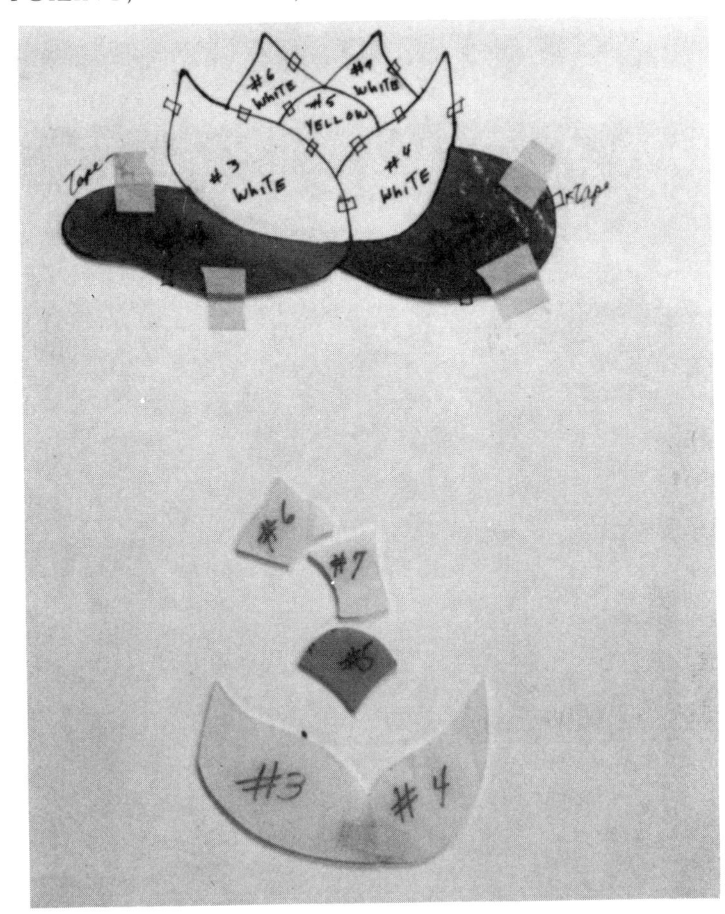

Illustration 3-1

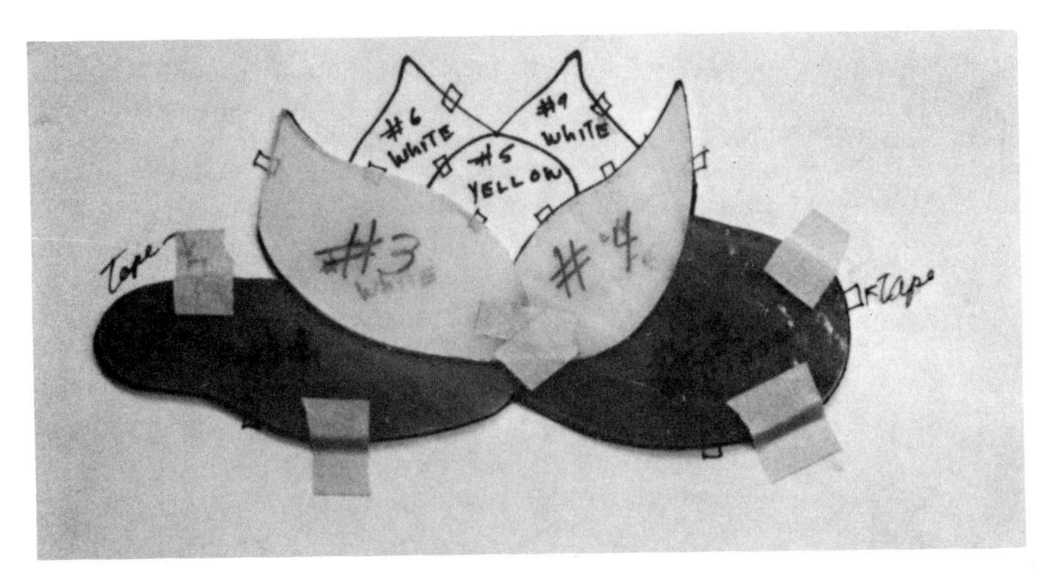

Illustration 3-2

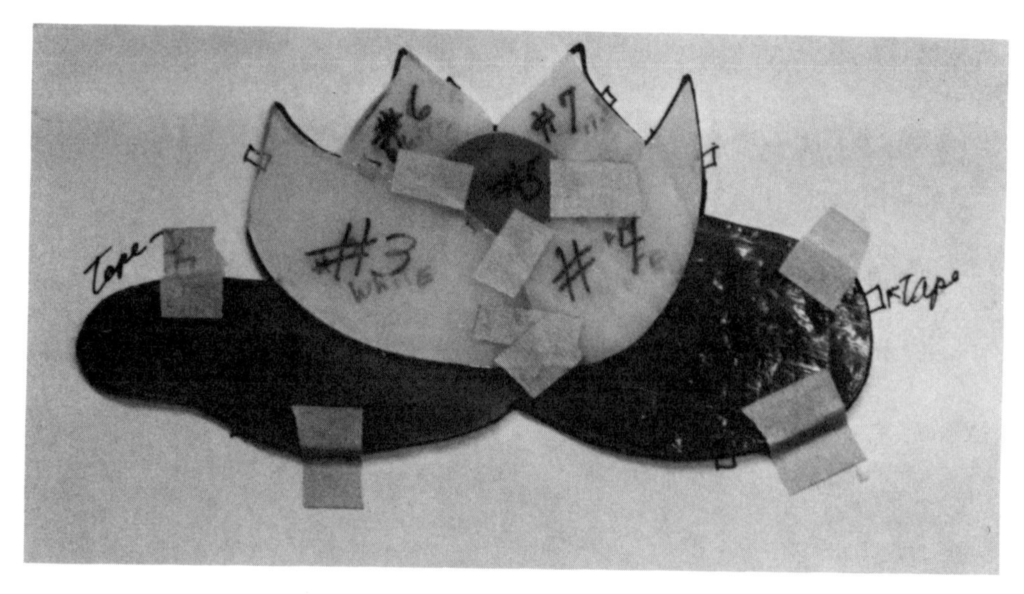

Illustration 3-3

Foiling Techniques

Now you're ready to begin foiling your pieces. Prepare your working surface and glass by going through the first four preparatory steps (pp. 31–33), making especially sure that there is no kerosene from cutting left on the glass (so be sure to thoroughly clean each piece with a cloth).

In addition to the general preparatory steps, you must also prepare the glass for foiling by marking (with your felt-tip marker) your foiling starting point on an *inside butting edge* of each separate piece of glass. This will prevent your beginning to foil on an outside edge. (*See* Illustration 3-4.) If you were to begin and stop on an outside edge, there would be a good chance that the foil (after soldering) would pull away from the glass. You always want to start and stop on an inside edge so that the foil will be soldered over on an inside joint of your project.

After you wipe clean your individual pieces of glass, you should be ready to do the actual foiling: (*See* Illustrations 3-5 through 3-14.)

1. Remove the backing from a small strip of foil.
2. Holding a piece of glass in your dominant hand, evenly line up your foil on the marked point on the edge of the glass, making sure that an equal amount of foil will be on either side of the glass. If it isn't centered in this way, the finished project will have foil seams at the butting edges that vary in width.
3. Begin wrapping the edges of the piece by pinching the foil between your index finger and thumb and over the edge, moving your pinched fingers and folding

Illustration 3-4

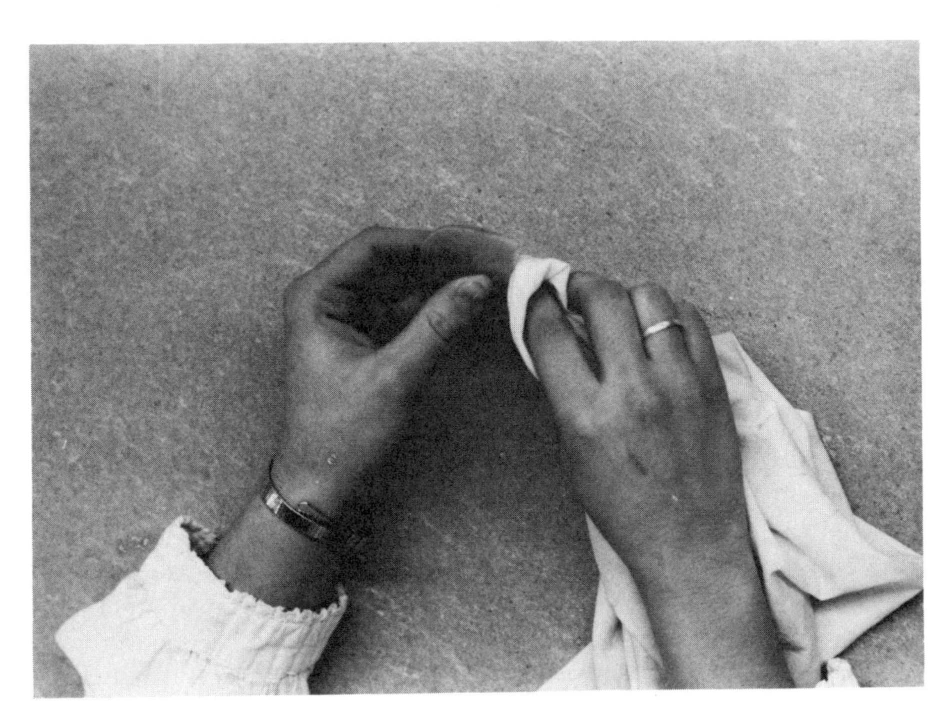

Illustration 3-5

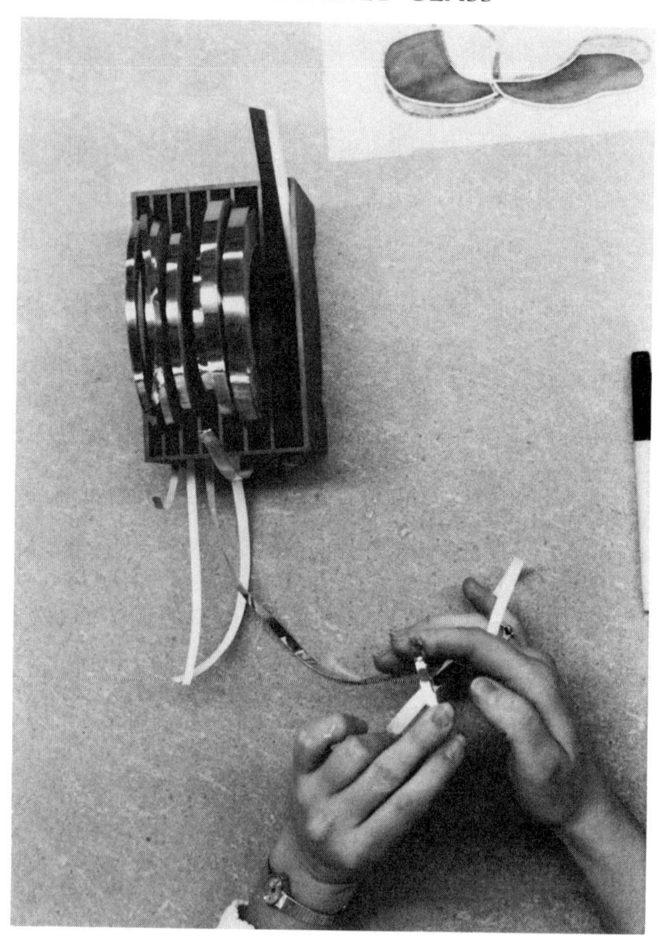

Illustration 3-6

down the foil so that it adheres to each surface (front and back). Wrap the piece completely, overlapping the starting point by ¼''.

Corners are folded down like packages, pressing down one side, then folding down the other side, over the first. This will give you a square wrap rather than a round one.

When you do an inside curve press the foil down *slowly*. This will stretch the foil slightly and avoid splitting the foil.

If the foil does split, solder will not flow over the glass at the split and the bead will not be continuous. If your foil should split, either place another small strip directly on top of the split (to cover it up) or strip all the foil and refoil the entire piece.

4. After completely wrapping the piece, take your Popsicle stick or pen or wallpaper seamer (or fingernail) and firmly flatten down the foil on both sides. This very important procedure will smooth out the foil for soldering and ensure total foil adherence to each individual piece and for the entire project, thereby strengthening the bond between the pieces that soldering will accomplish. We've seen too many projects break down and pieces of glass pull away from each other because this step was skipped or sloppily done.

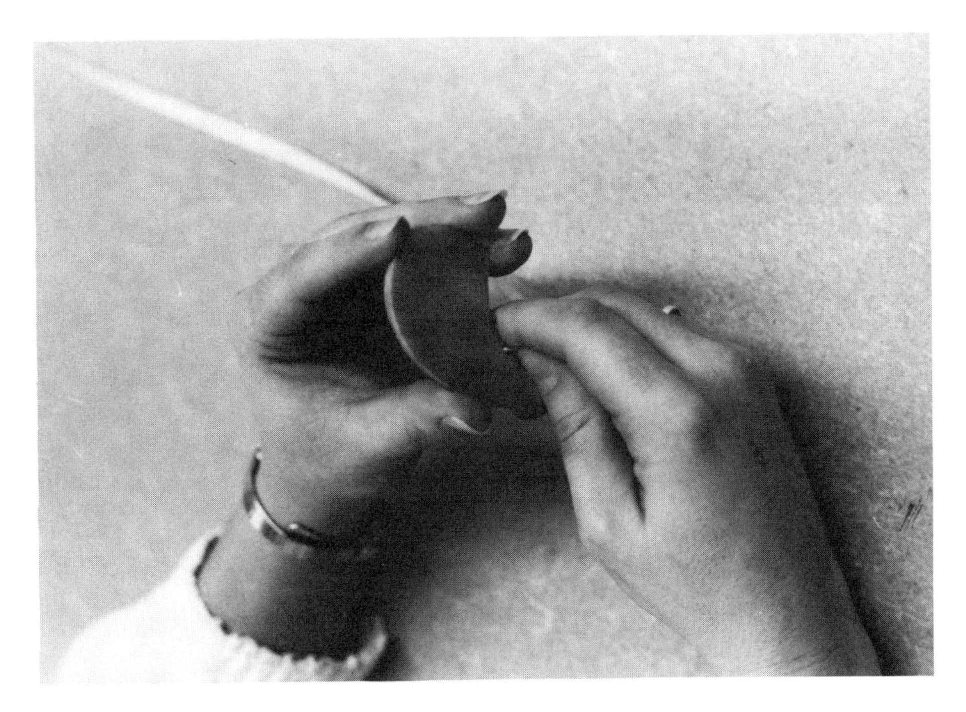

Illustration 3-7

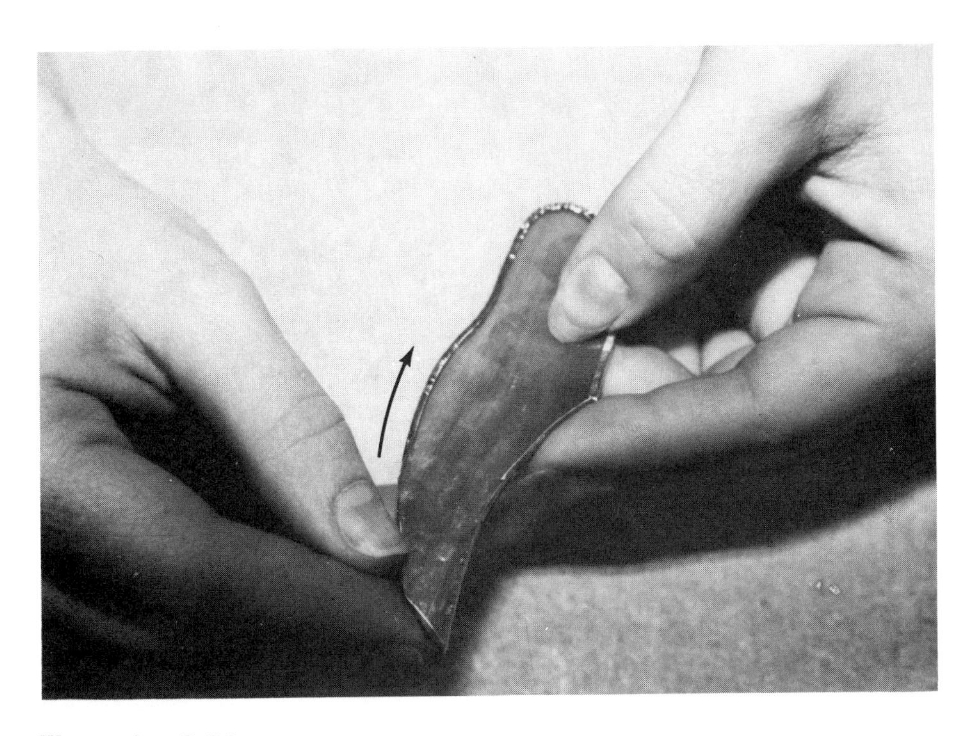

Illustration 3-8A

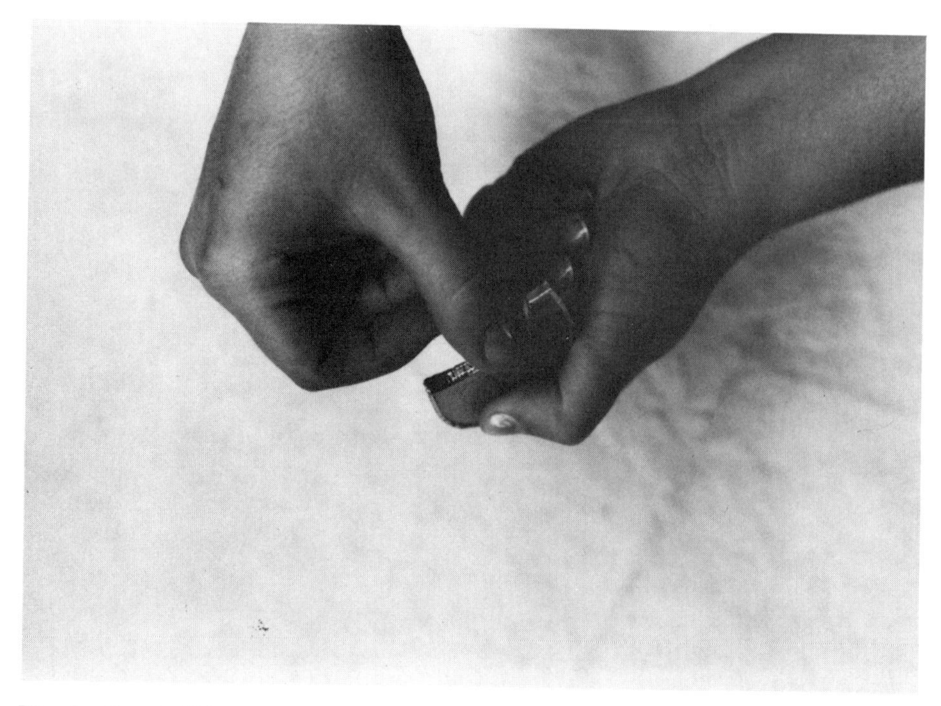

Illustration 3-8B

Illustration 3-8C

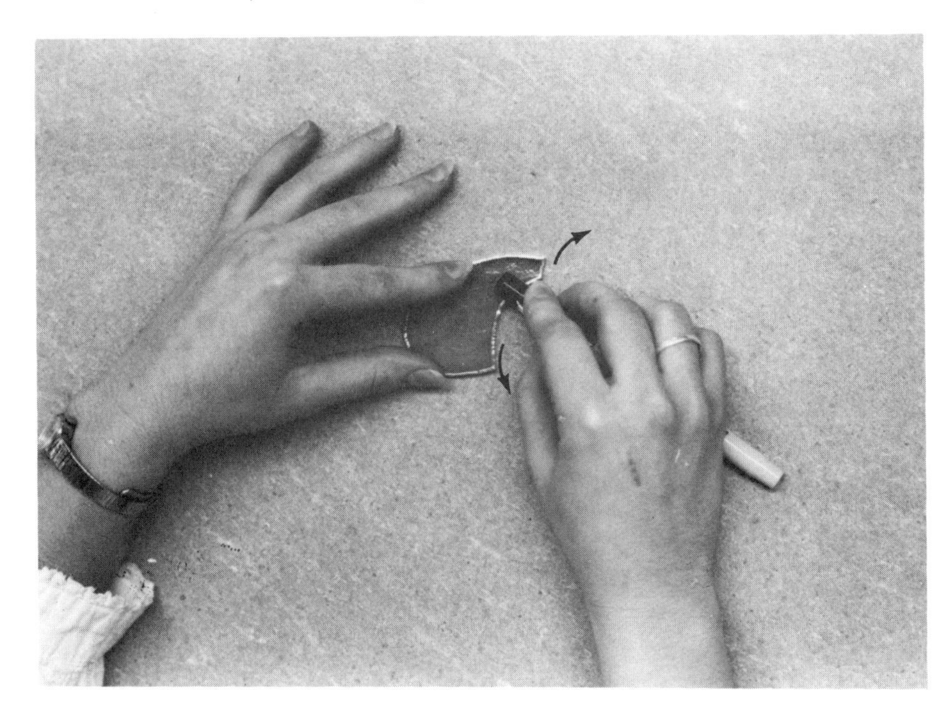

Illustration 3-9

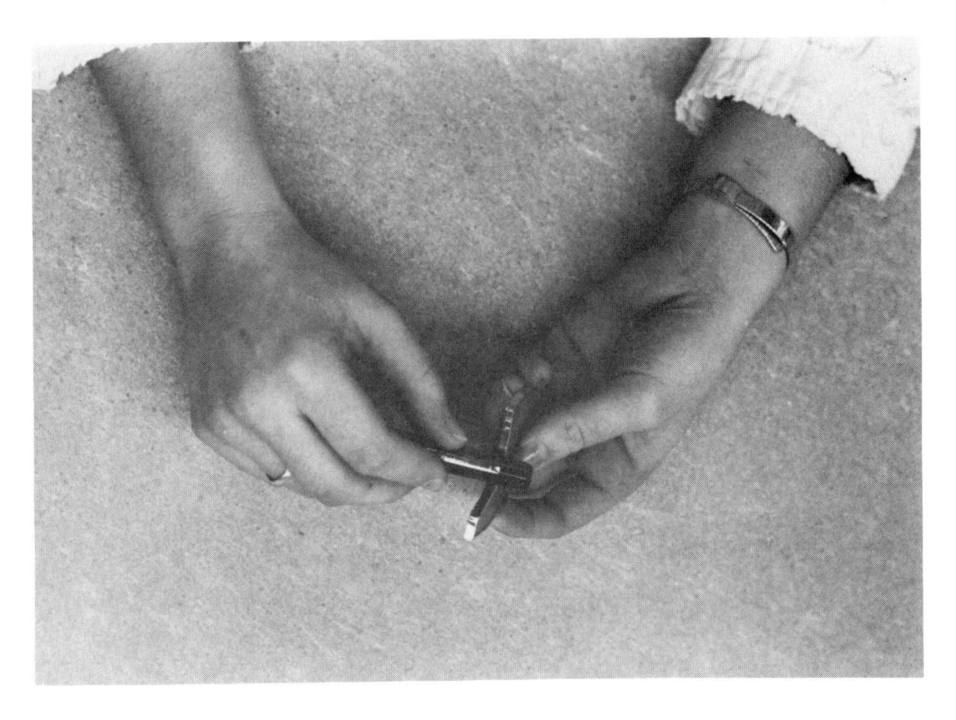

Illustration 3-10

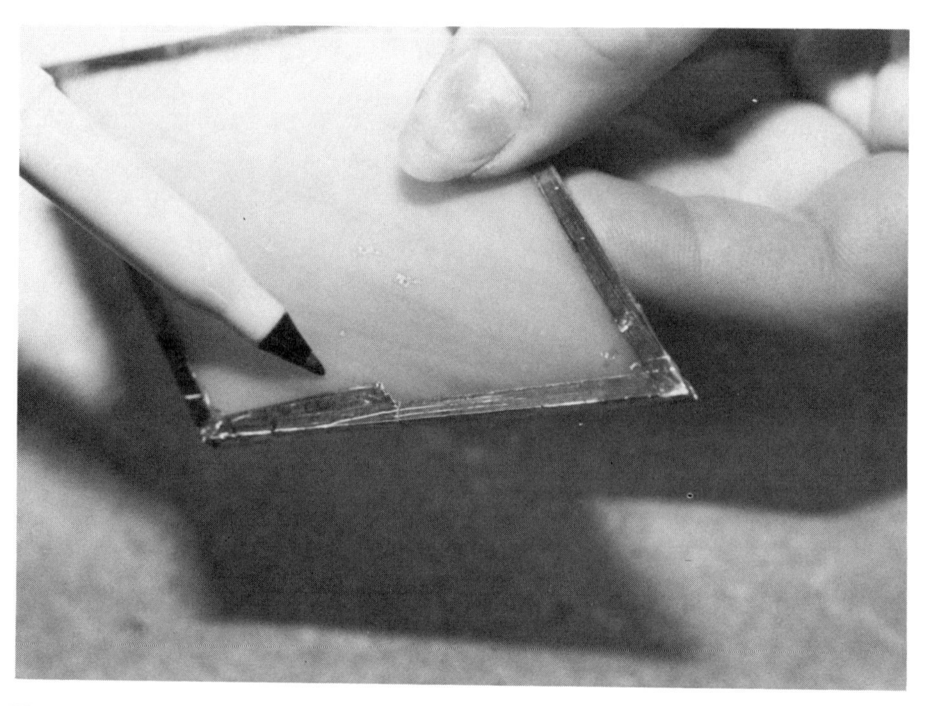

Illustration 3-11

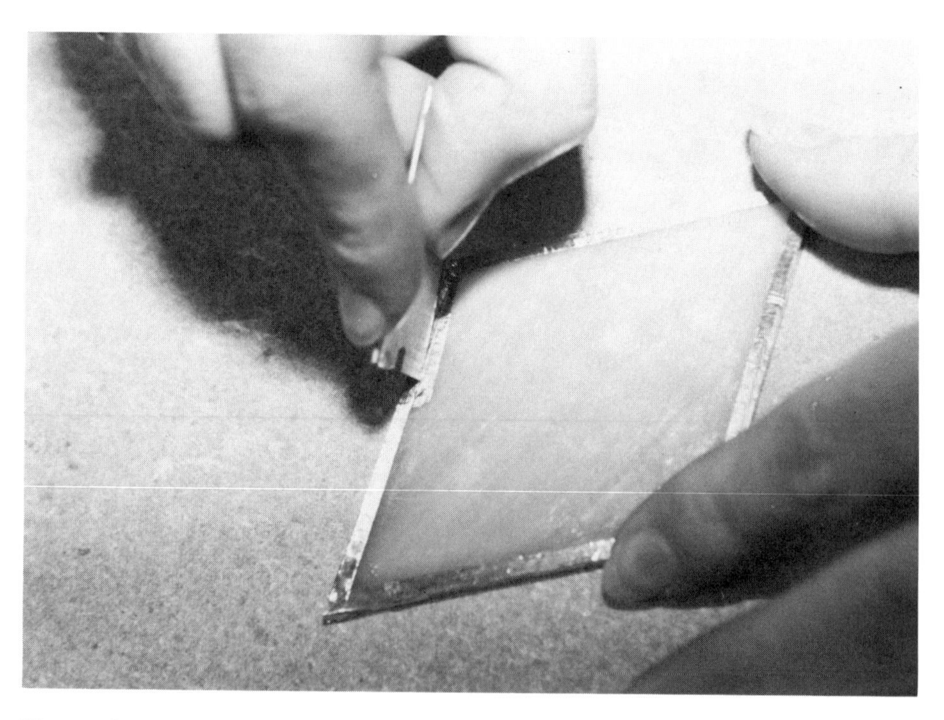

Illustration 3-12

Illustration 3-13

Illustration 3-14

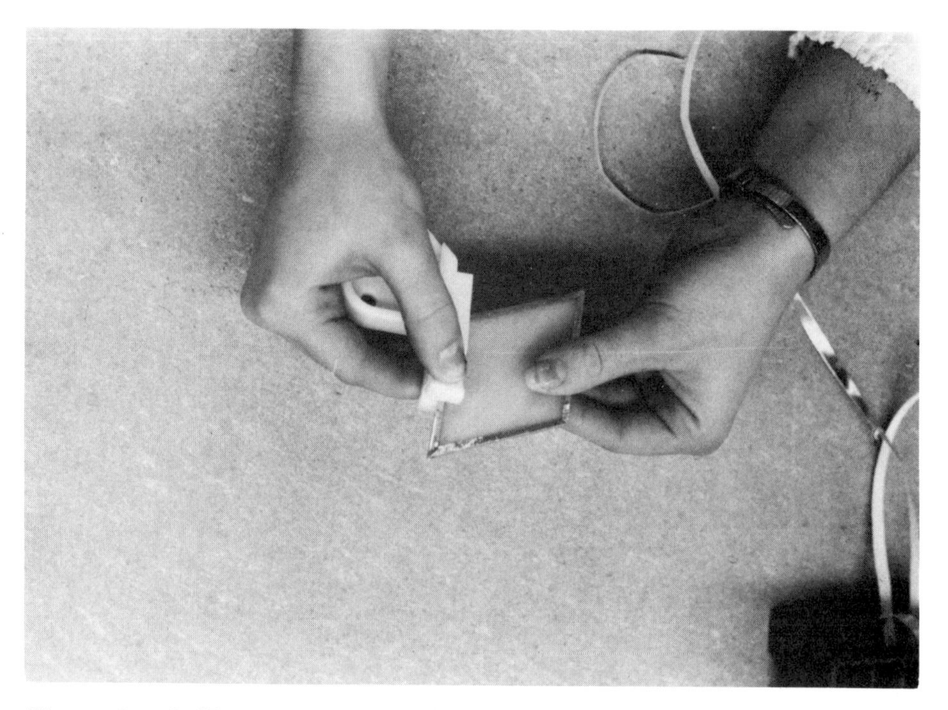

Illustration 3-15

5. When the pressing-down procedure is finished, check to see if there is any excess foil running over or exceeding the normal foil band (this especially happens at your overlap). Take your razor blade and remove any excess foil so that the seam will be the same width all the way around.
6. When the piece of glass is wrapped and foil pressed down, replace it in its position on the "good" or master pattern with the unwrapped pieces.
7. Repeat steps 1 through 6 with every single piece. After every piece is wrapped, the project is ready for soldering.
   NOTE: Never leave foiled pieces of glass around for any length of time without soldering them. The copper will tarnish and not accept the solder. If this should happen, use some extra fine steel wool or copper cleaner and wipe the copper clean.

There are various new wrapping tools and machines you can purchase from stained glass dealers that might make foiling and pressing down much easier. We use "the snail" (*See* Illustration 3-15) quite a bit and find it very useful, especially for pieces that have straight edges, e.g., rectangles, and it's relatively inexpensive. Other machines are generally much more expensive but could be extremely useful and time saving (which is a factor for justifying cost) when doing projects with many pieces (fifty or more), e.g., lampshades and panels. They could help those of us who find foiling boring to make it through this stage with less tedium. At any rate, as you develop your skills and do more complicated projects, you might consider purchasing one, although at this stage you do not need one.

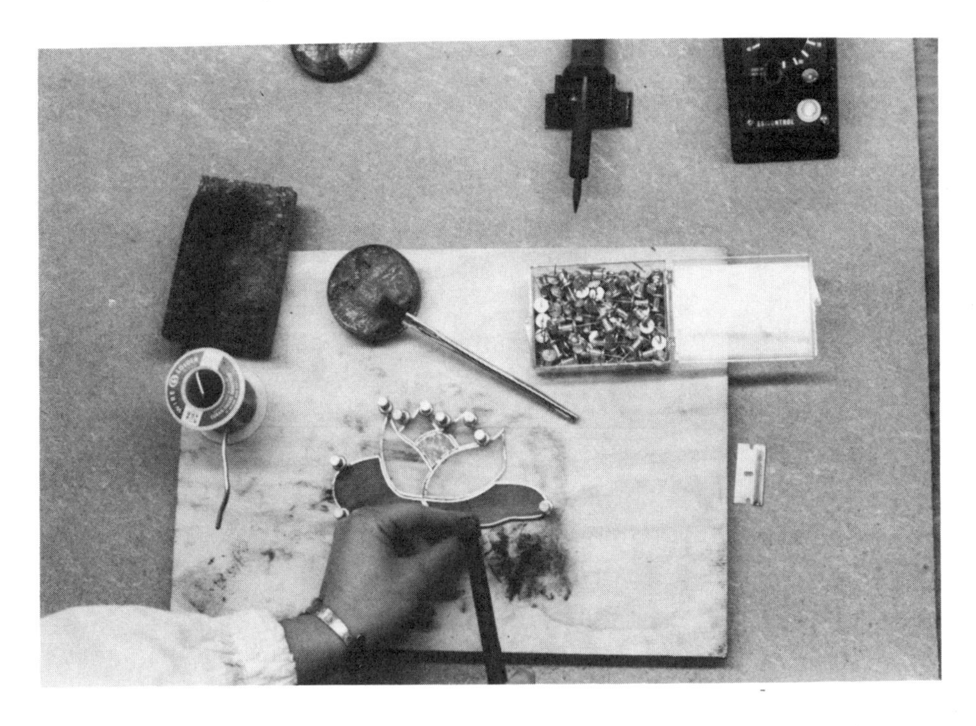

Illustration 3-16

Blocking and Soldering

To prepare and secure the unstationary individual pieces of glass for soldering we "block" our foiled sun-catchers by using push pins. This method not only prevents the pieces from moving, but ensures a tight butting which contributes to the roundness of the solder seams.

This is where you will need your plywood board. Put your lily on the board and proceed as follows:

1. Put your first push pin at the top, butting against the side of a project piece. Tap the pin into the board.
2. Place another pin an inch or so away from the first, butting it against another piece.
3. Continue all around the lily, pushing *and* then butting pieces together against the push pins. (*See* Illustration 3-16.)

You'll find this a handy technique for preparing the project for soldering, especially for projects with many more pieces than the lily.

Now the crucial soldering. Soldering techniques for foil are much different than the ones outlined for caming in Chapter 2. The goal is to make a round, even bead of solder on top of the copper foil seams in order to join the pieces together. It is in the finished solder bead that the precise workmanship of the previous tracing, cutting, customizing,

Illustration 3-17

and wrapping steps is reflected. Although the technique of creating a smoothly rounded solder bead is an art in itself and requires a great deal of coordination and patience, you won't have a chance of accomplishing this unless you've cut your glass as accurately as possible. As in our other processes, the success of soldering depends upon that first pyramidal fulcrum block: glass cutting.

Get your soldering tools together and proceed in the following manner: (*See* Illustrations 3-17 through 3-23.)

1. Since, in order to create good soldering beads, you need much more heat than for caming, set your control box at the extreme limit for your iron.
2. When your iron is ready, generously flux all the copper foil. As stated previously in Chapter 2, the flux allows the solder to adhere to the foil and flow smoothly.
3. Take the iron in your dominant hand, and the spool of solder with about an 8″ length of solder in the other. Always working with the iron *ahead* of the solder, place the flat part of the soldering tip very lightly on the copper foil, and slowly and lightly feeding the solder to the iron tip, run both the iron and solder along the seam, both hands moving in unison.
4. Continue applying the solder until you are about ½″ from the edge of the seam, then take away the solder, and continue off the edge with just your iron. This stopping will prevent "globs" of solder overhanging the edge.
5. Solder all the seams on one side.
6. Remove the push pins and solder all the foiled seams on the reverse side and the perimeter edges.

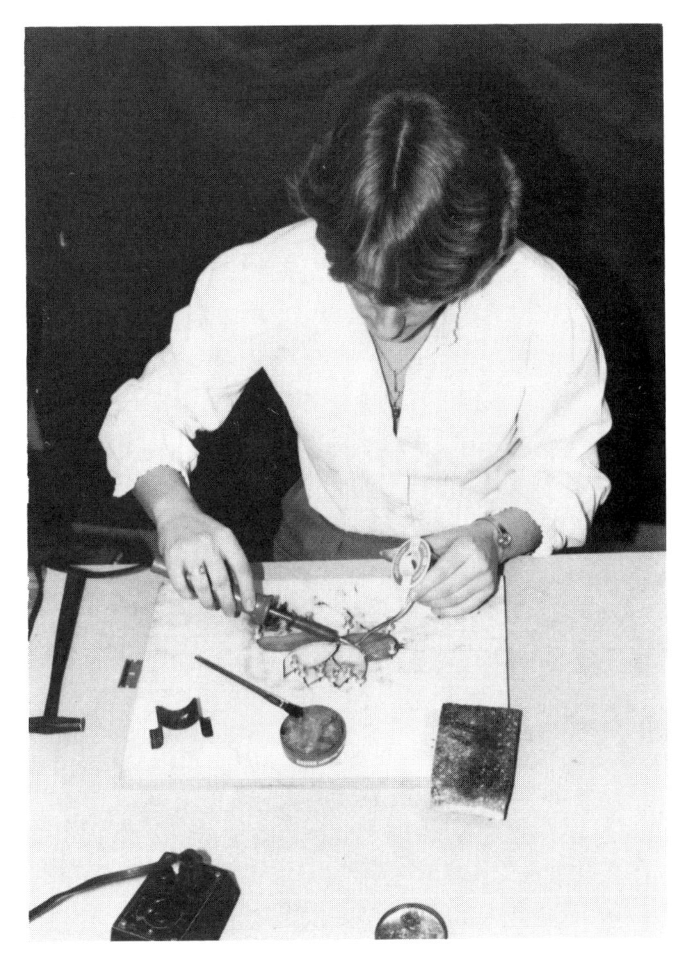

Illustration 3-18

7. Smooth out and round off the soldered seams by slowly drawing your iron over the soldered seam. Do not, however, do this more than two or three times. *NOTE:* When soldering over a "crossroads" section where two seams crisscross, stop and heat area for a few seconds longer and then continue on through.

The goal when soldering is, of course, to have everything go properly and have perfectly rounded and smooth seams. If things are not going quite right, consult the following troubleshooting list for correcting some of the common problems and undesirable soldering results:

a. If there is a section of your soldered seam with a wrinkle in it, take the corner of the soldering tip and place it on the crinkle for a few seconds and pull it out slowly. Put a dab of extra flux on the wrinkle to facilitate the smooth flow. Or, after the solder has cooled and has been cleaned, you can rub the solder wrinkle with fine steel wool until the wrinkle magically disappears.

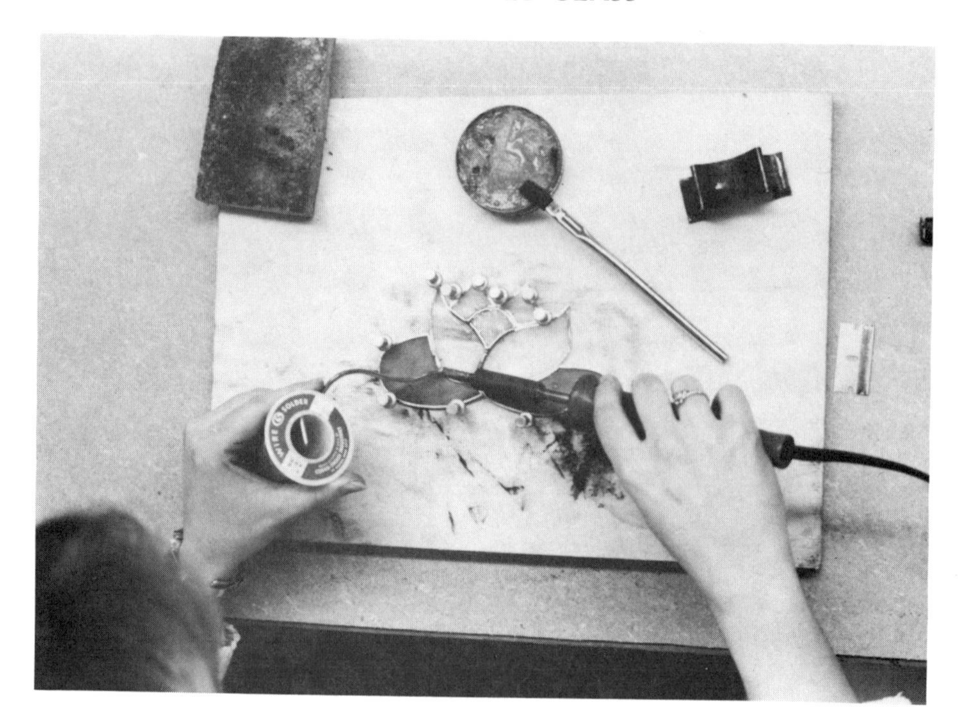

Illustration 3-19

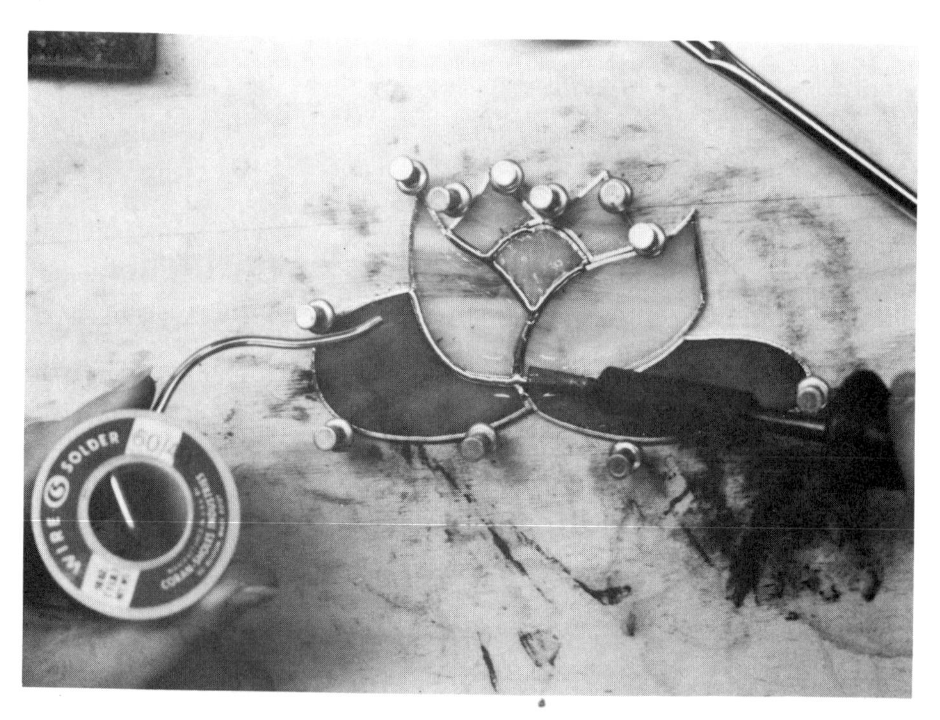

Illustration 3-20

Illustration 3-21

b. If you have a "glob" of solder in any one area, place the soldering iron tip on the glob, heat and drag or pull the excess solder to the outside of the seam quickly and shake the excess solder off onto the board by slightly lifting the entire piece allowing gravity to help you. You might have to repeat this before the bead smoothes out evenly.
c. If your bead contains a lot of pit holes, turn down your control box, wipe off the dirty flux, add new flux, and go over the area with some new solder.
d. If there is only one small area of your seam with a problem, take the tip of the iron, heat the area, and slowly pull away straight up in a "dabbing" manner.
e. If your solder falls through a crack and will not form a bead, it's generally because of one of two reasons: (1) either your iron is too hot, or (2) you have too large a space between your butting pieces of glass. To correct the problem, let the seam cool, turn down your control box, and add new solder. Then, reverse the project and remove the excess solder that fell through. Or, if it's impossible to recut one of the pieces of glass, you can place a narrow piece of copper foil, folded in half with the sticky part in, in the gap and solder over it. You may also place a small piece of copper wire in the gap, flux, and solder over.

• Soldering, like all stained glass activities, cannot be rushed. Patience and a desire for a perfect round seam are necessary personal virtues that are good prerequisites for this activity. It's a part of stained glass craftsmanship that is not easily learned; but with a certain amount of perseverance and fortitude and the proper instruction, you can become a competent solderer.

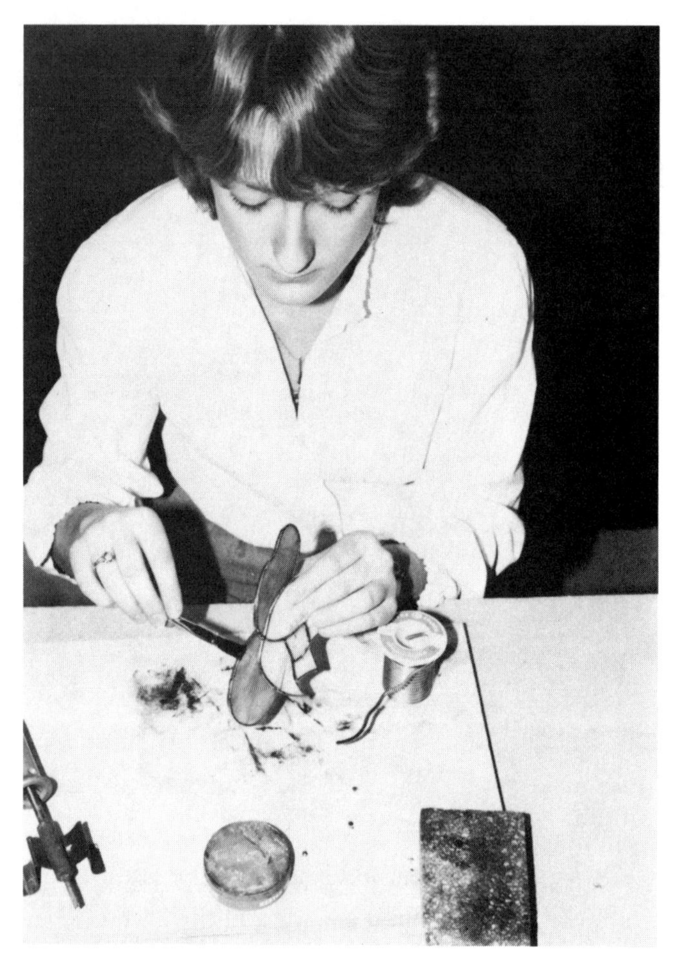

Illustration 3-22

• There's also a certain coordinated interaction and grace of motion needed between your hands, arms and shoulders and this generally takes a good deal of practice. To encourage the development of this coordinated skill, you should sit on a high stool when soldering; this will give you better leverage and help prevent your becoming tired.

• When soldering any project, use gravity to your advantage.* Always keep your project level unless you're trying to draw solder off (in that case, you'd turn your project on end to allow gravity to pull the solder down).

• Never flux your copper foil and leave without soldering the seam. When you come back to your project after a while, the flux and air will corrode the foil and the solder will not adhere to it.

• Pit holes in your bead are caused by dirty flux and too hot an iron. Turn down your iron and avoid using the dirty flux; scoop it out of the tin and use the clean portion. Also, frequently clean your tip on a damp sponge.

* We delve into this topic in much greater detail in our companion book *Challenging Projects in Stained Glass*, in our chapter on Lampshade Construction.

Illustration 3-23

REMEMBER: Copper foil soldering is a delicate, time-absorbing operation. All your painstaking work, from design through cutting and wrapping, will be diminished in quality if your soldering bead reflects sloppy workmanship. The itch to finish a project (especially a long and time-consuming one) should not be relieved at this crucial final stage by rushed or half-hearted soldering. Believe us, the self-satisfaction of a professionally finished bead-work will be well worth any sacrifice in regard to time and effort.

Finishing Techniques

Many people prefer the copper foil method because of the variety of "finishes" that can be applied with patinas to the soldered seams. The method for cleaning and applying the patina has already been outlined in Chapter 2, pp. 46 and 50. However, it is in the variety of shades that you can achieve with individually mixed solutions that gives the copper foil method its eye appeal.

You can buy bottled, premixed solutions (we recommend Allnova ® products) that will turn the soldered seams a variety of beautiful gray or copper shades. Also, some people prefer to mix their own solutions with copper sulphate crystals. Copper sulphate can be purchased at most stained glass supply houses, chemical supply houses, and even some hardware stores. If the crystals are large, we pulverize them into a powder that will mix more readily with water.

It takes some experimentation to find the best recipe of copper sulphate and water that will produce the right shade for you. Start with some scrap pieces of glass, wrapped with foil. Mix eight ounces of hot water with one tablespoon of copper sulphate powder and apply it to the soldered seams. If the copper shade is too light or not dense enough, add a tablespoon of copper sulphate and apply it to another soldered seam. The higher the concentrate of copper sulphate, the darker and denser the shade will be. Also, the more applications, the darker the shade will become.

After copper sulphating your entire project, and washing it again, you can apply polish. A German polish, Simichrome, does the best job. It is a tube of paste that can be bought at a clock shop, motorcycle, or automotive supply house. It will also brighten up your lead came. We've also found Twinkle®, Brasso®, and Glass Wax® (which also polishes your glass) turns your solder different shades with varying glosses. You should also repolish when you notice the copper tarnishing.

As with lead came, the patina process is *not* irreversible. If for some reason you don't like the finish, you can steel-wool your seams, wipe clean, solder again if necessary, and reapply your patina in different amounts to achieve the desired finish.

Of course, one very obvious alternative is not being mentioned here: You do not necessarily have to patina or polish your soldered seams. Some people prefer the au naturel silvery bright shine of the solder that can be enhanced with steel wool and polished. Some people prefer not to polish their patined solder, feeling that the unpolished copper lends a more "antiquish" appearance that belies its recent construction. The point is that personal taste best determines this final stage of finishing.

Combination Technique/Project

As a finishing sun-catcher project, which combines both fitting methods, we've provided a contentedly curled-up cat. (See Fig. 8.) You'll be copper-foiling the entire cat but lead-caming the outer edge.

It's a tricky little feline to cut out and we'd advise your practicing some difficult cutting (and reading Chapter 5) before attempting it. But, it's a challenging project that combines all the skills and steps involved in stained glass.

So, if you're confidently secure in your glass cutting skills, and willing to apply what you've learned so far with a minimum of direction (but don't be too proud to look back to our referrals) approach the cat in the following manner (*see* Illustrations 3-24 through 3-27):

1. Cut out all your pieces and fit and tape them according to the procedures outlined in this chapter.
2. Wrap with foil and block the entire cat.
3. *Except for the outer edges*, solder the cat on both sides, stopping your bead approximately ¼″ from the edge.

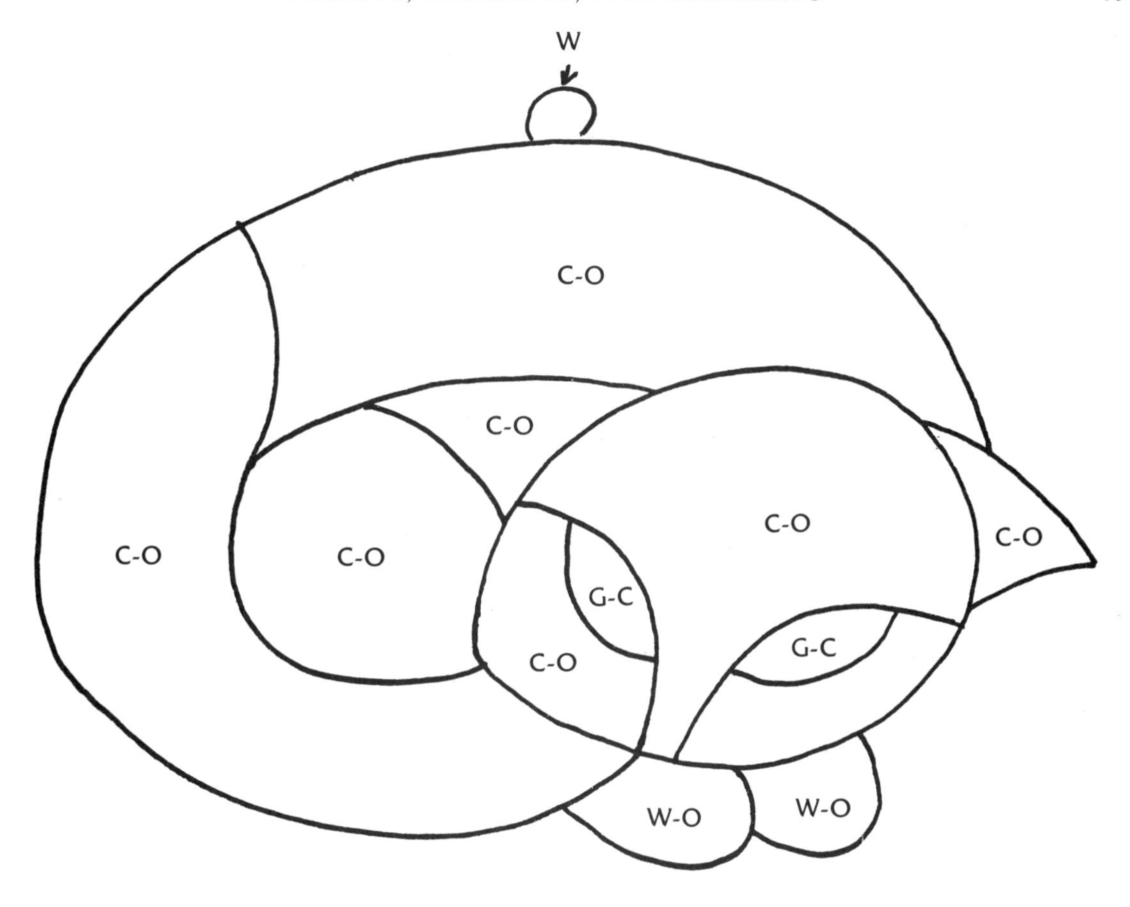

Materials
caramel opalescent (C-O)glass
white opalescent (W-O) glass
green cathedral (G-C) glass
1 roll, ¼″, 1.5-ml copper foil
1 lb. solder, 60/40
1 strip hobby U-came
1 can flux
1 strip wire (W)

Fig. 8

4. With a razor blade, scrape off the foil around the outer edges.
5. Take a strip of U-came and wrap it around the cat, tapping the lead to conform to the glass, mitering the two end points as usual (p. 35). If a bead of solder from one of your soldered seams impedes the glass edge from fitting into the lead groove, you'll have to draw the solder off so that the glass does indeed fit snugly.

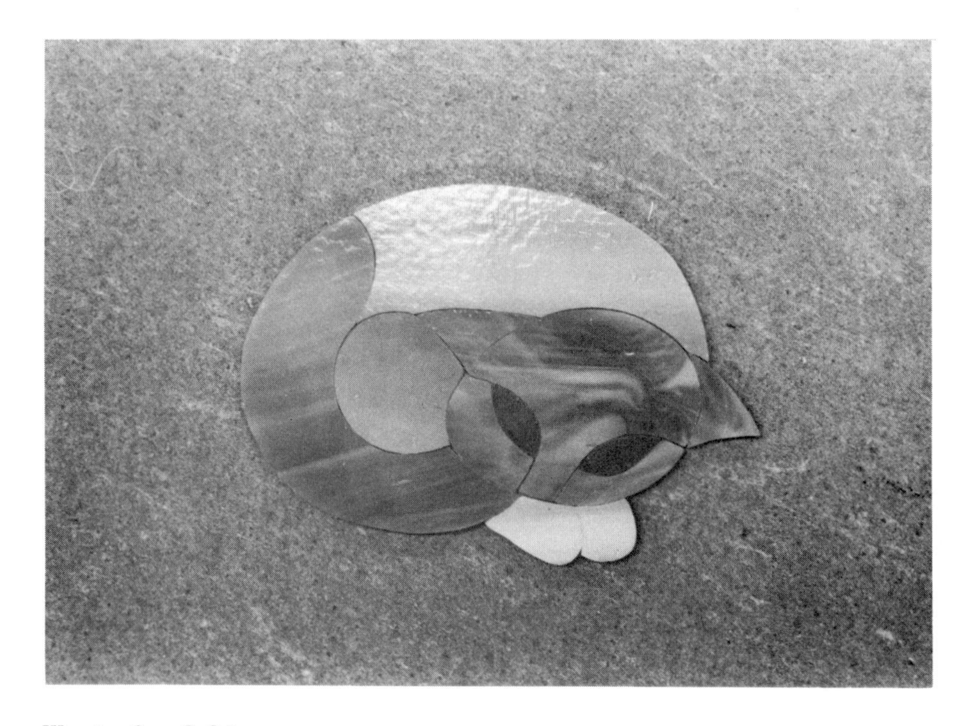

Illustration 3-24

Illustration 3-25

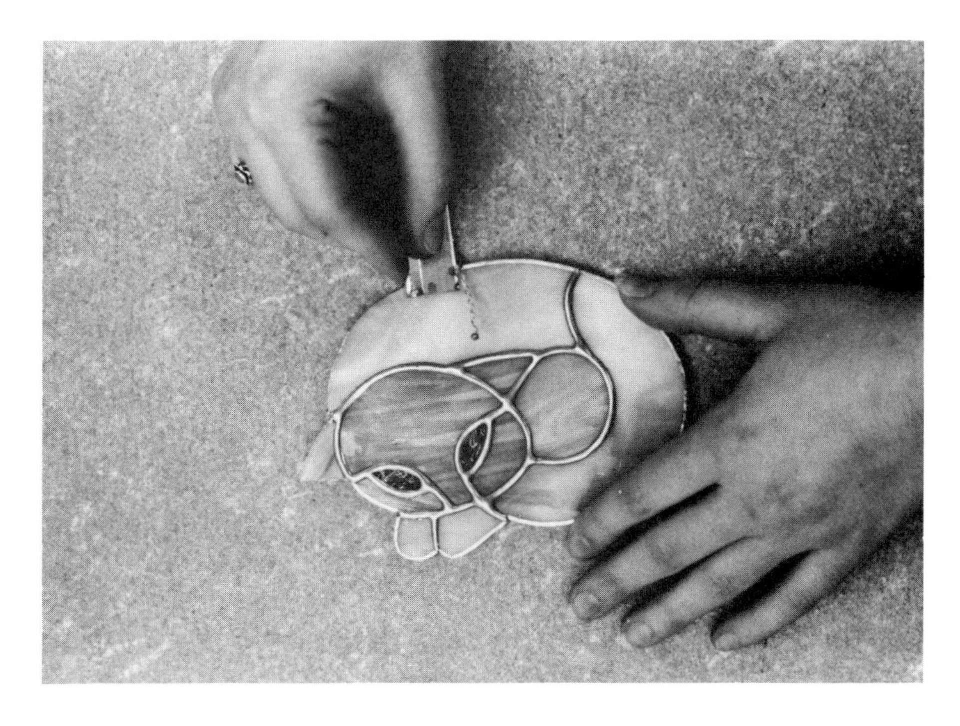

Illustration 3-26

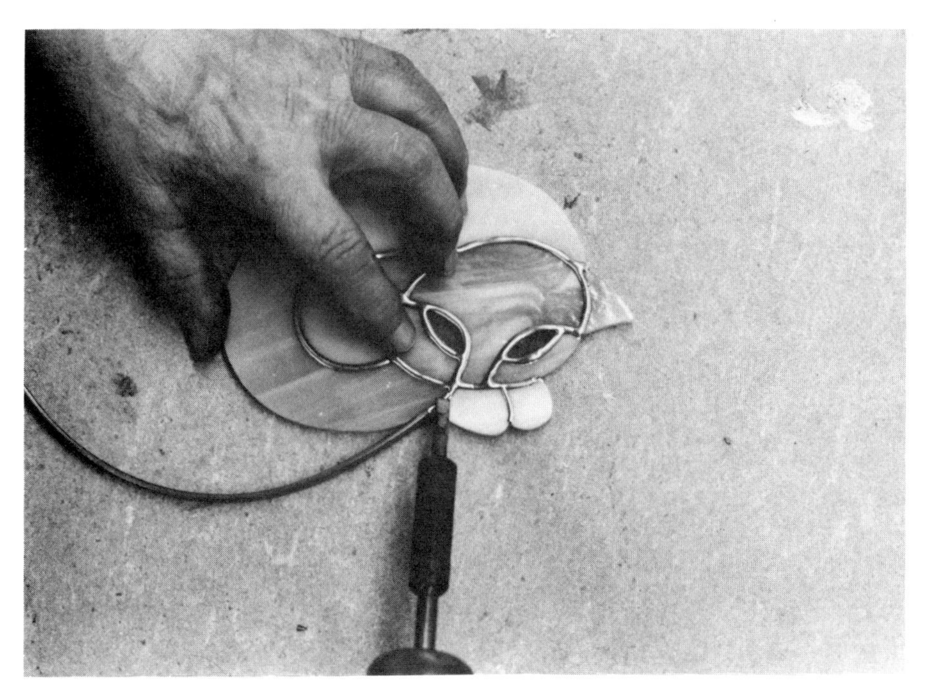

Illustration 3-27

6. Where each soldered seam meets the U-came, solder the came to the seam (you won't need glue in this case because there are enough seams to hold the lead to the glass).
7. Find your best point for a hook and solder one on (p. 44).

We think that for most foiled projects, the lead came adds a finished border that allows it to stand out more distinctly.

Summing Up

This chapter finishes off the first stage of your stained glass development as outlined in these first three chapters. Sun-catcher projects combine on an elementary level all the techniques you'll employ for all stained glass activities.

Our next three chapters will introduce other areas of stained glass work you should now concern yourself with, culminating with your introduction to panel and window construction.

Remember that practical reinforcement of all our techniques is a necessary component of all instruction. You shouldn't move on to the following chapters until you've completed other sun-catchers where you have repeated our techniques to the point where you can execute them with ease and which have prepared you for more difficult and challenging projects.

4

Glass, Color, and Pattern Design

Many people consider the design of the stained glass project to be the paramount consideration in stained glass. We do also in the sense that the stained glass artist needs to have an exact, life-size cartoon or blueprint before he or she can select the right glass and color combinations.

Those people who have an art background or who are artistically inclined will find stained glass the perfect medium for their creative talents. We probably can't help these people too much other than introduce glass as a concrete material for their ideas and discuss the individual properties and potential for glass.

However, there are many people who are weak in or feel inadequate about choosing designs, patterns, and color combinations. Although we can't "teach" these people to become great graphic artists, or give someone enough talent and/or training to draw or design his or her own patterns exactly as they would like, we can present guidelines, hints, and suggestions that should make them much more confident when choosing and developing patterns, glass, and color combinations.

Glass

The following description of the types of glass and their characteristics and project uses is a rather broad and "un-technical" generalization of glass that is available today. But it should give you enough basic knowledge to begin choosing and selecting glass without being at the mercy of the personal tastes and business considerations of your supplier.

CATHEDRAL

This is the domestic-made glass we've been recommending for all your beginning sun-catcher projects because it is a "soft" glass and is generally the easiest to cut for beginners. It comes in various colors: red, yellow, and orange are the "hot" colors and are priced much higher (usually twice as much) than the cool colors—blue, amber, green, clear, and lavender. Since the "hot" colors are produced using pure gold dust, their price fluctuates.

It is made with a variety of textures smooth on both sides, "hammered" (round indentations), or creped. Most companies make all the colors in a variety of hues (shades) and textures. Cathedral's properties lend themselves best to sun-catchers, bordering highlights, and terrariums.

TRANSLUCENT OPALS

This glass is characterized by heavy and light streaks (and sometimes white) running through it. It comes in various colors and hues but few textures. Generally, it is smooth on both sides. It is relatively "soft" like cathedral for easy cutting but it is priced slightly higher. These opals can be used in sun-catchers and terrariums but, are also, unlike cathedral, useful for three-dimensional objects where light is not a consideration.

DENSE OPALS (OPALESCENT)

Like translucent opals, there are many beautiful and bright colors available but few textures. It is a "hard" glass and difficult to cut, not only for beginners but all glass cutters. Unlike translucent opals, very little light will come through the glass. This is a good glass to use when constructing clocks, planters, lampshades, or three-dimensional objects that will either hang on a wall or when you don't want the hue or intensity of the glass to change because of the light.

SEEDY

Similar to cathedral in colors and translucency, its surface has tiny bubbles in it which make it difficult to cut for a beginner. The bubbles will cause the wheel of the cutter, when it occasionally gets "stuck" in the bubble, to deviate from the drawn pattern line on the glass. You can use this glass for just about any project that cathedral glass can be utilized for. However, when choosing this glass, the "seeds" could tend to distract the eye from the overall project.

FULL ANTIQUE

This imported glass is the most expensive but generally the most brilliant and beautiful in color intensity. It is difficult for a beginner to cut, not because it is a "hard" glass, but because it varies in thickness. When cutting antique, pressure is the most important consideration. Antique is best used in panels and sun-catchers, but not with lamps or three-dimensional objects.

SHEET OR SEMI-SHEET ANTIQUE

Very similar to full antique in color intensity, but less expensive, it contains internal prism-like lines which contribute to a texture-like appearance. It can be utilized for all projects to which antique lends itself.

Color Selection

For most people involved with stained glass, the colors have always held the most interest. Many of us first got interested in glass because we like the colors. Their hypnotic allure is still the driving force behind most of our activity in stained glass. Nothing can do more to create impact and excitement or dramatically detract from the design than the choice of colors.

Since the choice of color for any object—clothes, a house, a car, anything—is purely subjective, it would be foolish and presumptuous of us to tell you what the "best" colors are or in what combination to use them (a color wheel might be helpful to those of you who are at a loss in this respect). But we can offer guidelines that generally work best with stained glass. Following is a random list of what you should keep in mind when engaged in this most critical color determination activity:

1. *Take your time*. Be absolutely sure that whatever colors you choose will be right for you and your purposes. Before you even go to the supplier, get an idea of the general colors you want by coloring in your design with crayons. Make a number of copies and try different color combinations until you're positive that you know exactly what you want. All your hard work will be for nothing if you quickly tire of and regret choosing the colors in your project.
2. Depending upon your project's design, keep the idea of *balance* in mind. You want the viewer to immediately notice the most important part of your project—the focal point. At the same time, you do not want to divert attention from it. Since the eye is usually attracted to brighter colors, the use of hot colors—red, orange, yellow—should be restricted. Draw attention to your focal point by using these colors for your center of interest, and balance your project by distributing any other bright color in small proportions and away from your main subject.
3. The *value* (lightness or darkness) of a repeated color can have an effect on your overall color scheme. Whether you choose to contrast different colors or complement different values of the same color, which will add depth, remember that your project needs balance.
4. When you go to your glass supplier with your colored pattern, you must *look at the glass you choose through light*. The color of the glass will change as the light changes. This is what makes stained glass such a unique and difficult art form. Put all the glass you're going to choose on a light table and make sure that the hue and value is exactly what you want.

   Also observe the color of the glass with natural light coming through it. The glass will not have the same value with artifical light as it will with natural light.

   When selecting colors, there is no hard, fast rule as to mixing types of glass. Generally, you'll do your beginning projects using the same type throughout. But some types complement each other very well. For instance, the combination of cathedral or antique as a "background" glass with opalescent utilized in your main subject adds the illusion of depth to panels. And, conversely, using just a little cathedral when the rest of your project is opalescent will illuminate a small flower or border.

5. When choosing colors (and glass) do not let an impatient supplier or clerk hurry you or talk you into any color or glass before you yourself have made up your mind. We've all spent hours choosing glass for a project. Don't buy until you select exactly what you want.

These guidelines are not "rules" and are not written in concrete. What we want to emphasize is that you will need to experiment with and consider different combinations of color and glass type as your stained glass skills develop and you begin to do larger projects. But in any case, *think* these areas through *before* you buy any glass and begin cutting.

Patterns and Design

There are many original pattern books available on the market for stained glass projects at studios, book stores, and libraries. But there are many other sources for patterns that lend themselves to stained glass work, among them:

Greeting cards	Coloring books
Paintings	Altair® design books
Bath towels	Logos
Quilting and embroidery patterns	Dictionaries

When adopting alternate sources or existing patterns for stained glass, you must scrutinize each line and detail to determine the adaptability of the lines for both cuts and design. You may have to subtract or add lines to facilitate your cutting. You'll also have to consider the aesthetics of the line or pattern you are working with. The lead lines should not detract from the design in the sense of its being too busy; nor should there be too few lines that would threaten the security of its structure.

Many patterns which you may want to use (especially panel patterns) will probably be too small and will need enlargement. Most manuals suggest the use of graph paper and corresponding one-inch blocks. We prefer to transfer the pattern onto a clear transparency (acetate) and project it with an overhead projector onto a large piece of paper taped to a wall. You then can enlarge the pattern to the dimensions you want by moving the projector closer or farther away from the wall.

Most office supply stores or copying centers have the clear transparencies. You can buy the overhead projector (or opaque projector) at a school supply store but, unless you do a great deal of enlarging, the cost may not be worth it. However, rental centers like Taylor Rental have overheads available and a large number of enlargements could justify a minimal cost for one day's work. The time saved and accuracy of copying are other factors which make this method so attractive.

These important considerations of glass, color, and design are in many respects just as important as the execution of your project. Some would maintain that they are the most important. Without getting into a rhetorical debate, we'll terminate this chapter by saying that the materials, aesthetics, and execution are interdependent and reciprocally influential in determining the quality and lasting satisfaction of your work.

5

Difficult Glass Cutting

You should be at the stage now where you've developed both the fundamentals of glass cutting and a comfortable familiarity with your tools. (For this chapter, you'll use the same tools as listed in Chapter 1.) You're probably anxious to get into more difficult and complicated projects and patterns. In this section, we're going to provide instructions and techniques for difficult patterned cutting and for making specific common cuts that you'll have to master in order to continue to work with stained glass. Remember our pyramid: We're still positioning the fulcrum block for the rest of this stained glass structure; and believe us, that careful positioning (through repeated practice) will make stained glass work that much easier and satisfying and less discouraging. This, as well as the first glass cutting chapter, make up the key to the entire system.

Most manuals suggest that you make certain difficult cuts in stages; we feel that, in most cases, you should try to continue with one continuous score which will eliminate tiny "nipples" at each breaking point. For this reason, positioning glass becomes important in regard to body motion. For all cuts that are long or complicated, you should perform a "dry run" with your cutter, making sure that you can score the glass in one continuous, fluid motion, while giving your body an ample turning radius. If you can't do this, reposition the glass or yourself until you can ensure one continuous stroke.

Let's get right into the types of cuts we want you to practice and master because you will need to use these techniques for the lighthouse panel in the next chapter (panels).

The Straight Line (Fig. 9). You'd be surprised to see how often you'll need a truly straight cut and won't be able to do it. You'll obviously need a steel ruler or square that has a rubber or felt backing (p. 4). *Do not* trust your eye when attempting a straight cut.

The technique for cutting a straight line is as follows: (*See* Illustrations 5-1 through 5-9.)

1. Place your straightedge on the glass, at least ½'' from the edge. Make sure the length of your straightedge exceeds the length of the score and make sure you have an equal length of the straightedge hanging off either end of your piece of glass. In other words, you must center the glass underneath your straightedge to prevent the straightedge from rocking back and forth.
2. Position your body at the opposite side of the straightedge so the armpit of your dominant arm is directly over the straightedge. This will prevent your elbow from hitting your stomach and causing you to shift in mid-score;
3. Place your spread fingers of your free hand on the upper edge of the ruler applying even thumb-and-finger pressure on the straightedge;

PRACTICE EXERCISES

#1

Fig. 9

4. With your kerosene brush, and with only one stroke, apply a liberal amount of kerosene along the cutting line.
5. Begin your score *at the top* (cutting toward yourself for straight lines only), using normal cutting pressure, butting the side of the cutter to the side of the straightedge slowly proceeding downward. *Important:* Do not exert so much pressure with your cutter against the side of the straightedge that it causes the straightedge to move off line. No more pressure is needed against the straightedge than what is required to draw a straight line with a marker.
6. When the score reaches your thumb of the hand on the ruler, stop your score but do not relax cutting pressure. Then creep your fingers on the ruler down the ruler, somewhat like a caterpillar, shifting pressure to your fingers and sliding your thumb down again. Then proceed with your score, advancing your cutter another five or six inches, executing normal pressure.
7. Continue this procedure until you reach the bottom of the ruler.*
8. Pull the glass apart immediately.

Practice cutting straight edges until you can do them easily.

Sometimes you will need to cut an exact 90-degree angle. All you need here is a square with rubber backing. Merely place the square right on top of the glass and trace, at least ½'' from both edges, the outline of the *outside* of the square, then take your straightedge and make two straight cuts using the method described in the above procedures.

In conjunction with straight cuts, we should mention the importance of a proper and exact *measuring technique*. You'll especially need to know how to do this when making repeated bands of glass of the exact same width and length, e.g. with borders, frames, and panel lamps. The method is as follows:
(*See* Illustrations 5-10 through 5-13.)

1. Always make sure you have a piece of glass with at least one 90-degree angle.
2. Take your ruler and place it flush against the edge of the glass at the 90-degree angle.
3. Bend over closely and place a dot on the 1'' mark.
4. Further up the glass, place the straightedge flush against the edge, and repeat step 3.

* For left-handers: When you try to cut a straight line, most lefties have a tendency to pull away from the straightedge at the bottom of the score causing a "hook" in the straight line. To prevent this: When you are approximately two inches from the bottom, take one small step to your right maintaining the same cutting pressure and continue scoring to the edge.

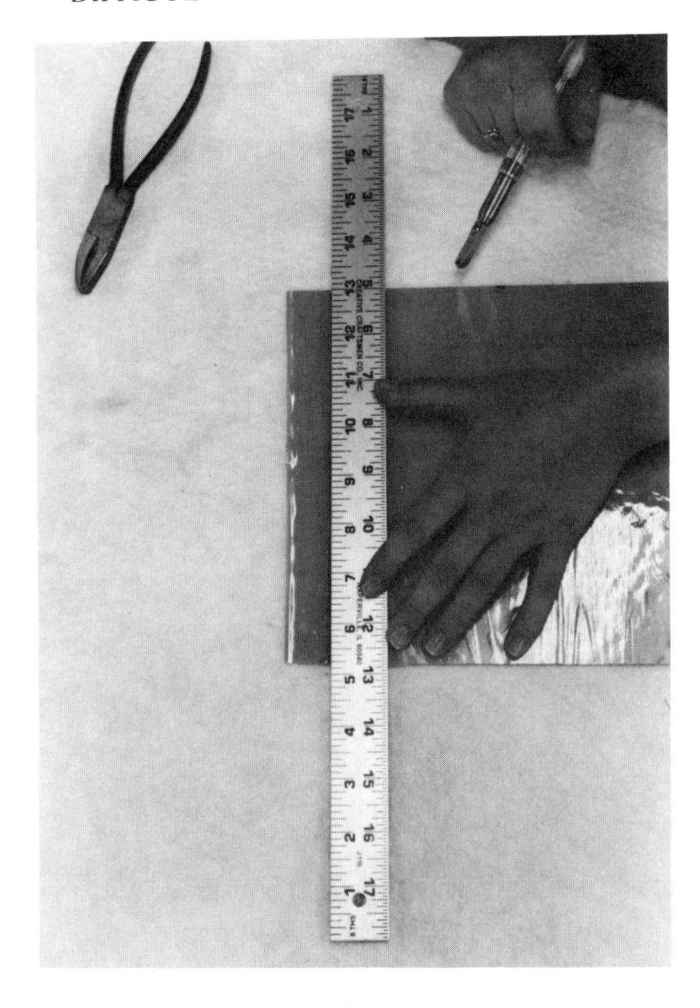

Illustration 5-1

5. Line up your straightedge beside the two dots.
6. Pick up your cutter, lining up the wheel with the center of your bottom dot.
7. Repeat step 6 at the top; however, reverse your cutter to allow you to see the mark more clearly.
8. Make your score.

Cut five or six strips in this manner to see how well you measured. All your strips should be the same size.

An *Inside Curve* (Fig. 10) is a common problem-cut that can be made simple by following our suggestions. After tracing Pattern #2 on a piece of glass (mark the "good" piece with tape as we have), proceed as follows:
(*See* Illustrations 5-14 through 5-18.)

1. Try a few dry runs in order to position yourself and/or the glass so that you can make one continuous cut.

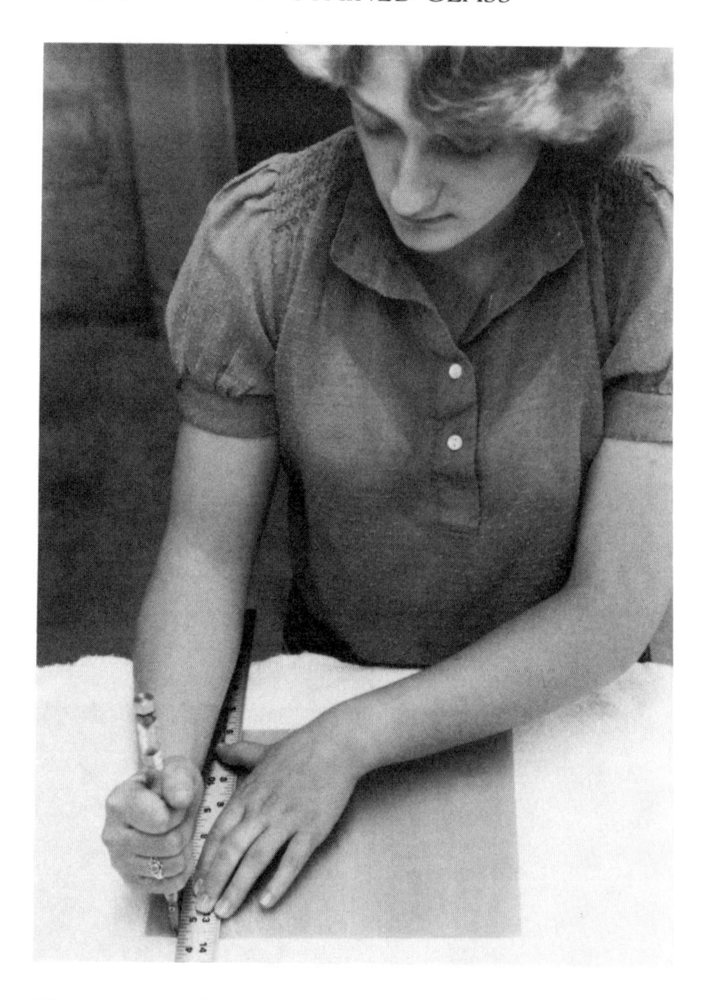

Illustration 5-2

2. Trace your flux brush dipped in kerosene from your jar over the pattern line on the glass.
3. Score the glass in one fluid, continuous motion, *turning your body*, not your hand, if necessary.
4. Separate the pieces by using cut/run pliers and then "teasing" the glass apart.
(a) First, try to use your cut/run pliers, running them on both ends of the score. Listen for that little "click" and watch the fracture as it runs down the score.
(b) If the glass does not come apart, then try to "tease" the glass apart by positioning your hands as closely as possible on either side of the score. *Gently*, move your thumb and hands little by little along the fracture, working one side up and down with your thumb until you pull the "good" piece free.
5. Wipe the glass clean of kerosene.

Now the tricky part: What do you do if a piece needs *both* an *inside curve* and an *outside curve*? A *rainbow Band* (Fig. 11) is a perfect example of this type of cut: You must "save" the entire middle piece, or band, from being broken at a number of vulnerable

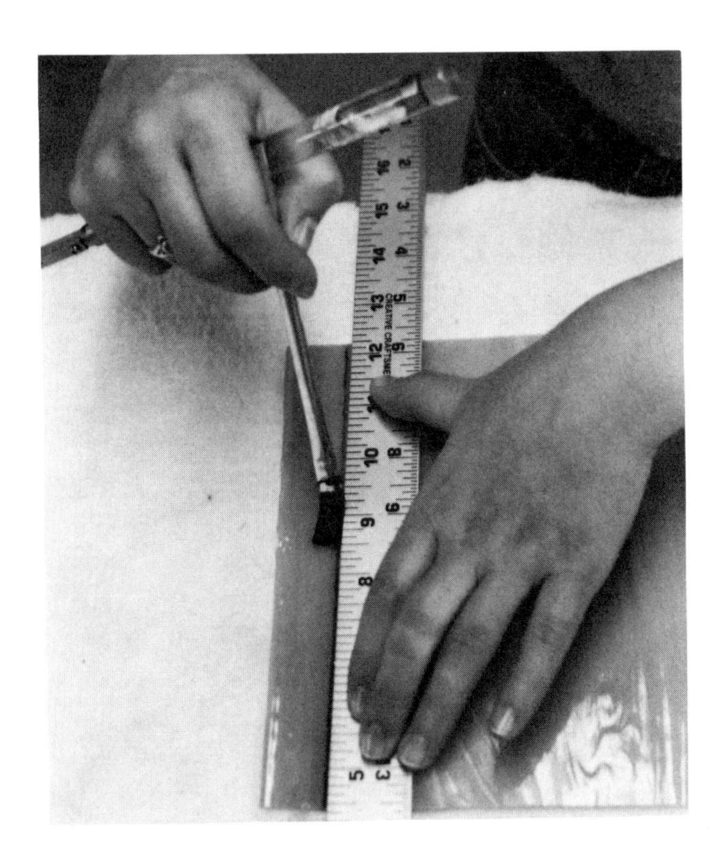

Illustrations 5-3 and 5-4

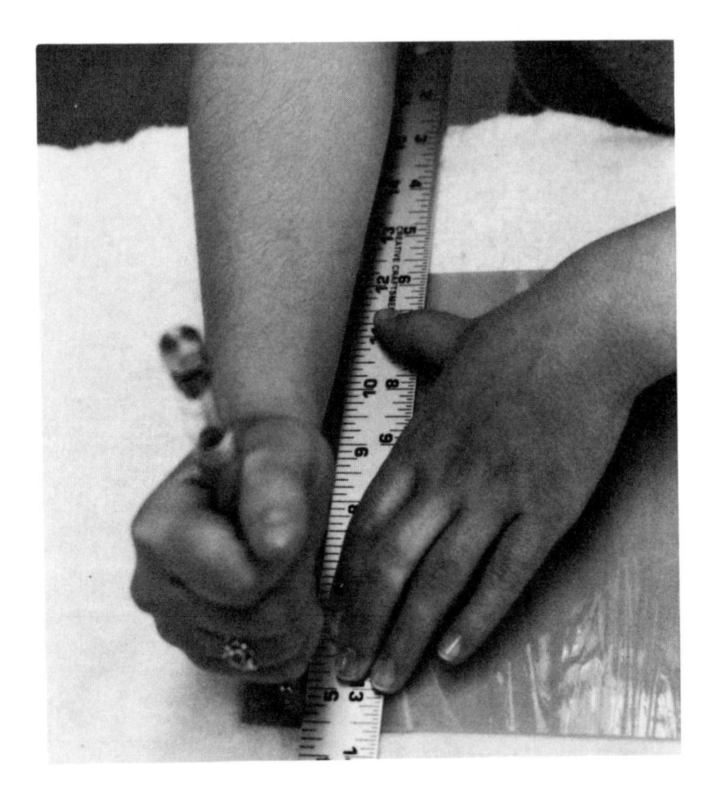

Illustration 5-5

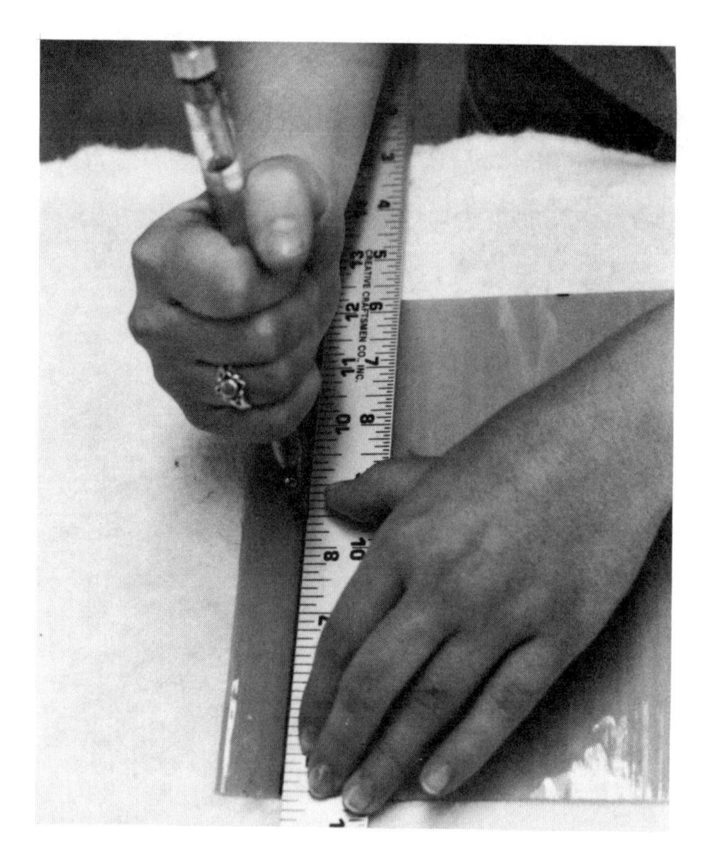

Illustration 5-6

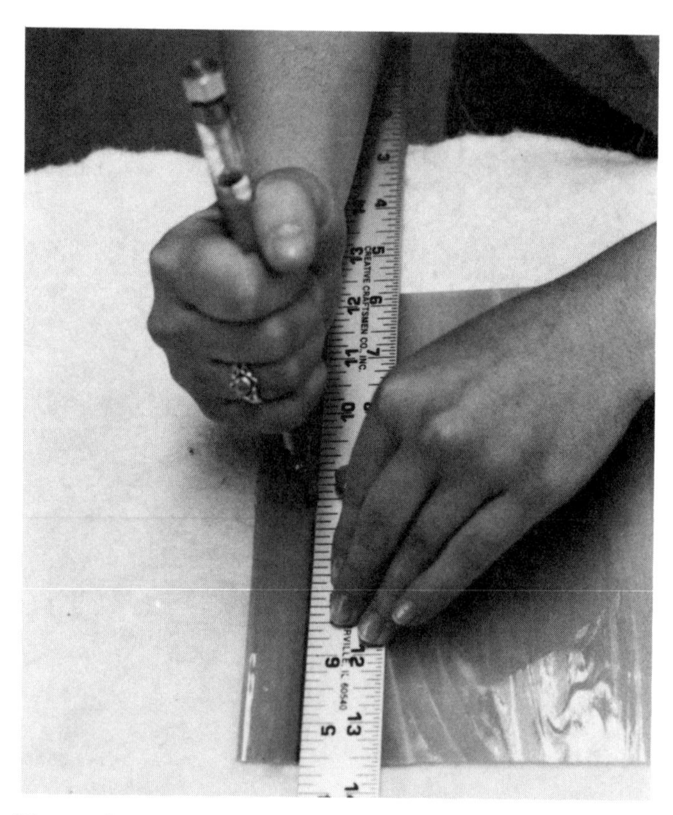

Illustration 5-7

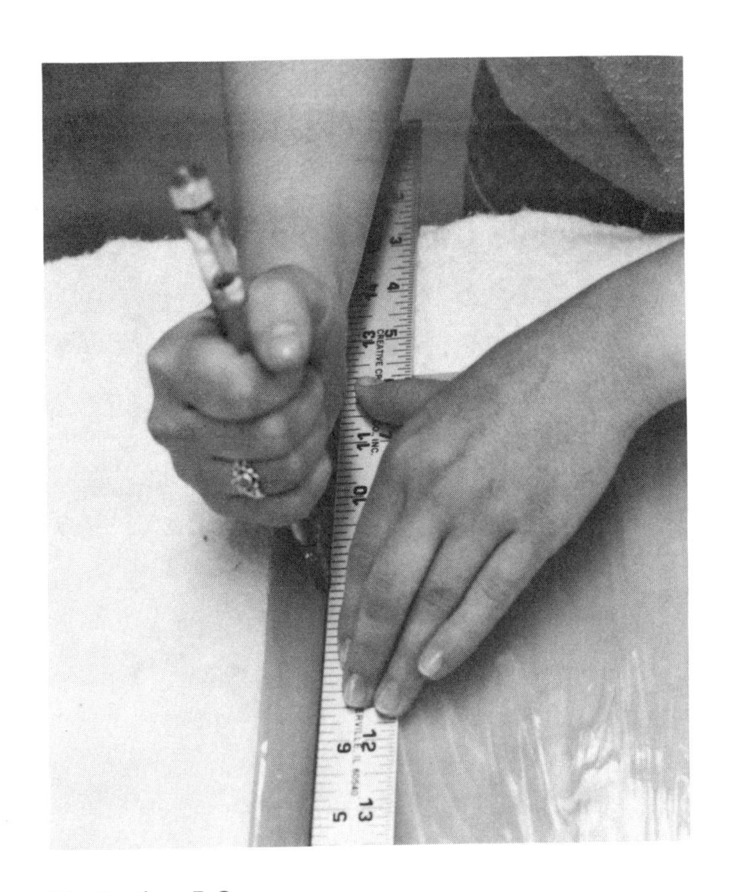

Illustration 5-8

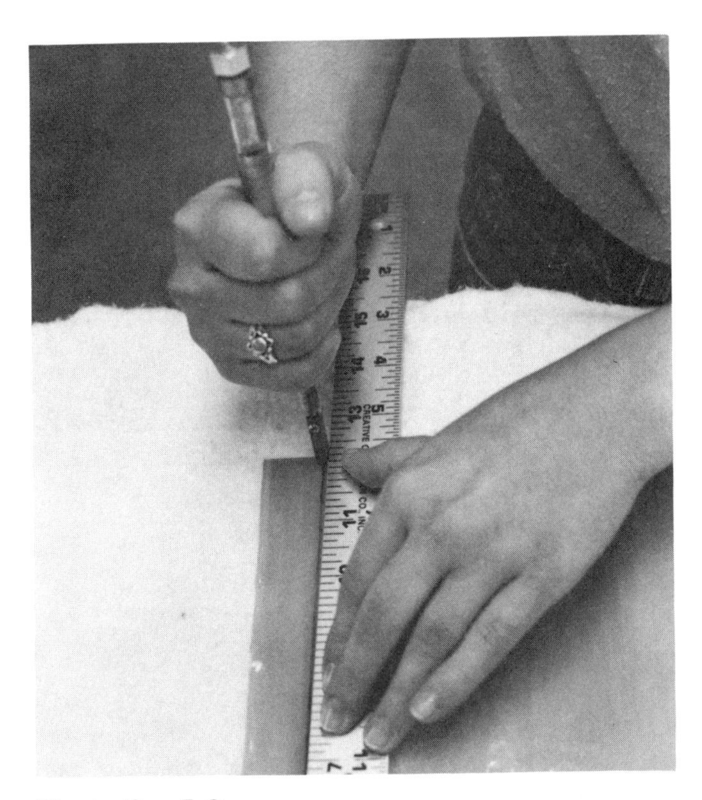

Illustration 5-9

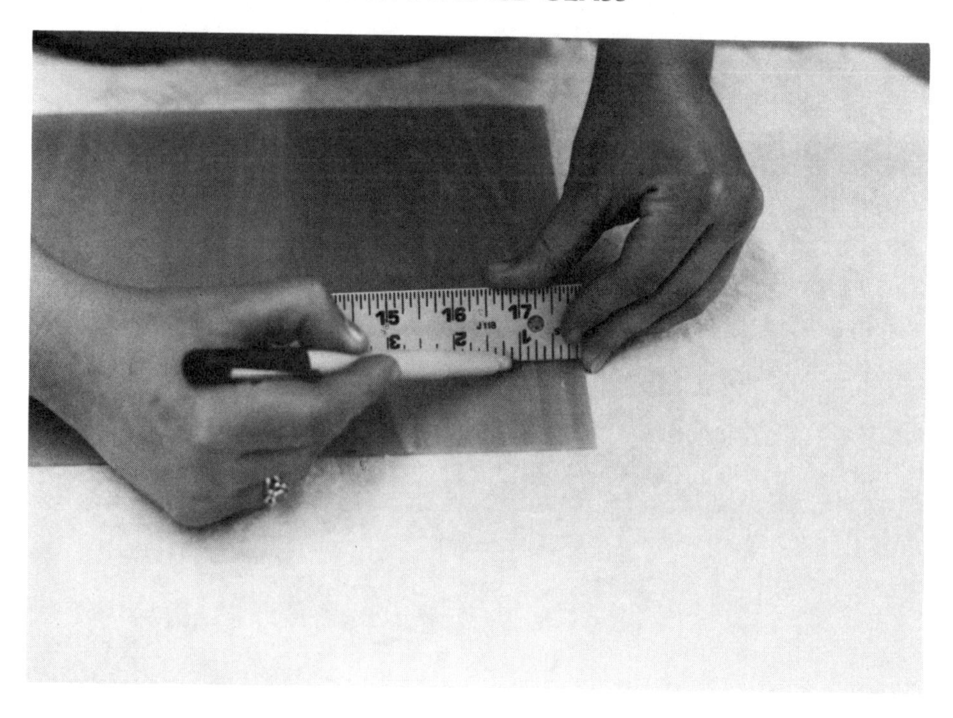

Illustration 5-10

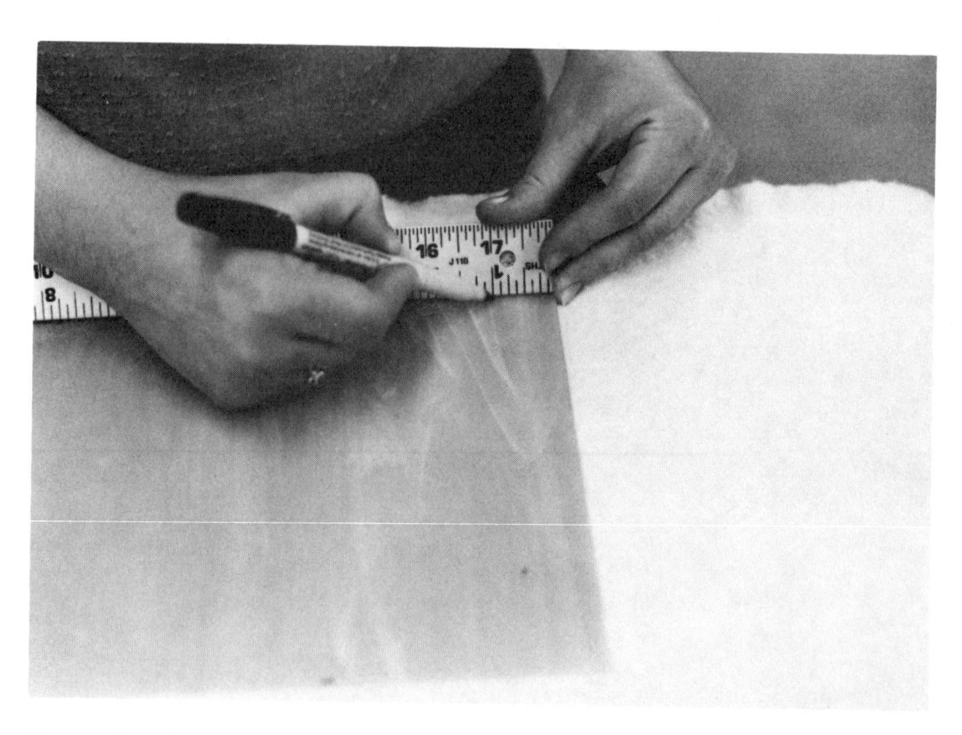

Illustration 5-11

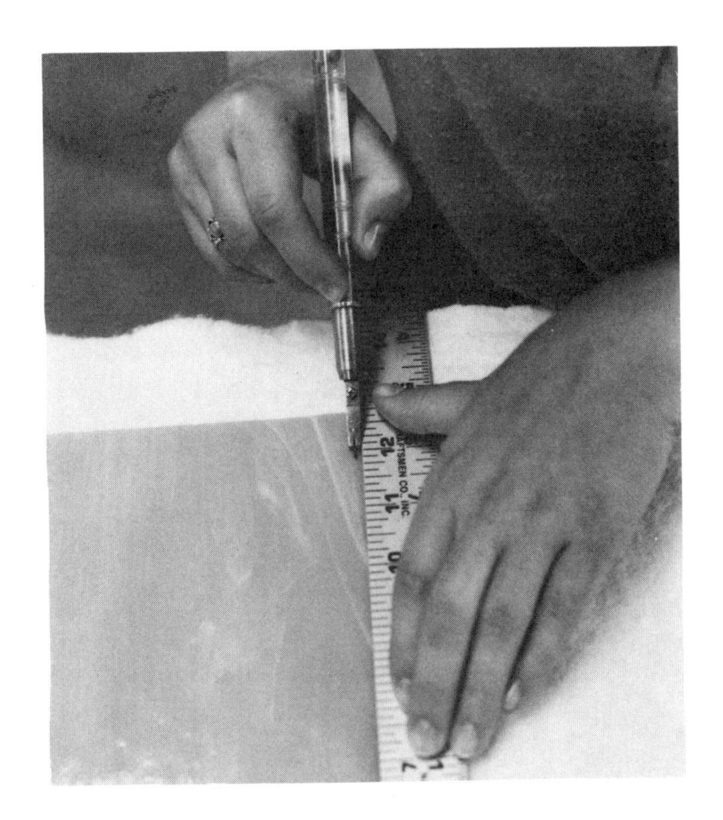

Illustration 5-12

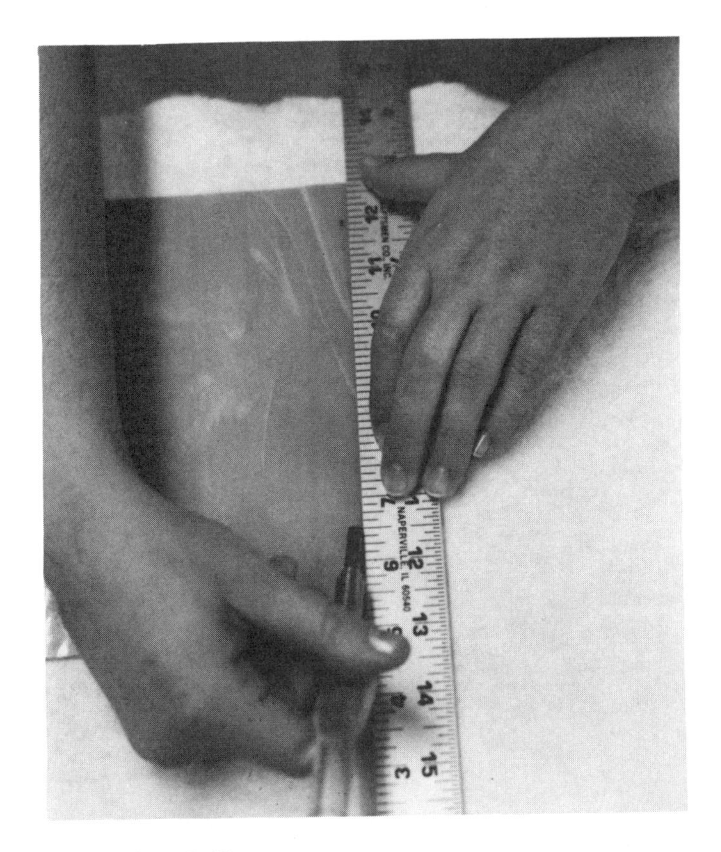

Illustration 5-13

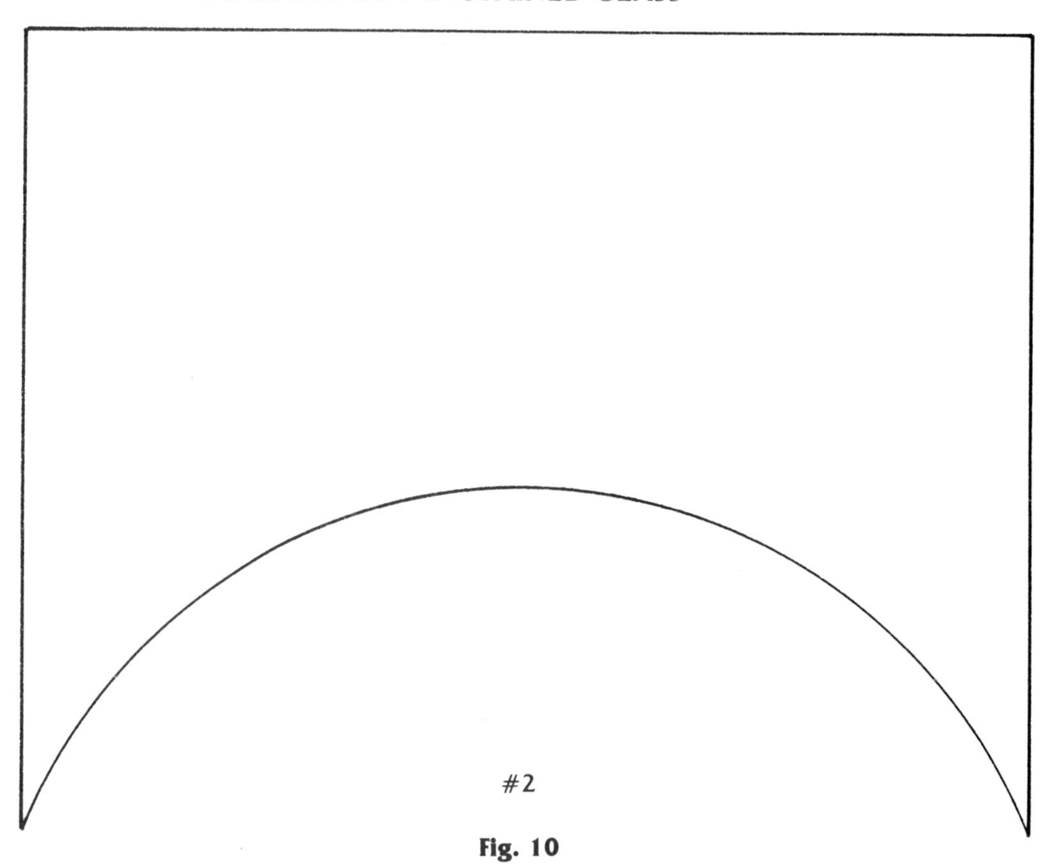

Fig. 10

Illustration 5-14

Illustration 5-15A

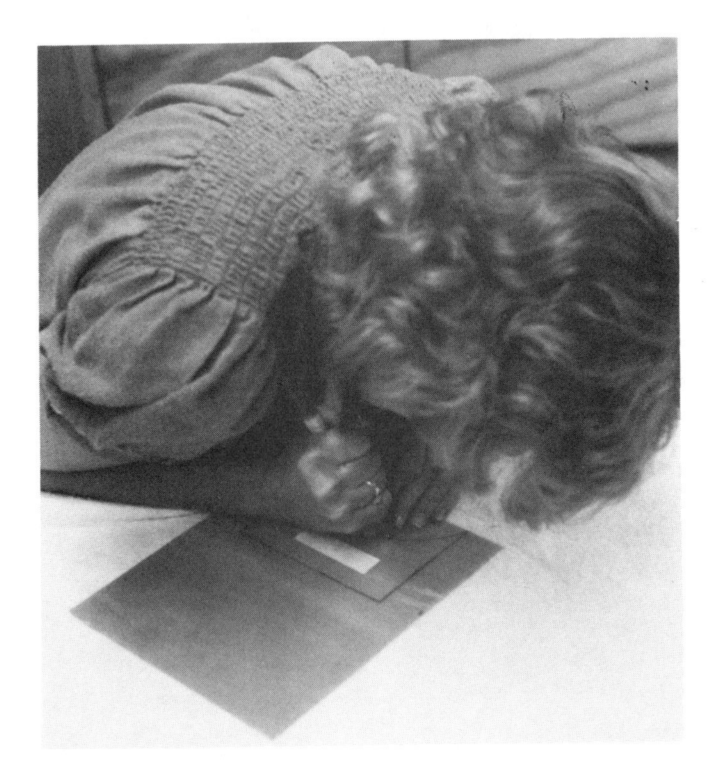

Illustration 5-15B

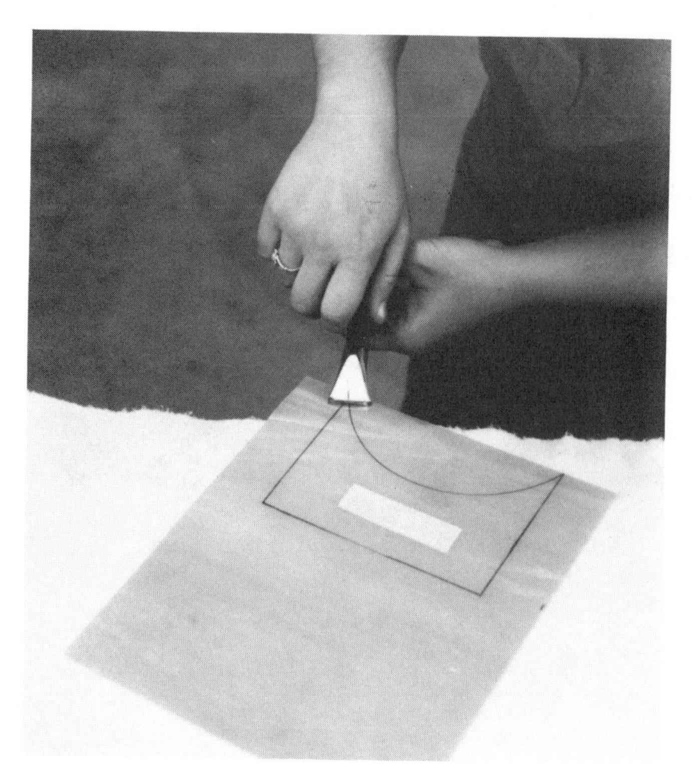

Illustration 5-16A

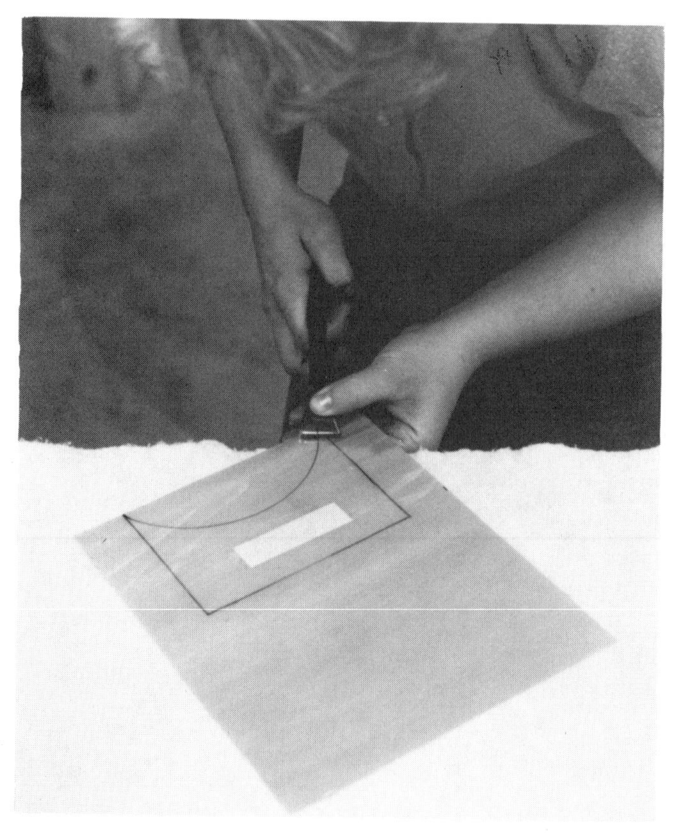

Illustration 5-16B

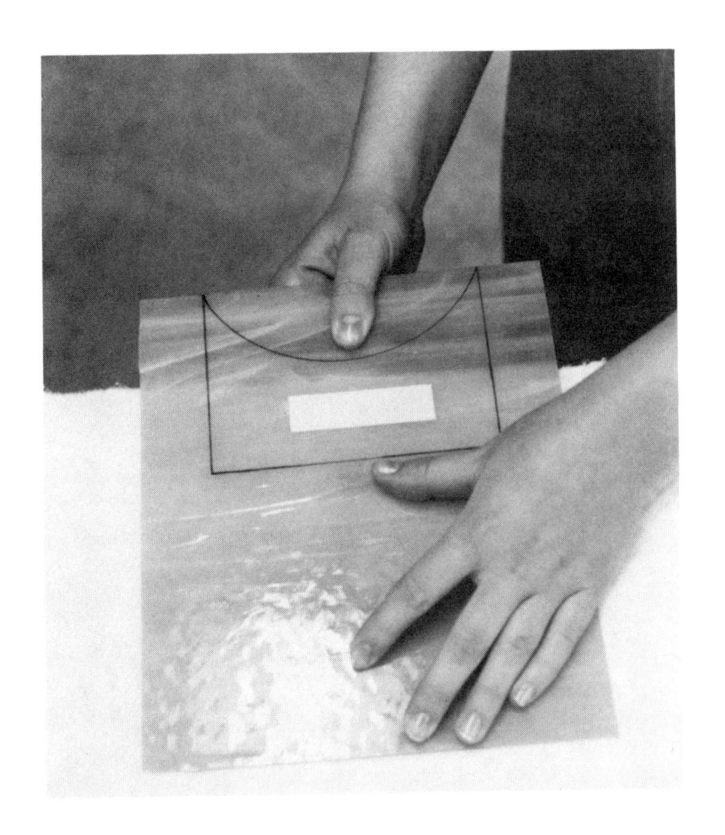

Illustration 5-17

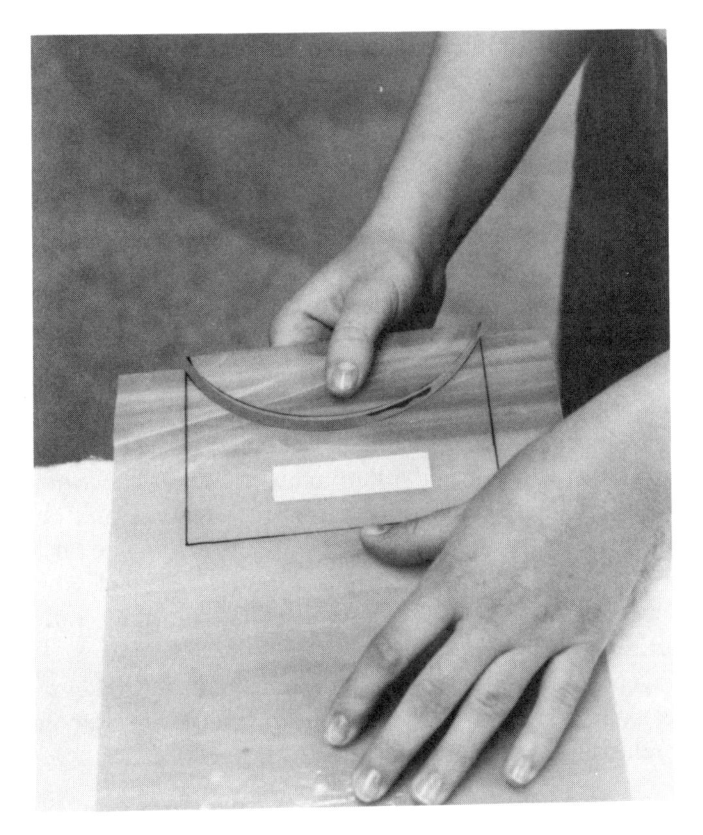

Illustration 5-18

PRACTICE EXERCISES

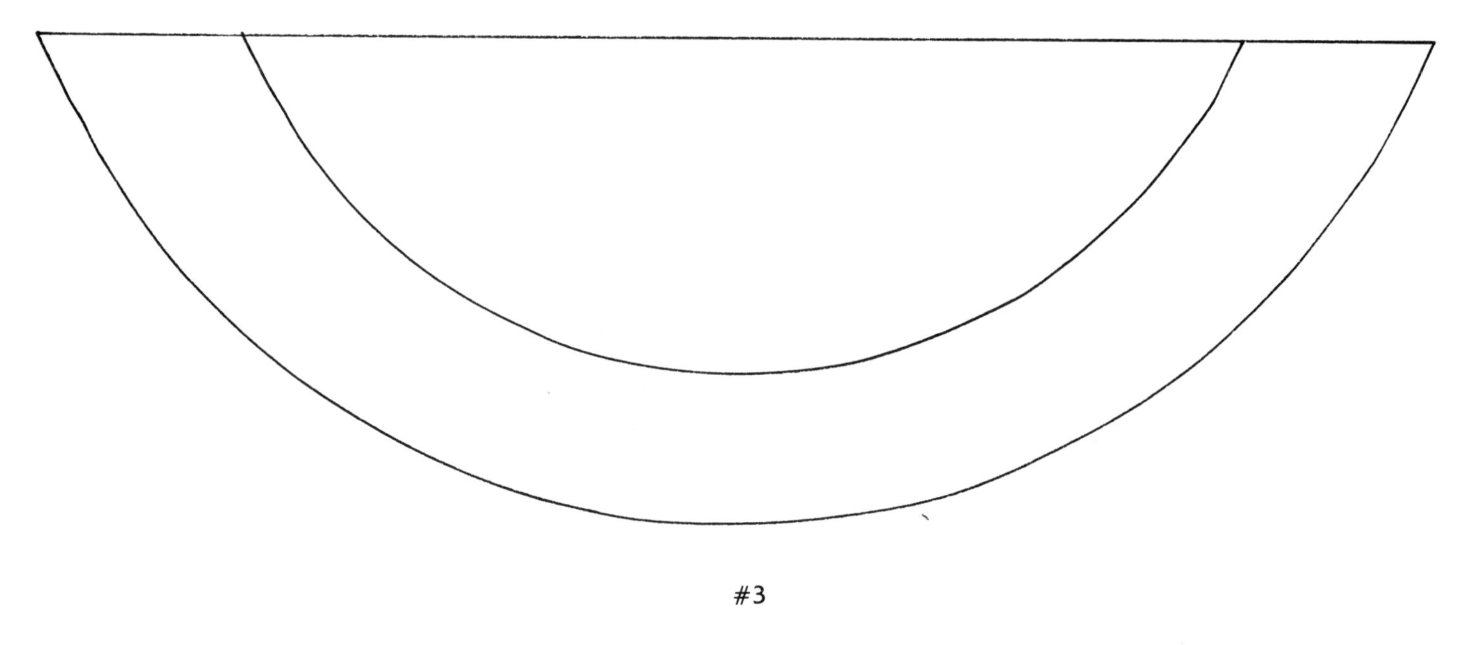

#3

Fig. 11

points. The best way of approaching this cut is as follows:
(*See* Illustrations 5-19 through 5-24D.)

1. First, make your dry run, and position yourself accordingly.
2. Score the *inside* cut first with one continuous score.
3. Use your cut/run pliers at both ends, listening for the "click" and watching the fracture.
4. Tease the glass very gently and very slowly, *wiggling the glass from the edge into the center*. It might take a minute or two before the glass comes apart, but it will—*just have patience*.
5. After you have the "inside" piece out in one piece, you need to get the other outside piece free.
6. Make your outside score and *immediately*, while the score is "hot" . . .
7. Use your cut/run pliers on both ends and teasing technique to disengage the "good" rainbow band in one piece. *Remember*: Don't chop down with your cut/run pliers trying to have the fracture run from one side to the other. This is how you break glass. Take your time and tease the glass and in ninety percent of the cuts, the "good" piece will come out whole rather than as a jigsaw puzzle.
8. If the piece refuses to come out, you'll need a few relief points running in the same direction as the score. Follow the method as described in our discussion of relief cuts and outside curves (Chapter 1, p. 13).

Some people freak out when they have to *cut a Circle* (Fig. 12). Some never attempt projects that require this type of cut; others will go to the unnecessary expense of buying

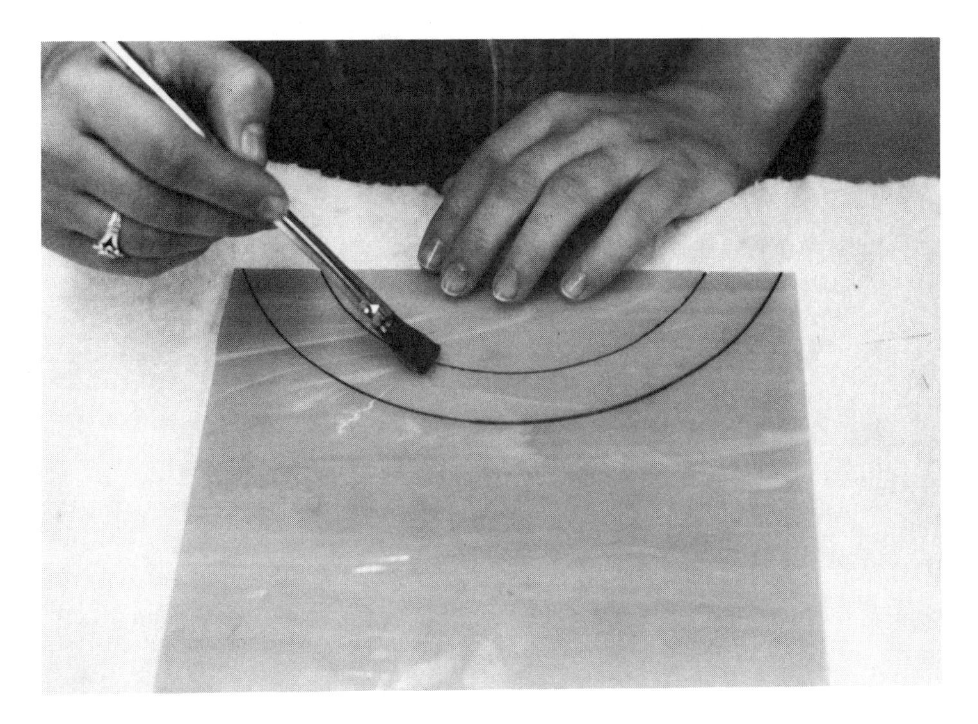

Illustration 5-19

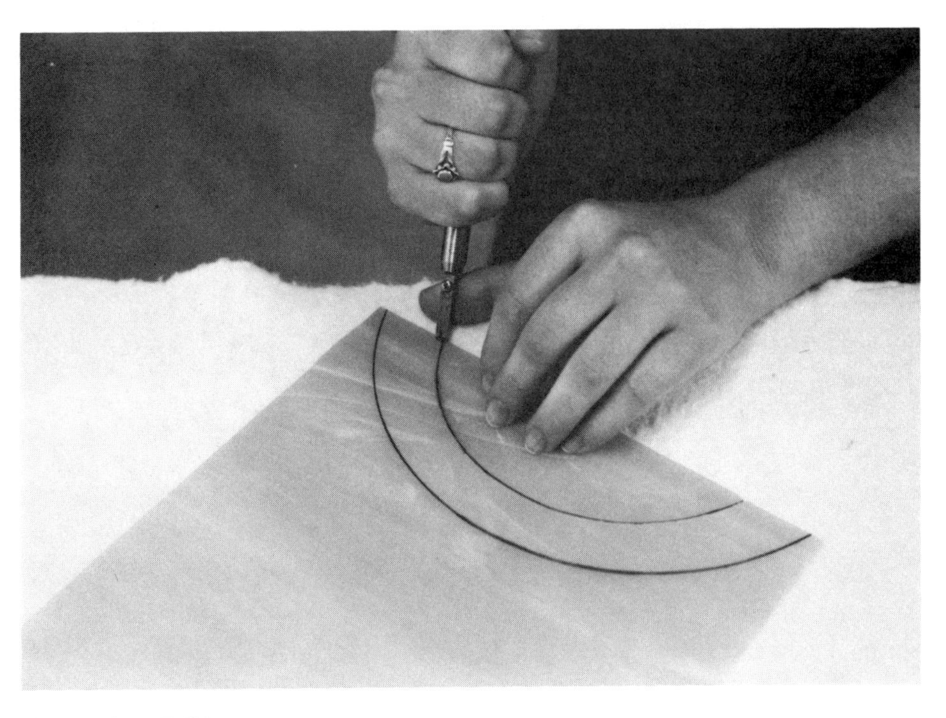

Illustration 5-20

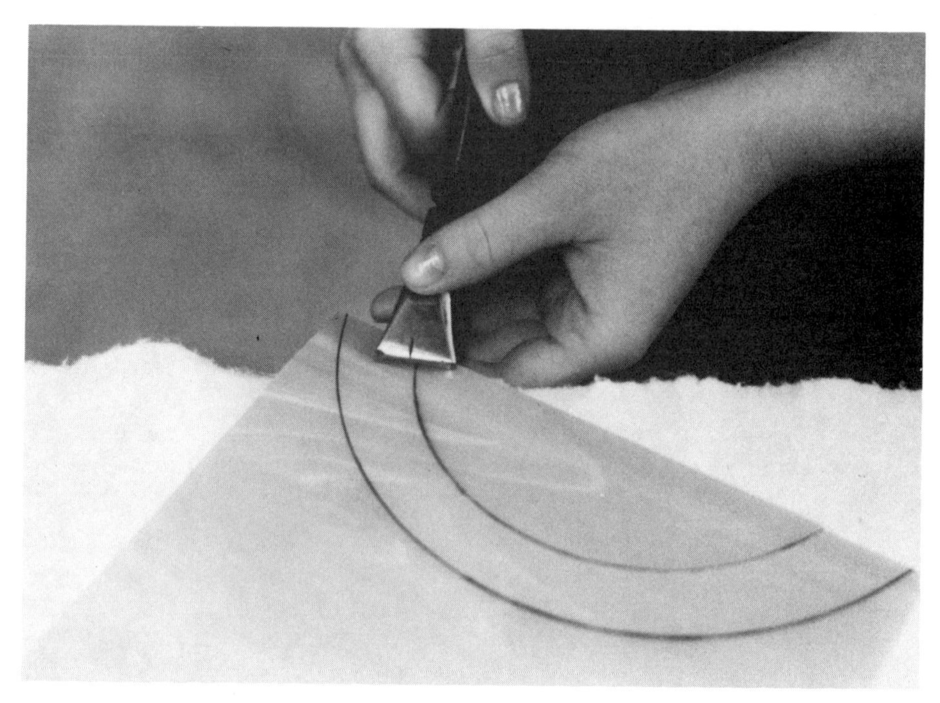

Illustration 5-21A

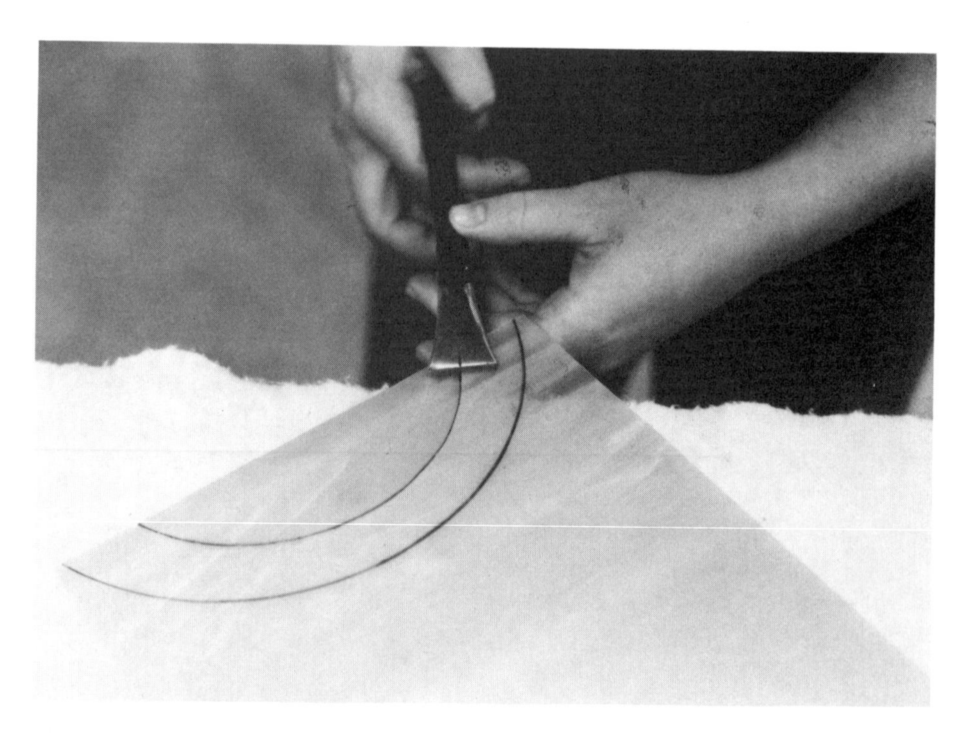

Illustration 5-21B

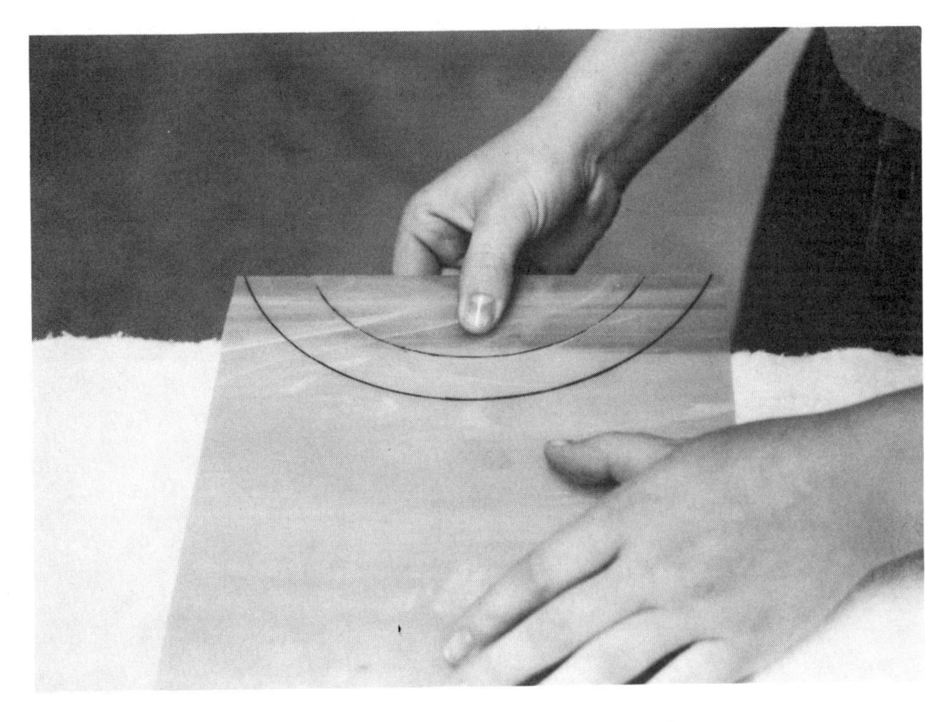

Illustration 5-22

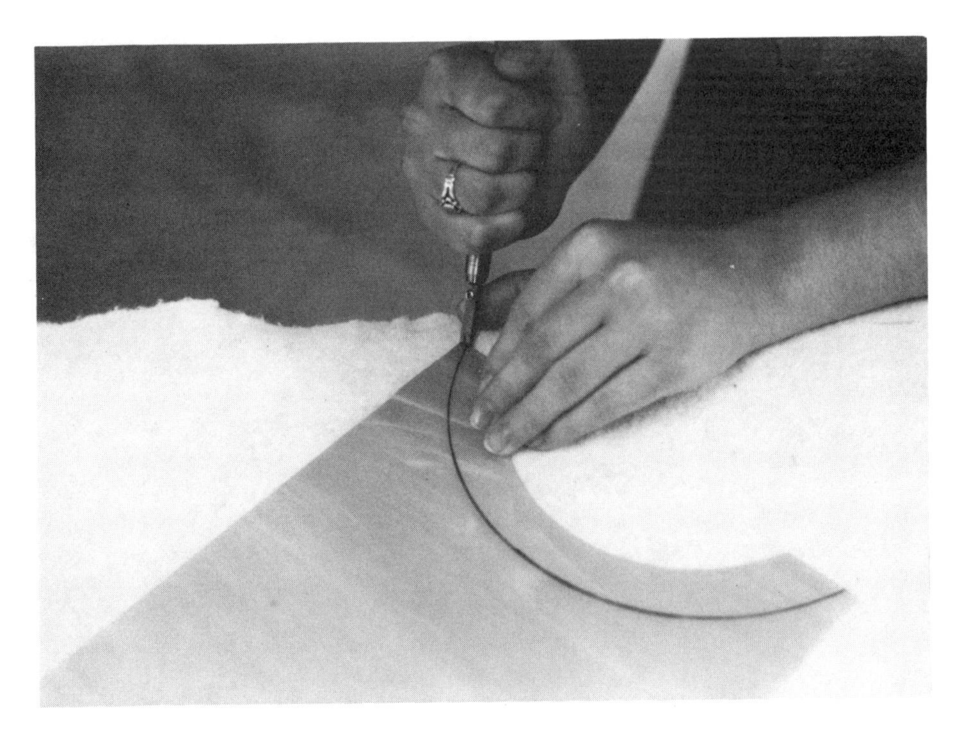

Illustration 5-23

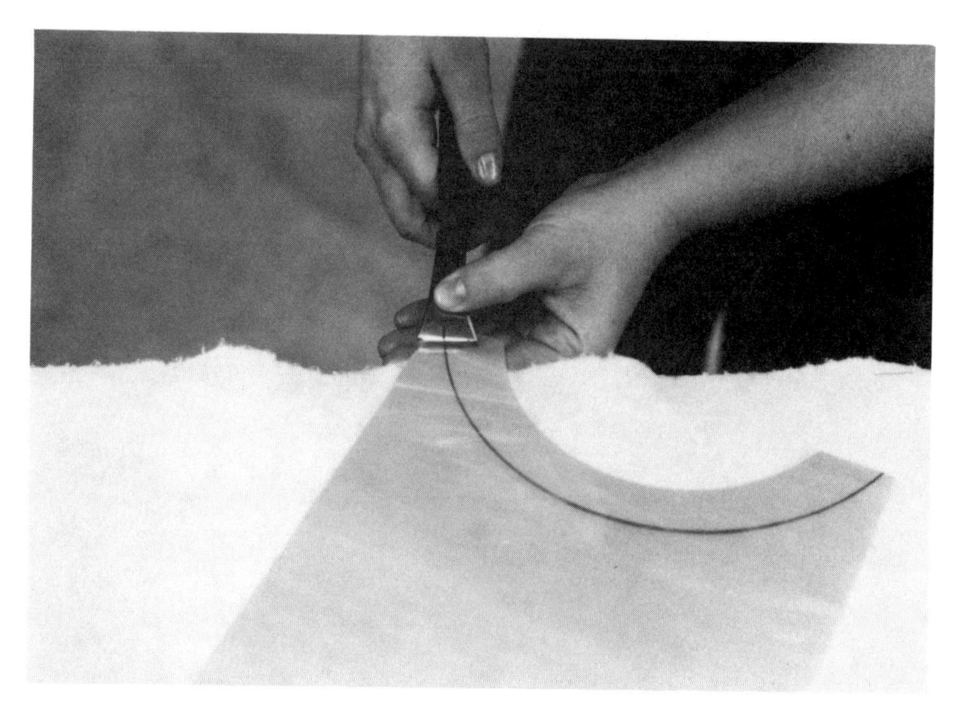

Illustration 5-24A

Illustration 5-24B

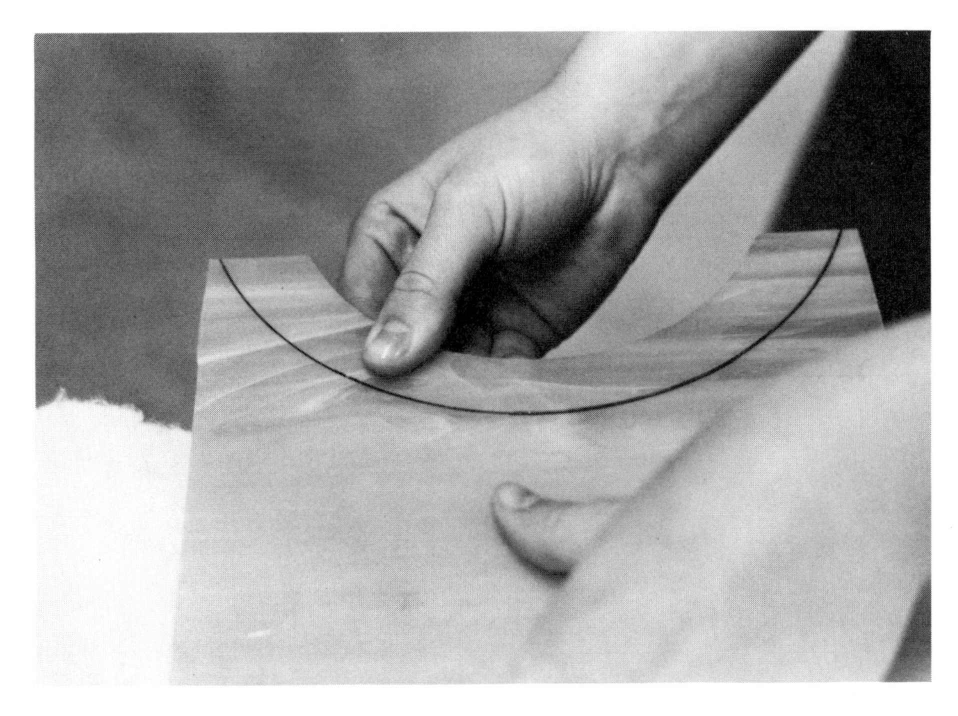

Illustration 5-24C

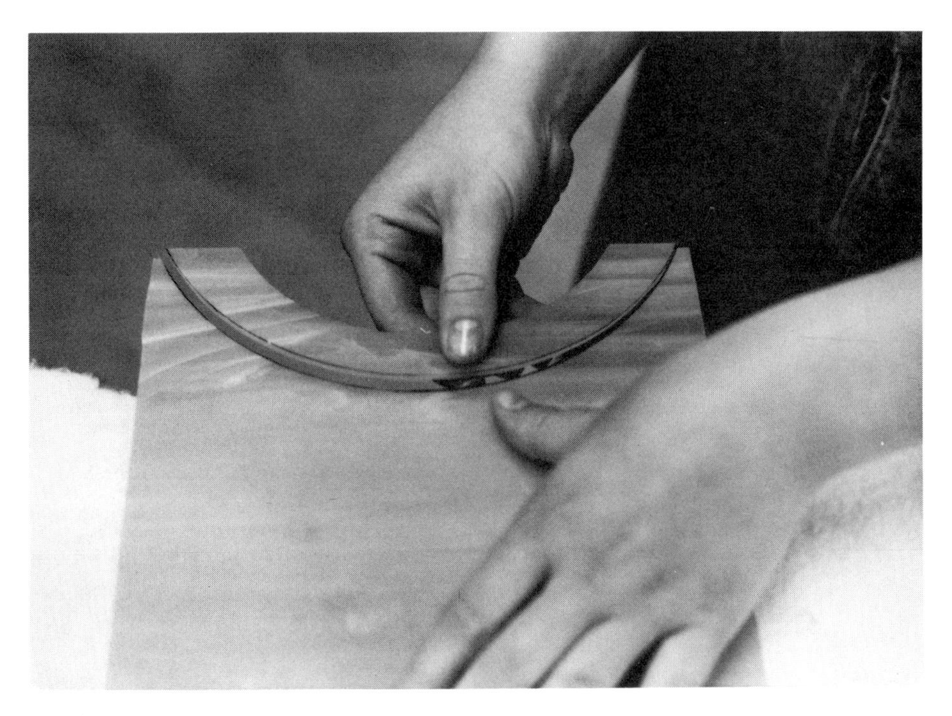

Illustration 5-24D

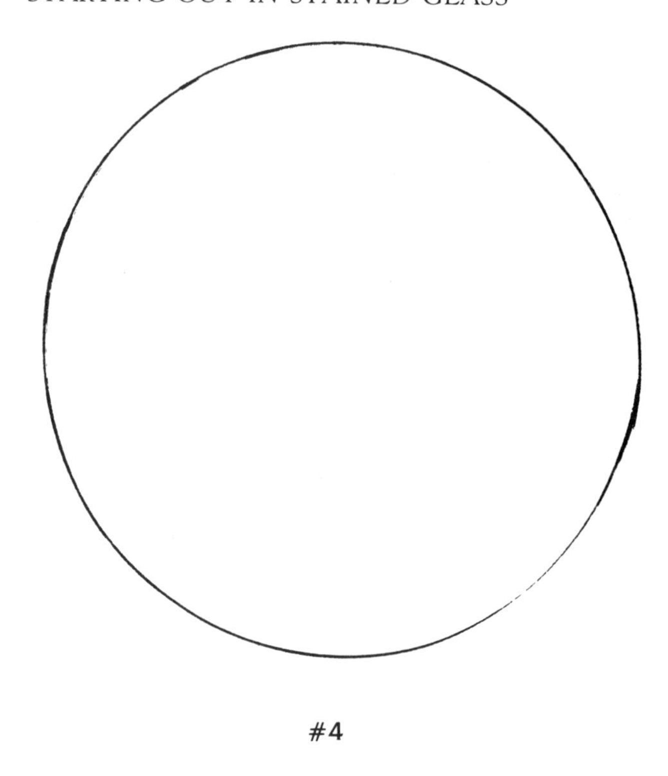

#4

Fig. 12

a circle cutter. An easy method of cutting a circle is as follows:
(*See* Illustrations 5-25 through 5-32.)

1. Draw the circle on the glass, making start/end lines, halving the circle from edge to edge, and . . .
2. Trace your kerosene brush around all lines.
3. Take your cutter, and beginning at the *end of one relief mark*, score the glass in one continuous motion (moving your body if necessary) halving the circle to the other relief line and off the edge of the glass.
4. Use your cut/run pliers on both ends of the relief cuts and tease the glass apart (as described on p. 96).
5. Score the remaining half of the circle.
6. Fracture each end of the circle with your cut/run pliers.
7. Tease the glass and pull the circle free.

You should now have a good circle with two tiny nipples at each half-mark (arrows). Remove these nipples with your carborundum stone using the technique outlined on page 23.

One final cut that you will find yourself needing to master, especially for terrariums and lamps, is the *Extreme Point* (Fig. 13). When attempting this cut, many times the

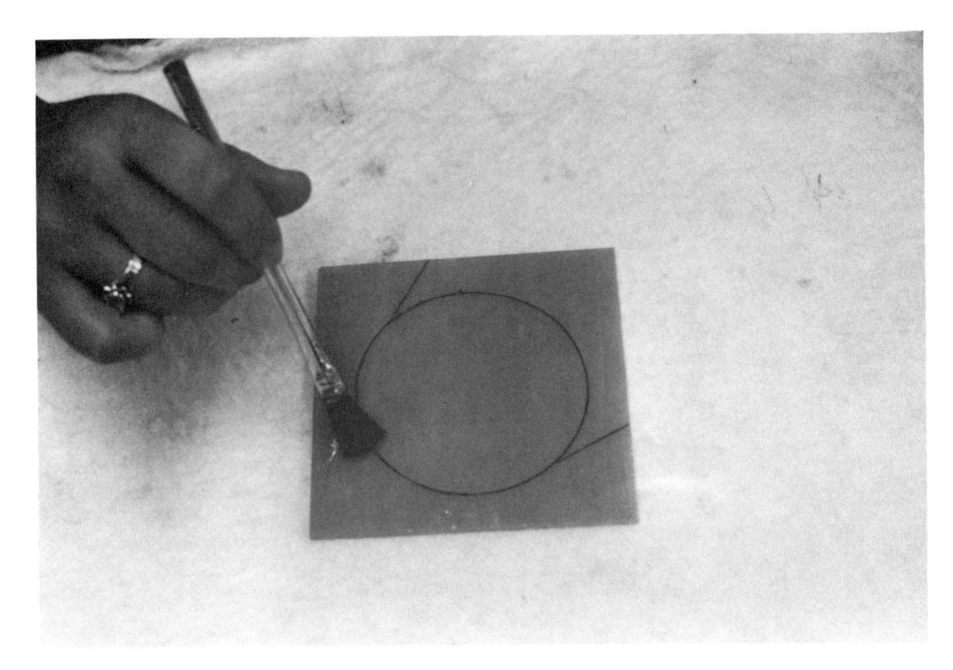

Illustrations 25 and 26

Illustration 5-27A

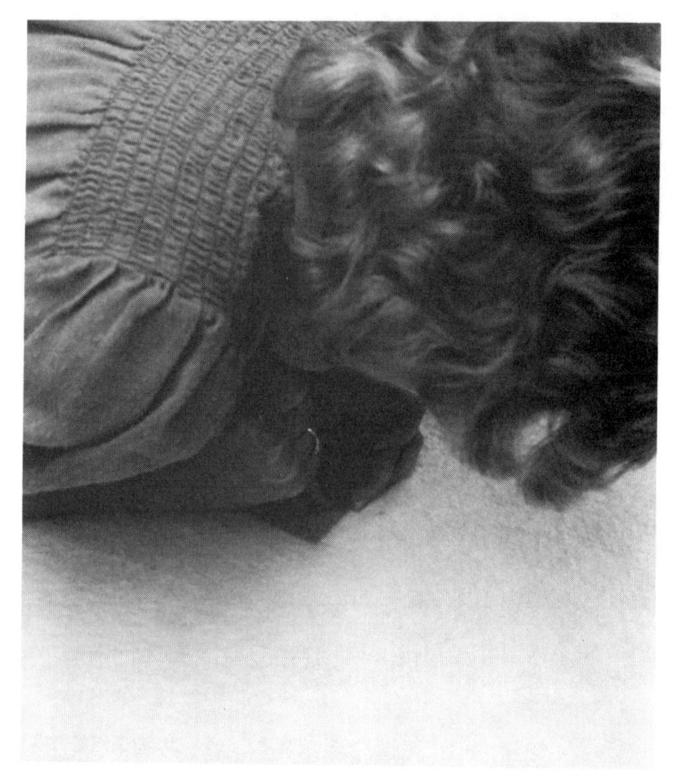

Illustration 5-27B

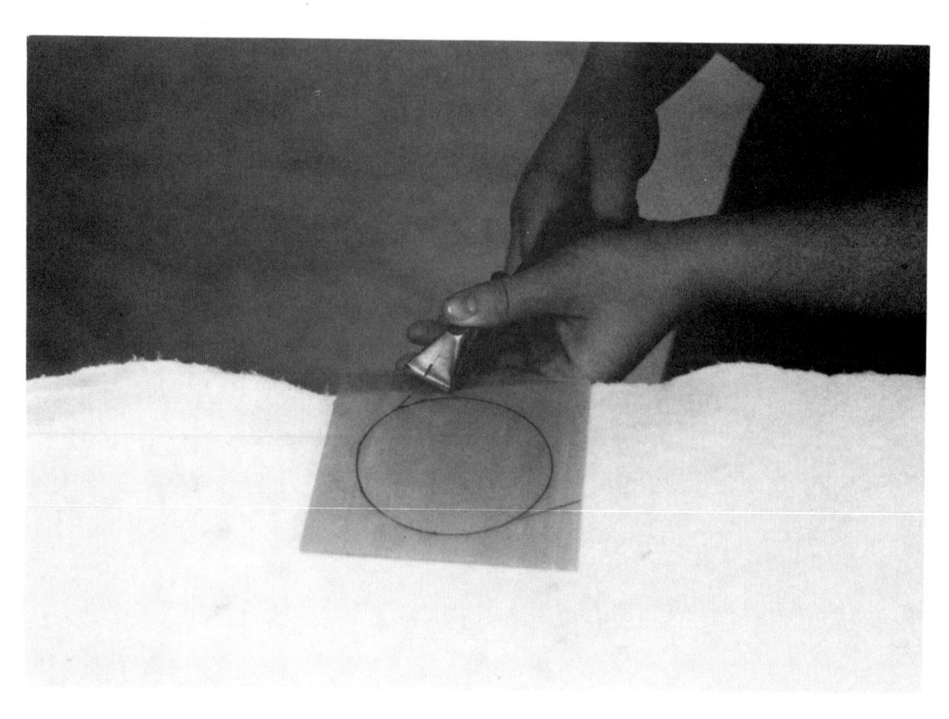

Illustration 5-28A

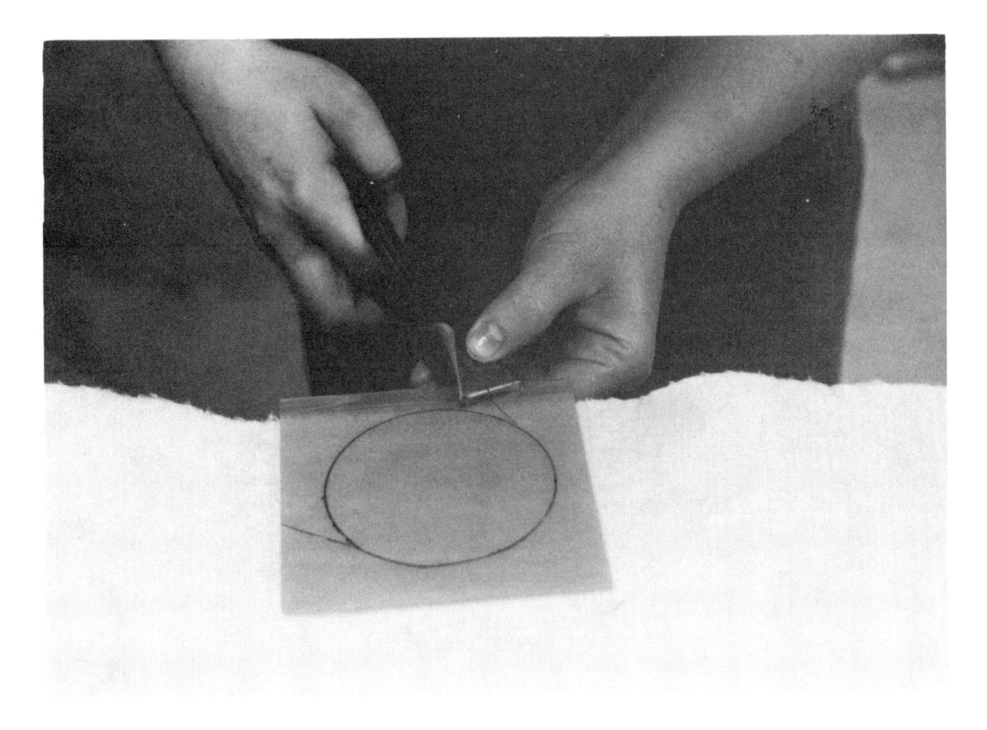

Illustration 5-28B

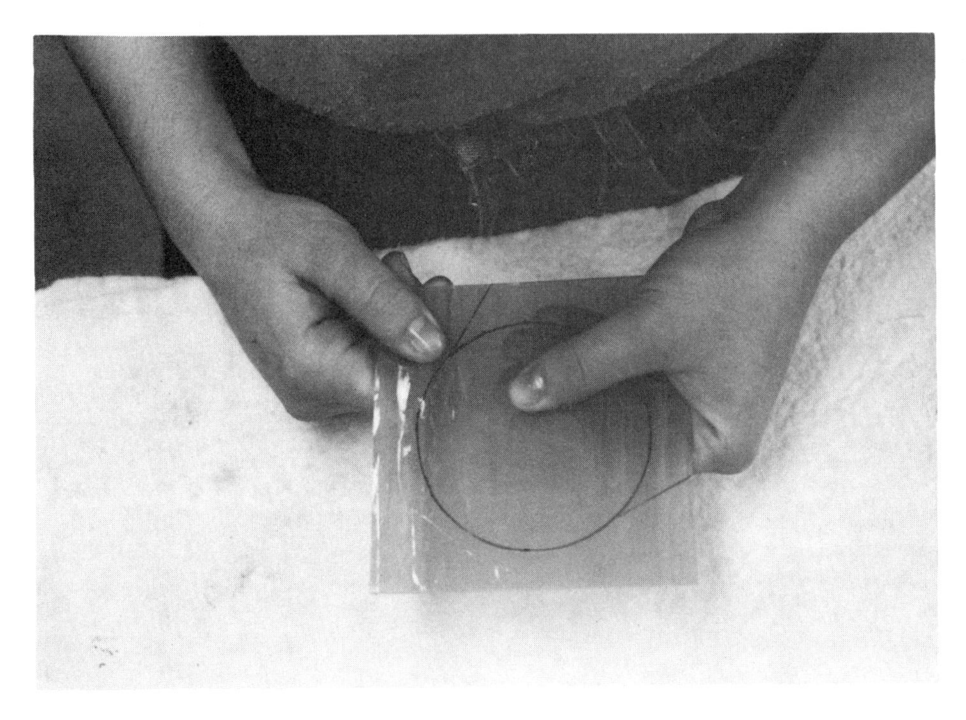

Illustration 5-28C

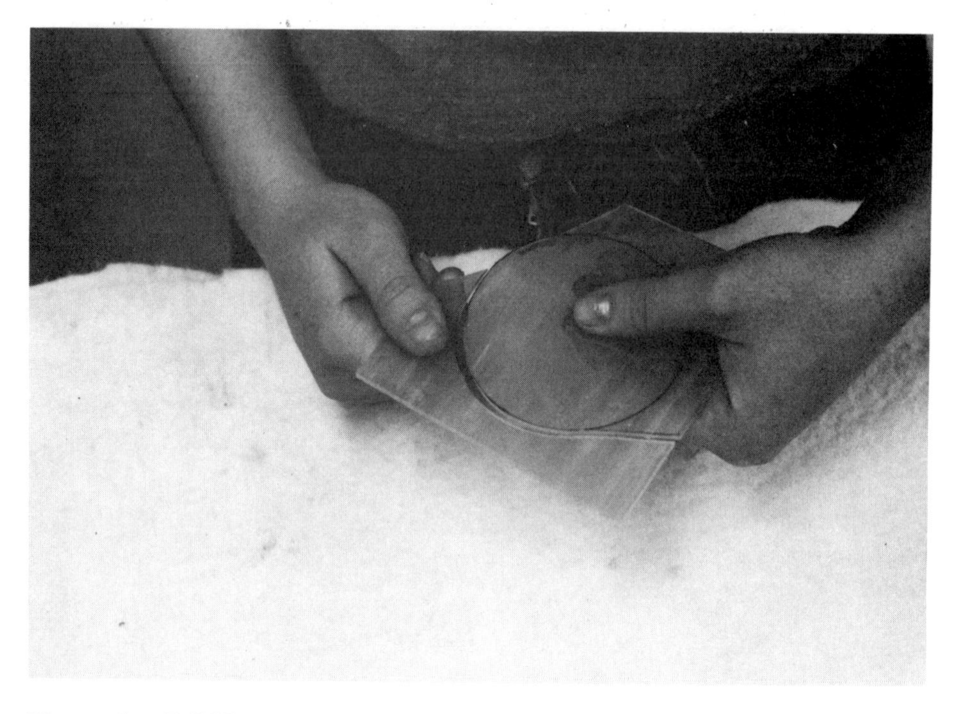

Illustration 5-28D

Illustration 5-28E

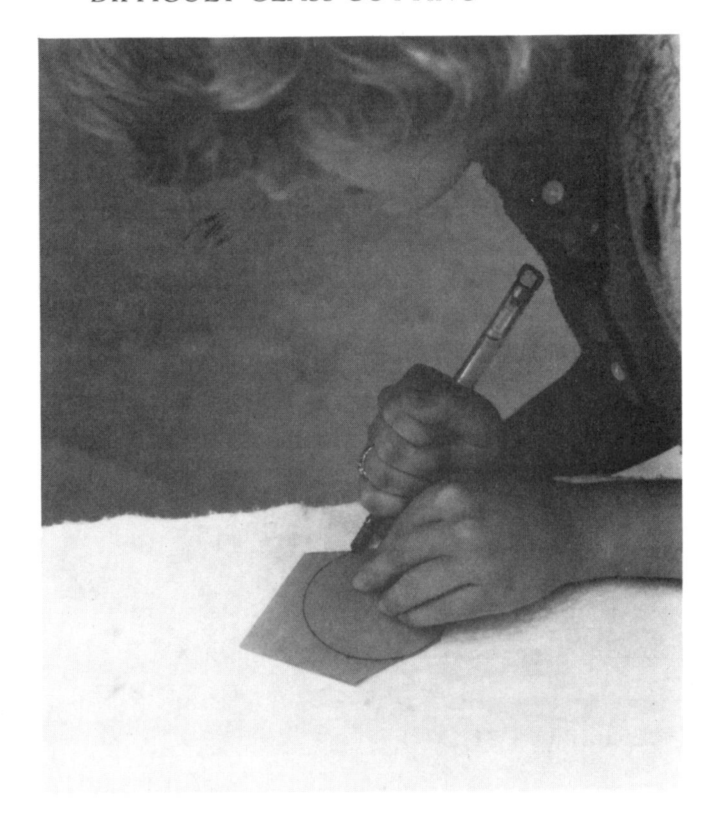

Illustration 5-29

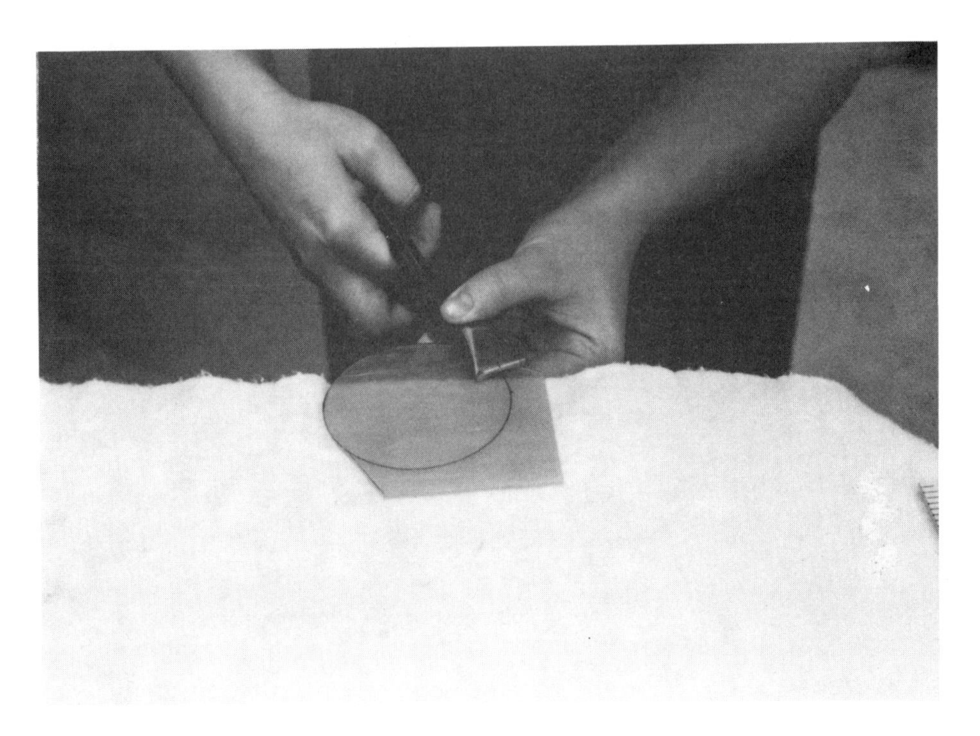

Illustration 5-30

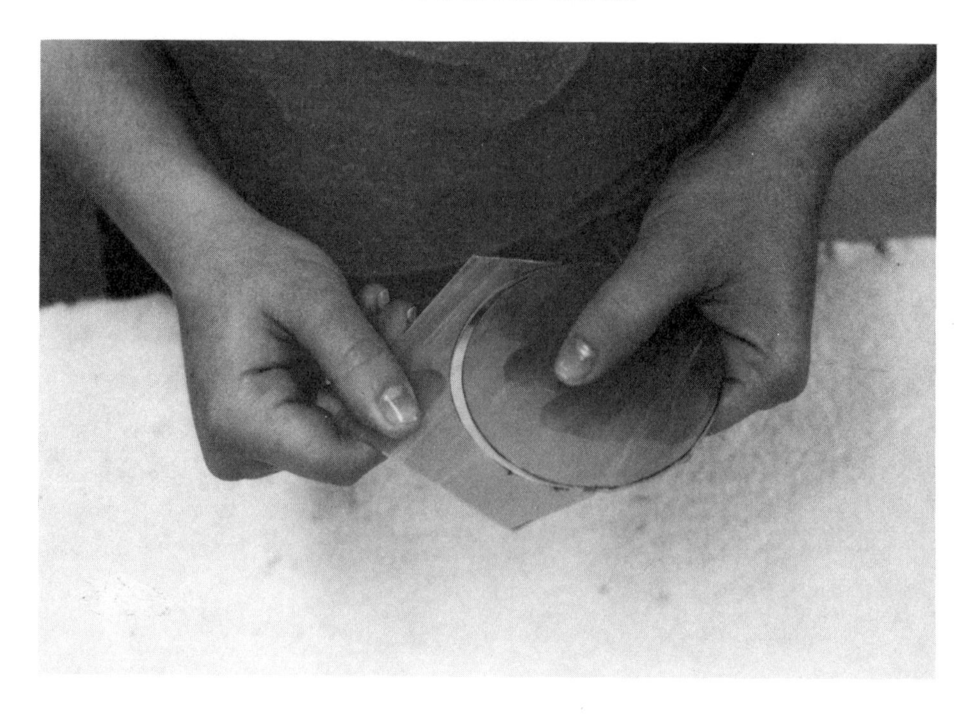

Illustration 5-31

Illustration 5-32

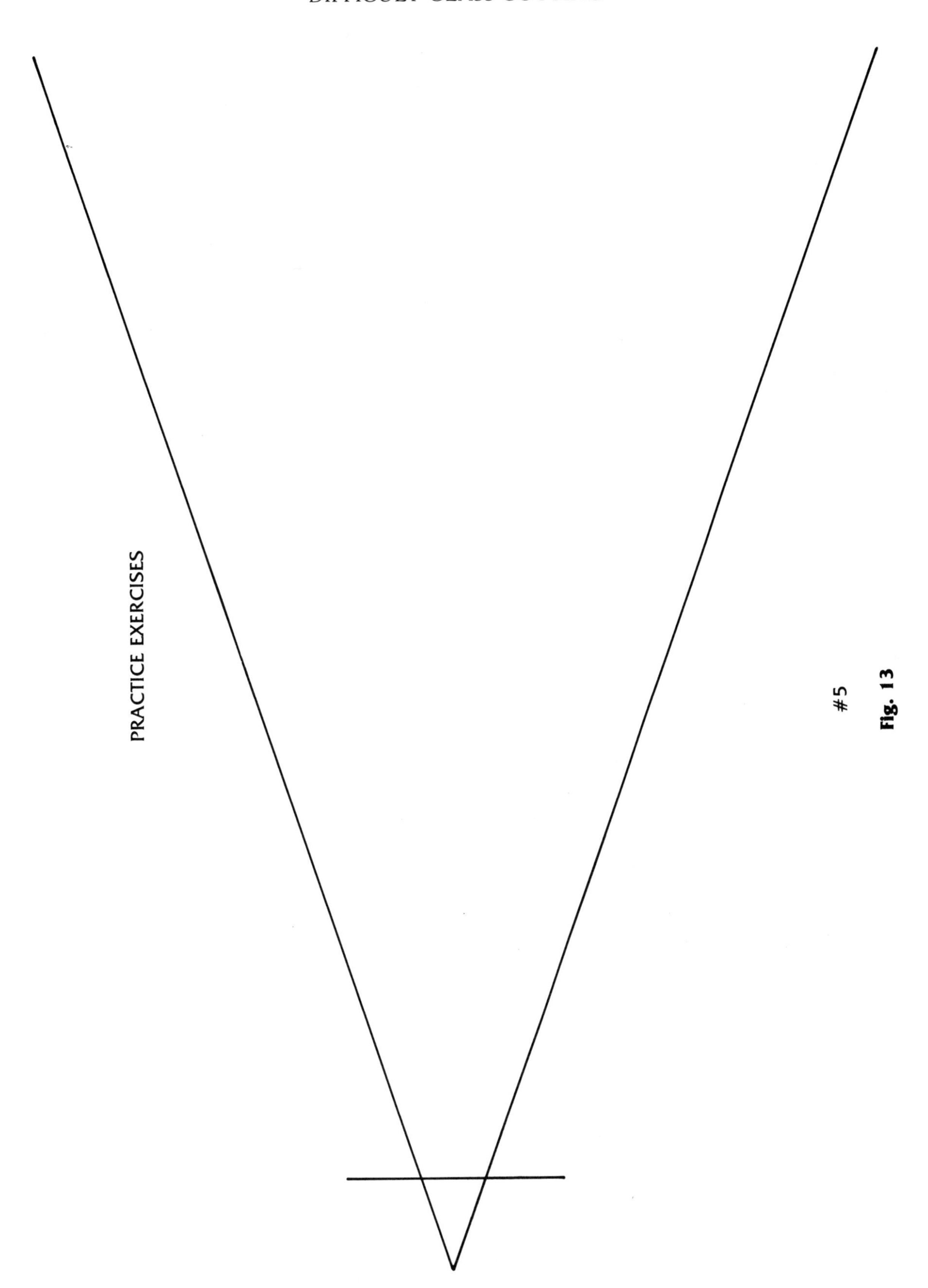

Fig. 13

Illustration 5-33

point will break off. Our unique technique for this cut will guarantee that in ninety-nine out of a hundred tries, the point will not be lost. Here is what you do:

1. Place our pattern on the glass, point up. Make a horizontal mark ½'' from the tip of the pyramid intersecting both pattern lines. (*See* Illustration 5-33.)
2. Using your straightedge, score the right side of the pyramid following the method outlined for straight line cutting on pp. 93–94. (*See* Illustration 5-34.)
3. Pull the glass apart but *save* the unwanted piece.
4. Position the "good" piece of glass so the point is down or facing you and replace the unwanted piece in order to stabilize the straightedge for the ensuing cut. (*See* Illustration 5-35.)
5. Place your straightedge on the inside of the pyramid.
6. Bend down close to the glass and, with normal pressure, score the glass only as *far as the extra horizontal line*; then *ease up* and *relax pressure* at this point for the rest of the score. (*See* Illustrations 5-36A and 5-36B.)
7. To pull the glass apart, *pull at the larger end* of the pyramid, not at the pointed end. (*See* Illustrations 5-37A and 5-37B.)

This technique should give you a sharp, clean point.

All of the cuts in this chapter require practice. You probably won't cut them out the first time you try; but keep at it. You'll need to know in your mind that you can make these cuts in order to execute the project in the next chapter. This chapter and the next are your introduction to the unparalleled artistic satisfaction of accomplishing a challenging task.

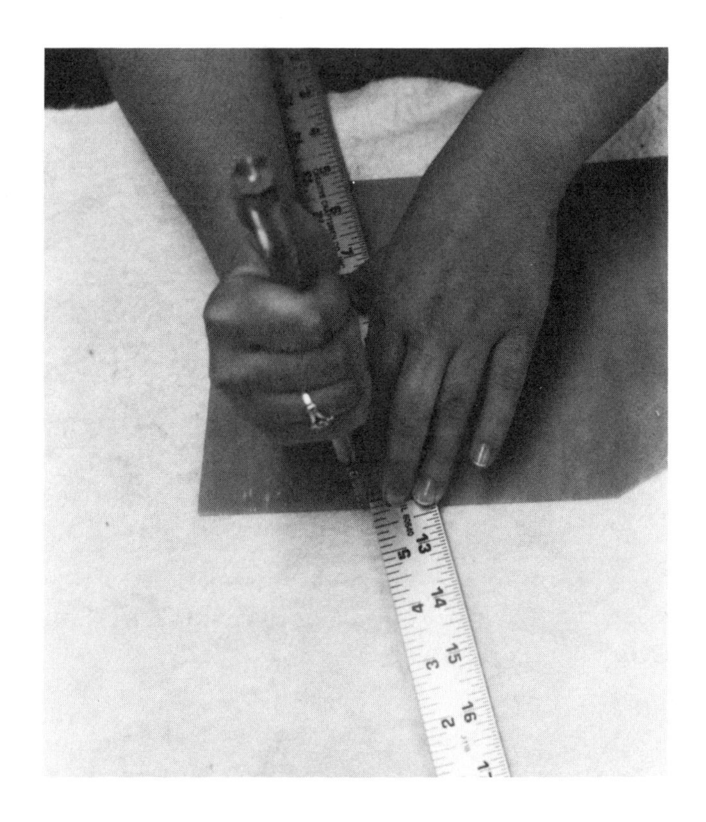

Illustration 5-34

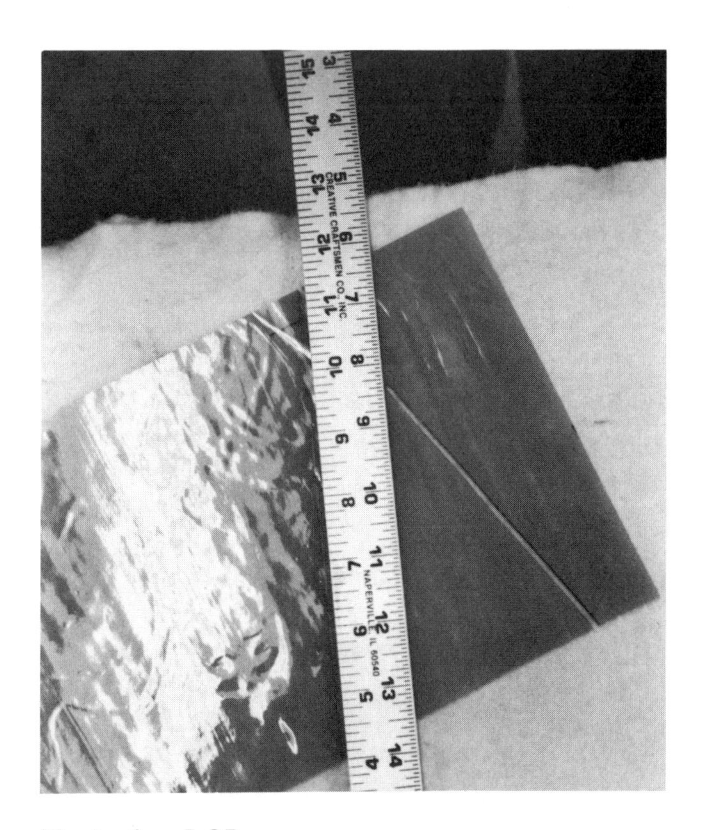

Illustration 5-35

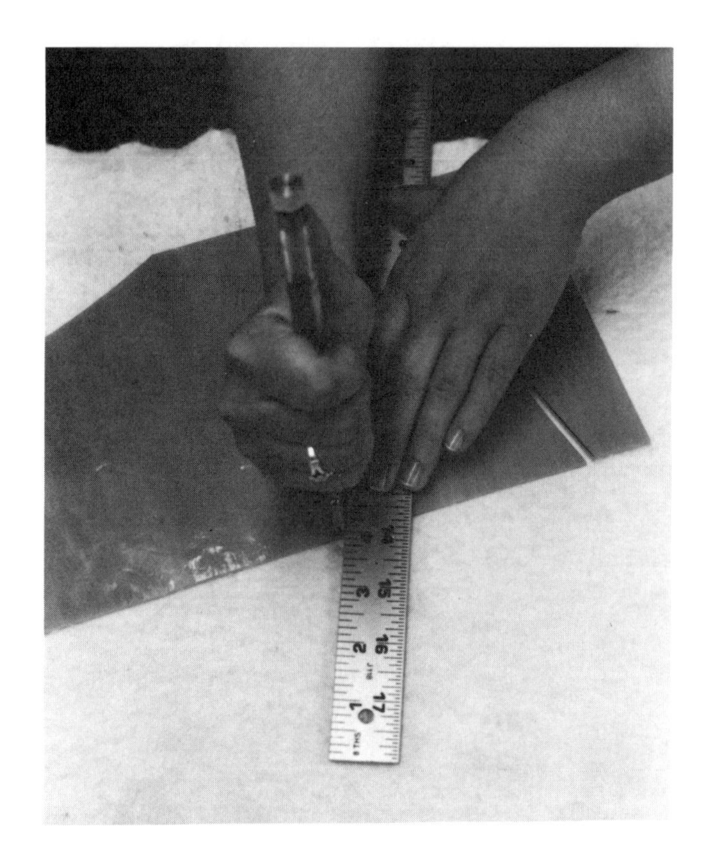

Illustration 5-36A

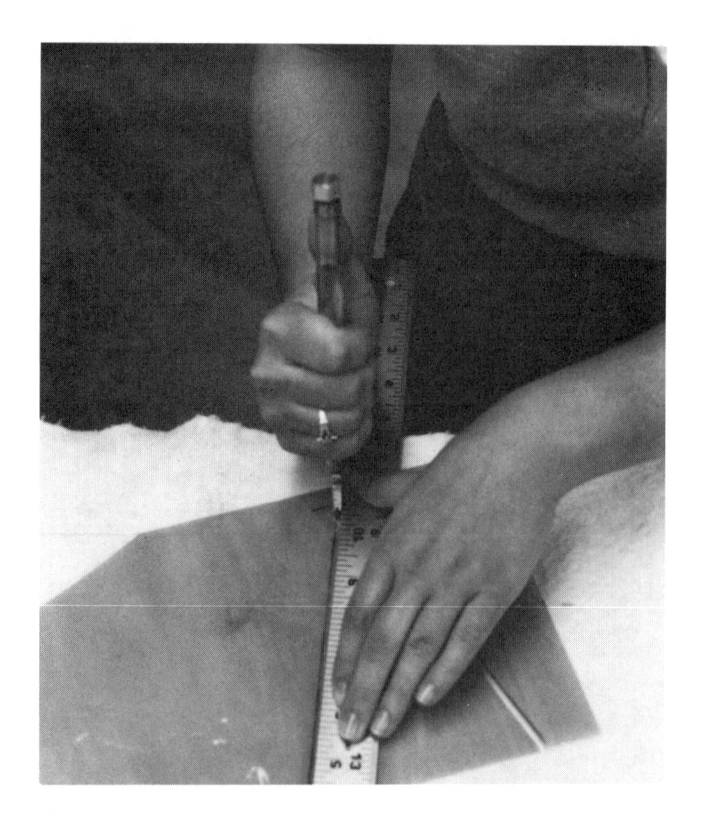

Illustration 5-36B

Illustration 5-37A

Illustration 5-37B

6

Panels

It is in the construction of a panel or window that the techniques and processes of the previous five chapters become thoroughly integrated. Although a panel or window is certainly a much more complicated project than a sun-catcher, the foundation for its construction has already been laid. If you've methodically and carefully followed our advice and techniques, and practiced them, we feel that you should be ready. Now it should be more of a matter of persistence and the exercise of your personal virtues (and, of course, skill) rather than inexperience or lack of confidence that will best determine the success of your first panel.

We've provided a small-sized panel project that will utilize the copper foil method. After you've accomplished this project in foil, and gained more glass experience, you may want to attempt it (or another one of similar size) with lead came. We prefer doing panels with foil because we believe the foil method is easier (at this stage) to accomplish, creates a stronger panel, and offers a more delicate lead line than using lead came. We feel that in many cases, with leaded windows, a structurally essential horizontal bar or two distracts the eye from and interferes with the design. By simply soldering brass rods into your foiled seams, you can reinforce any size copper foil panel, if needed, without detracting from the design. (We've constructed 6′ x 3′ windows with copper foil using this reinforcing method).

So, here is where everything comes together and your pyramid of techniques builds your first traditional project.

Tools and Materials

In addition to all your cutting, soldering and foiling tools and materials, you'll need the following:

Glass. In choosing the glass colors for this panel, you do not necessarily have to be realistic with your colors. What you're looking for, obviously, is bright *color*. If your sky glass is blue and white, you shouldn't make your lighthouse blue. A contrasting color—red, for instance—would be a better choice because of its naturally complementary combination. In addition, as mentioned in Chapter 4, a brighter color will direct the eye to the center of interest in the panel. At this stage, you might want to experiment with colors or glass other than what we've recommended.

Foil. One roll of 1½ millimeter, 7/32'' thickness. It's time you started to see what a finer lead seam looks like.

Batten Strips. Border or frame the panels with these strips so that the cut pieces will not move beyond the limits of the pattern.

Blocking Board. A ½'' or ¾'' piece of plywood, at least 2' x 2' , will be needed in order to nail down your batten strips and upon which to place your cut pieces.

Glass Router. A router is a filing or grinding machine that has a high-speed, upright, diamond (commercial) cylindrical bit that allows you to shape the glass more accurately. (*See* Illustration 6-1.) There are many routers on the market today but we prefer the *Glastar*® Company which makes various sized routers.

While a router is really not dangerous to use, you should use safety glasses or purchase an eye shield that fits your router to protect your eyes from errant particles.

Although the router is not a dire necessity (in the same sense that a soldering iron is) to do panel work, you'll find that the time and effort saved will justify the expense. Besides, you'll find a router to be invaluable when you move on to the most difficult of stained glass projects—a lampshade.

Lead Came. One 6' strip of #25 U-came for a finishing border.

Methods

To prepare your patterns and work station for the panel, you must first do the following:

1. Trace two patterns, as usual, one for a master and one for a working copy. (See Fig. 14.)
2. Place your blocking board on your work table (2' x 2') and lay your master pattern in the center of it. (*See* Illustration 6-2.)
3. Border your pattern with your ½'' batten strips, 1/16'' *into the pattern.* (*See* Illustration 6-3.) This will allow for any expansion caused by foil and for the bordering lead. Also, make sure that the batten strips are at right angles at the corners by measuring them with a square.
4. Nail them down after you've verified the 90 degree angle.

You must block your panel in this manner to prevent the glass from moving and to allow you to compare and adjust your individual pieces as you cut and place them within the framework.

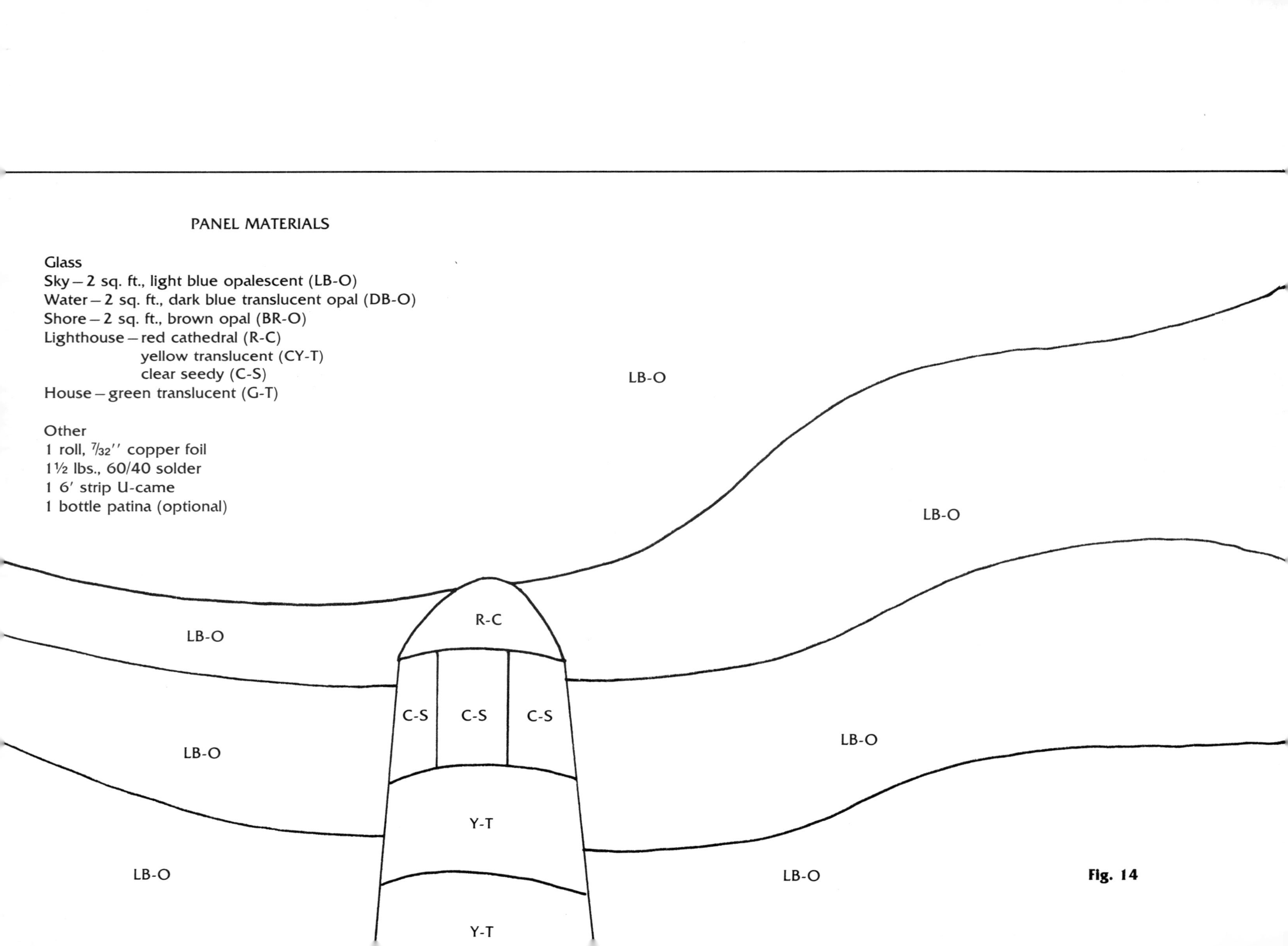
PANEL MATERIALS
Glass
Sky – 2 sq. ft., light blue opalescent (LB-O)
Water – 2 sq. ft., dark blue translucent opal (DB-O)
Shore – 2 sq. ft., brown opal (BR-O)
Lighthouse – red cathedral (R-C)
yellow translucent (CY-T)
clear seedy (C-S)
House – green translucent (G-T)
Other
1 roll, 7/32'' copper foil
1½ lbs., 60/40 solder
1 6' strip U-came
1 bottle patina (optional)
LB-O
LB-O
R-C
LB-O
C-S
C-S
C-S
LB-O
LB-O
Y-T
LB-O
LB-O
Y-T
Fig. 14

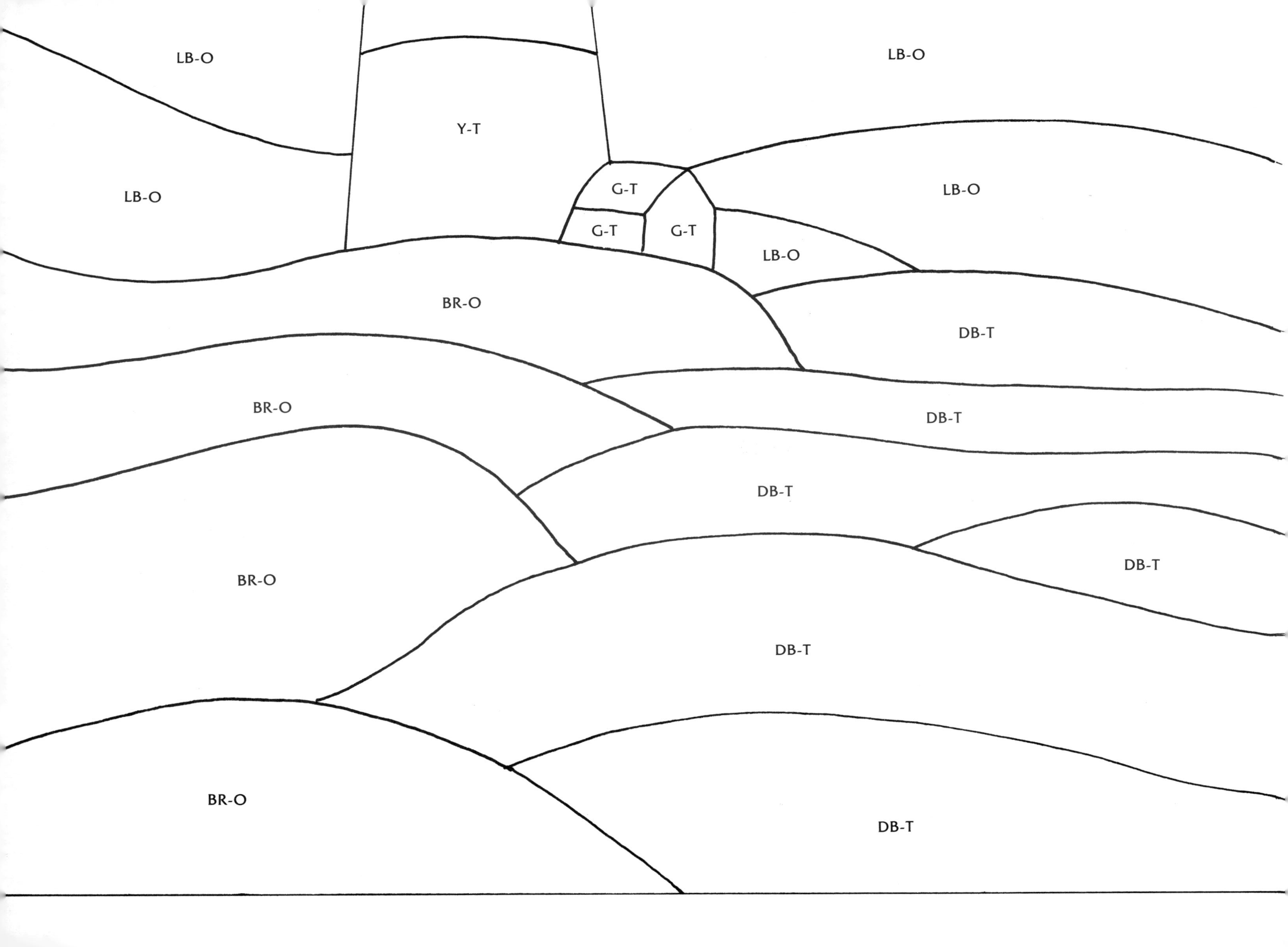
LB-O
LB-O
Y-T
LB-O
G-T
LB-O
G-T
G-T
LB-O
BR-O
DB-T
BR-O
DB-T
DB-T
BR-O
DB-T
DB-T
BR-O
DB-T

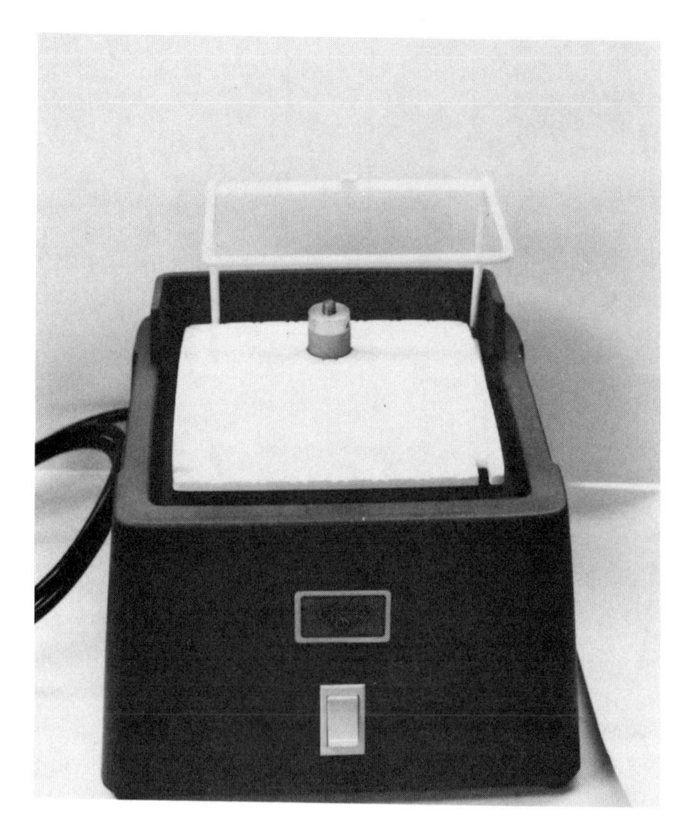

Illustration 6-1

Illustrations 6-2 and 6-3

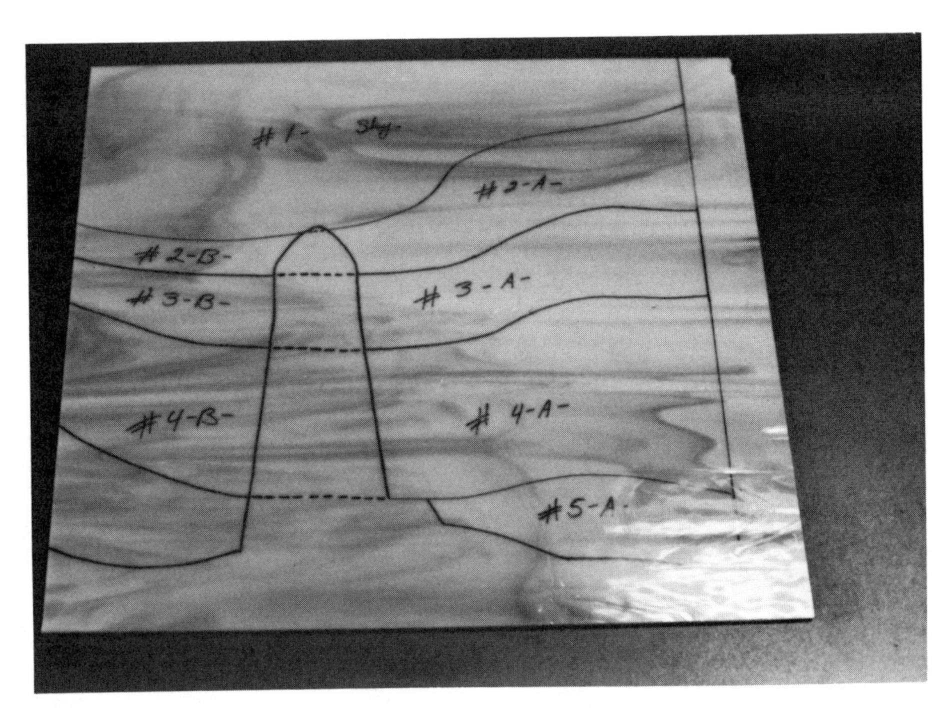

Illustration 6-4

We'll begin the cutting with the sky pattern first (we usually commence our panels at the top corners and proceed down). Cut out from your working pattern just the sky portion. If you use our recommended opalescent glass, take note of the "grain" or horizontal white swirl in your glass. Trace your sky pattern and its individual sections (as indicated below) right on the glass, making sure it naturalistically flows with the swirls to reflect the true positions of clouds. (And also make sure that the glass itself has 90-degree angles at the corners to match up with your frame.) Draw the dotted line as we have to follow through the space where the lighthouse will be inserted. (*See* Illustration 6-4.)

After tracing your pattern, approach the cutting as follows:

1. Cut your straight sides first, with a straightedge, if you have not lined up the sides against the edge.
2. Begin with piece #1. Cut through the bottom line from one end to the other.
3. Separate using your cut/run pliers.
   NOTE: As you cut each piece, if any should have a "flashed" edge—a razor-thin excess strip of glass—remove it by grozing or filing with a carborundum stone. If you don't remove it when you foil the piece, the seam will split at worst and give you a variable-width seam at best.
4. Place your cut piece into the appropriate section within your framework. (*See* Illustration 6-5.)
   Continue cutting the pieces in order, cutting through the dotted lighthouse lines. (*See* Illustration 6-6.) If one of your pieces breaks incorrectly, be sure that the replacement piece has the same horizontal cloud flow as the rest of the sky.

Illustration 6-5

Your sky should now be cut out and in place, *unfoiled*. (*See* Illustration 6-7.) The lighthouse is your next section. In order to guarantee that the cutout lighthouse will fit into this open area where it should, customize your pattern by placing a white piece of paper underneath the blue glass and drawing a new pattern, tracing against the blue glass. This will allow for any deviation as a result of the sky cutting. Cut all the lighthouse pieces just as you did for the sky, and place appropriately.

Continue cutting the other sections of the panel—the ground first and then the water. Approach the ground in the same manner as you did the sky: (1) Draw the pattern on one large piece of glass, working from top to bottom, scoring through the pattern lines; and (2) after cutting the ground, and setting it in place, customize the adjoining water by redrawing the pattern, just as you did the lighthouse. This will ensure that the butting pieces conform to one another as closely as possible.

You should now have a glass jigsaw puzzle held in place by your batten strips. (*See* Illustration 6-8.) Look over all the pieces, checking for "flashed" pieces or butting pieces that don't fit properly.

Once you are satisfied that the pieces fit together well enough, remove a side batten strip to allow for the slight expansion caused by the accumulation of foil, and replace with push pins as you foil and replace the pieces. Begin wrapping the pieces, starting from the top down. Although this is a relatively small panel (thirty-one pieces) you might still find yourself getting bored with the tedious wrapping. But remember what we

Illustration 6-6

mentioned in the third and fourth chapters: The linear structure aesthetics are an integral part of your project. It is imperative that you wrap each piece carefully and correctly so that the foiled seams are properly prepared for soldering. The finished solder seams have to complement and enhance the glass and overall design. Don't allow yourself to become careless at this stage.

After all pieces are wrapped, you're ready for soldering. Make sure all the pieces butt as tightly as possible without their buckling. (*See* Illustration 6-9.) Soldering, *which should be accomplished at one sitting*, should follow the usual procedure:

1. Flux the entire panel.
2. Begin soldering, bottom to top, and continuing along the horizontal seam, *stopping just short* (¼″) of the edge.
3. At each intersecting solder seam, follow the technique outlined in Chapter 3, p. 44, for ensuring smooth, rounded intersections.
4. After completing the front side, turn the panel over and repeat steps 1 through 3.
5. Thoroughly clean the panel.

(*See* Illustrations 6-10 through 6-13.)

Illustration 6-7

Finishing Steps

We recommend that you finish all foiled panels by framing with a lead came strip. This tends to give the panel added stability and strength. The wrapping of the came is similar to the technique for sun-catchers, outlined in Chapter 3, p. 85, with these additional exceptions and instructions:

1. Evaluate all the edges of the panels, looking for internal soldered seams that continue to the edge.
2. Remove all the solder that hits an edge to a distance of approximately ¼''. (*See* Illustration 6-14.)
3. Strip all the foil around the four sides with your razor blade. (*See* Illustration 6-15.) Do not remove any copper foil from the edge of the glass where an

Illustration 6-8

Illustration 6-9

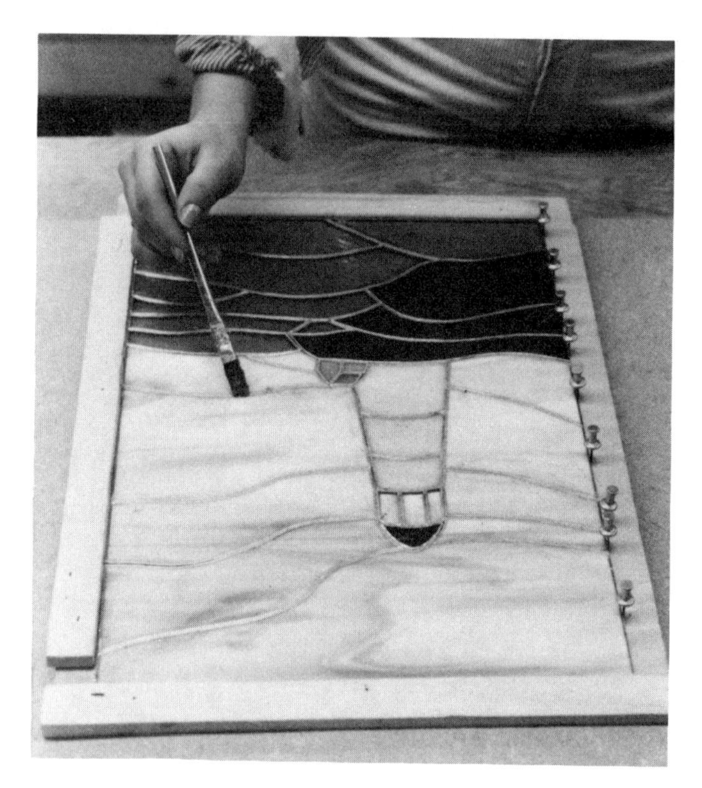

Illustration 6-10

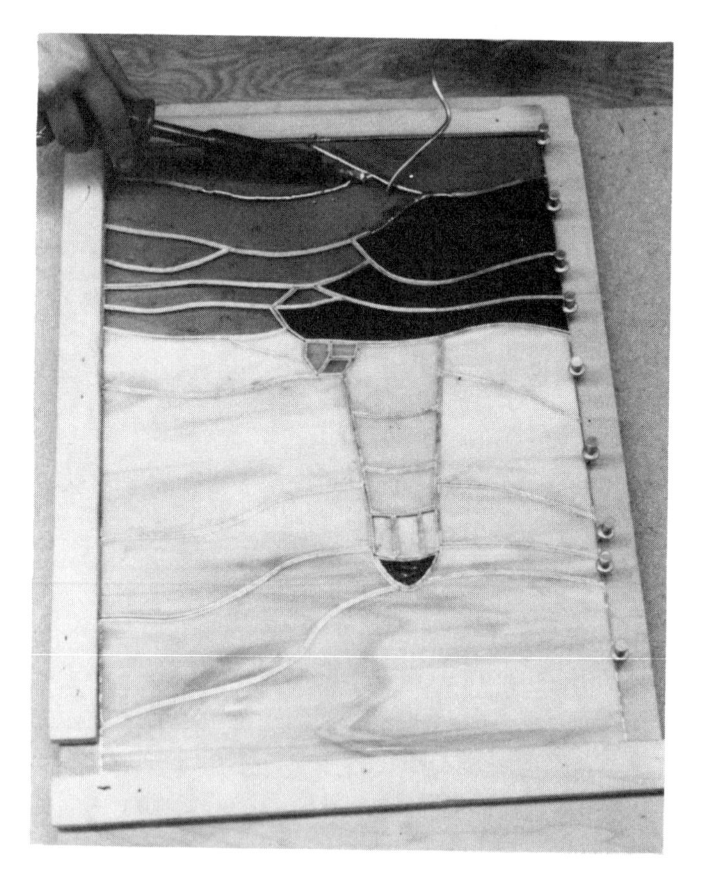

Illustration 6-11

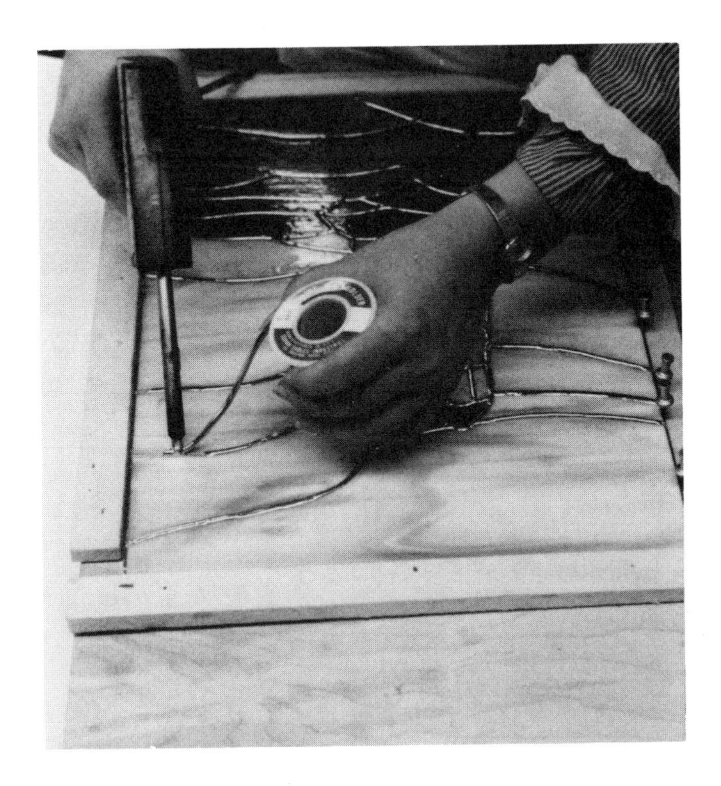

Illustration 6-12

Illustration 6-13

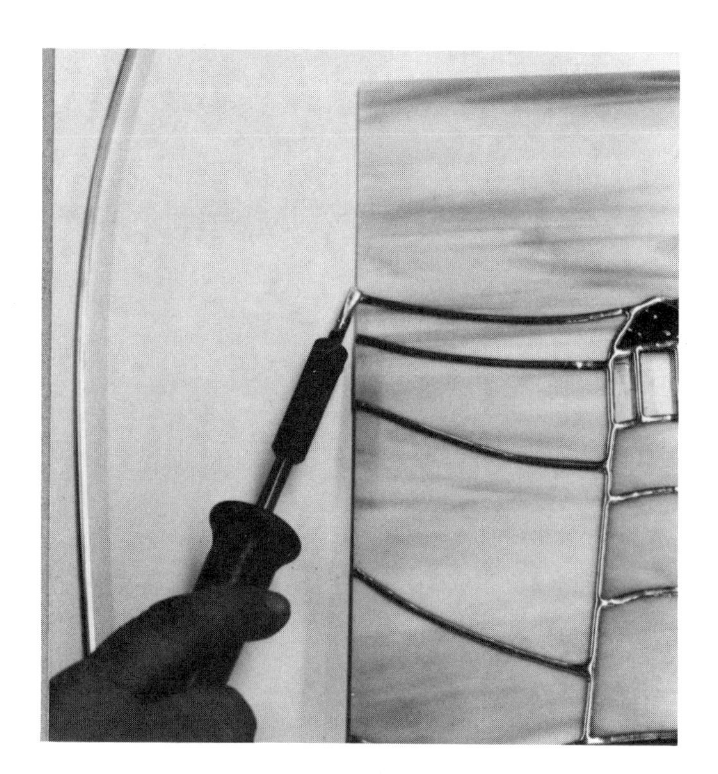

Illustration 6-14

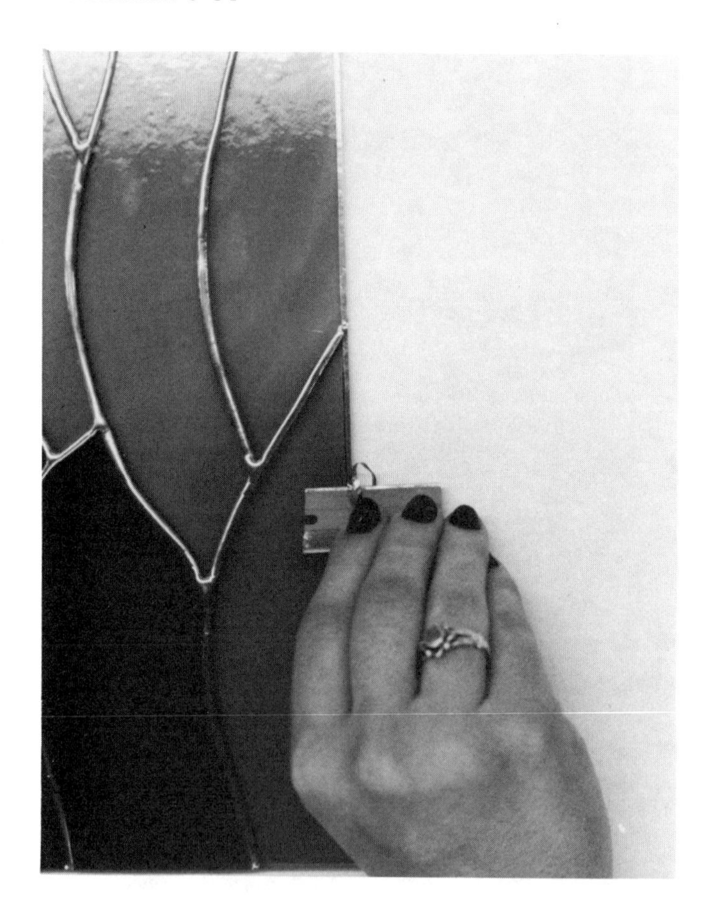

Illustration 6-15

ILLUSTRATION #1

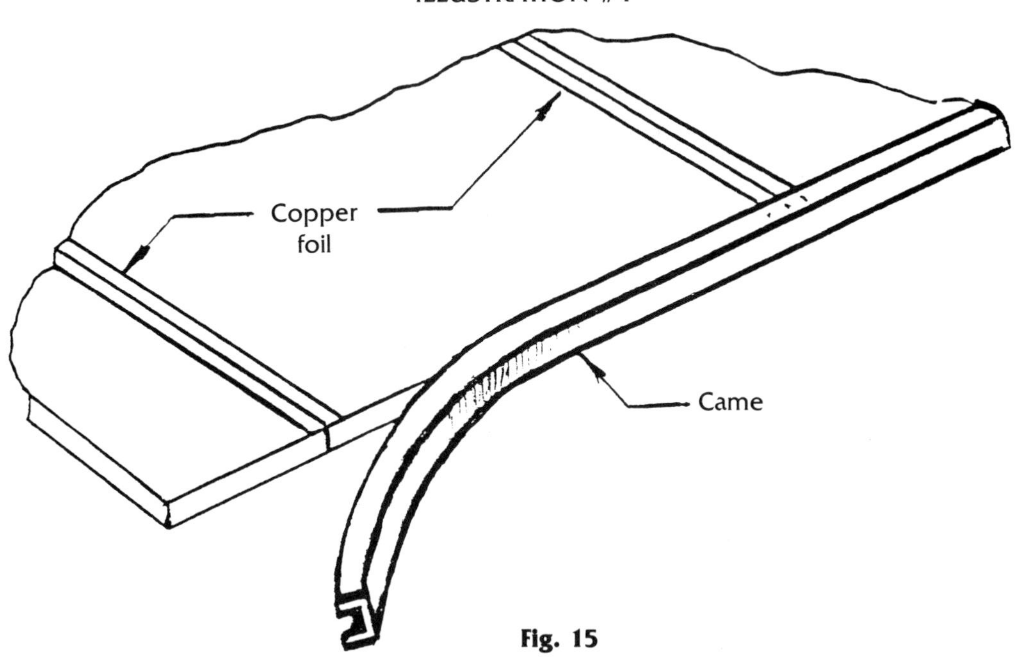

Fig. 15

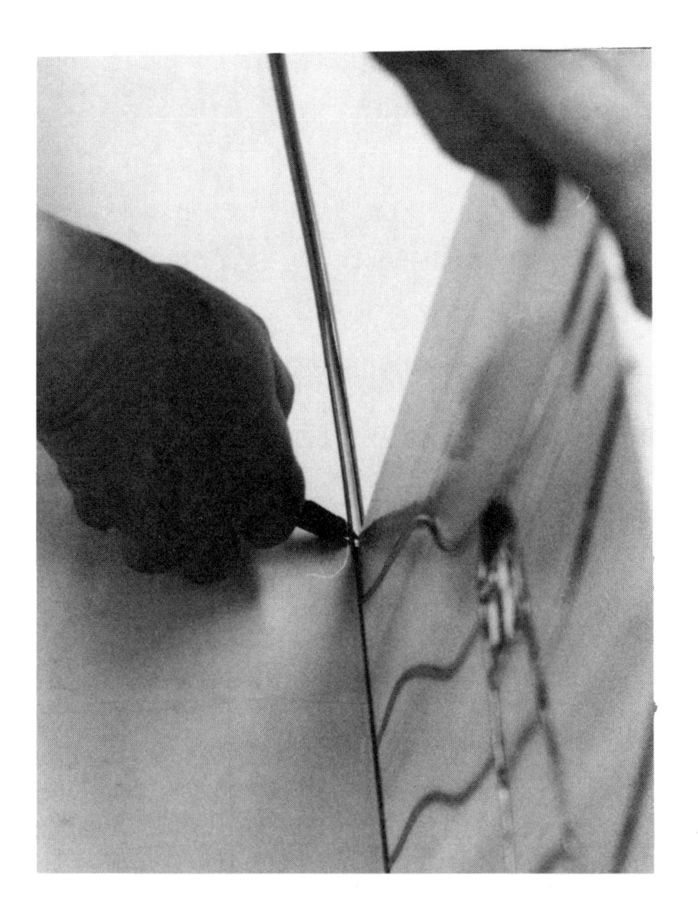

Illustration 6-16

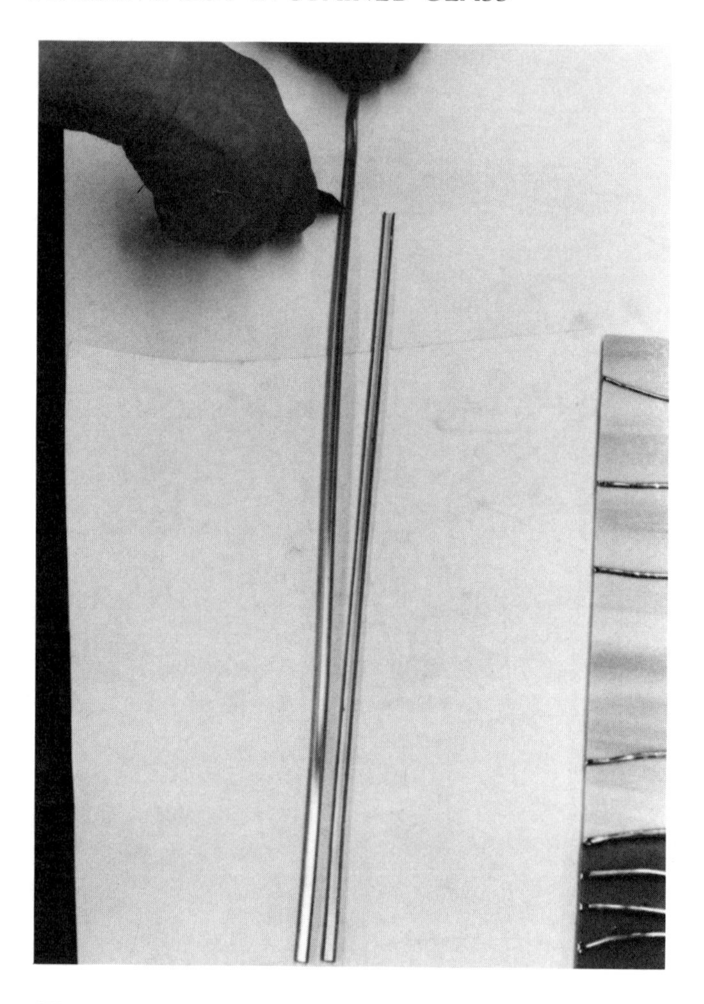

Illustration 6-17

internal solder seam will meet the border came because if you remove the foil, it will be impossible to solder the came to the seam. (*See* Fig. 15)

4. Stretch your strip of U-came, square off your edges, and lay it flat, groove up.
5. Insert one side of your panel, measure, mark (with a pencil or pen), and cut off two strips (one for the opposite side) the same length. (*See* Illustrations 6-16 and 6-17.)
6. Do the same with the remaining sides.
7. Miter all four strips and lay them on their sides, next to their respective glass sides, groove facing in. (*See* Illustration 6-18.)
8. Begin assembling, one edge at a time, starting with the *right* side, by placing the came on the edge, gently tapping in place with your rubber hammer, until the came is snug. (*See* Illustration 6-19.) *Do not solder yet.*
9. Tap the bottom came snugly into place. (*See* Illustration 6-20.)
10. Flux and solder the two cames together at the *corner*. (*See* Illustration 6-21.)
11. Fit and attach the left strip of came at the corner.
12. Tap, flux, and tack solder all the joints where a copper foil seam and the lead meet. (*See* Illustration 6-22.)

Illustration 6-18

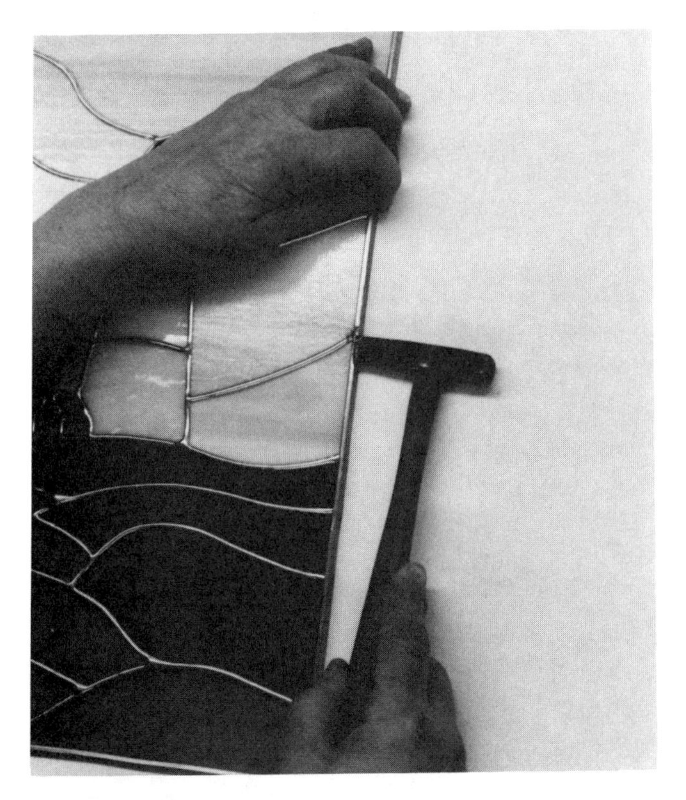

Illustration 6-19

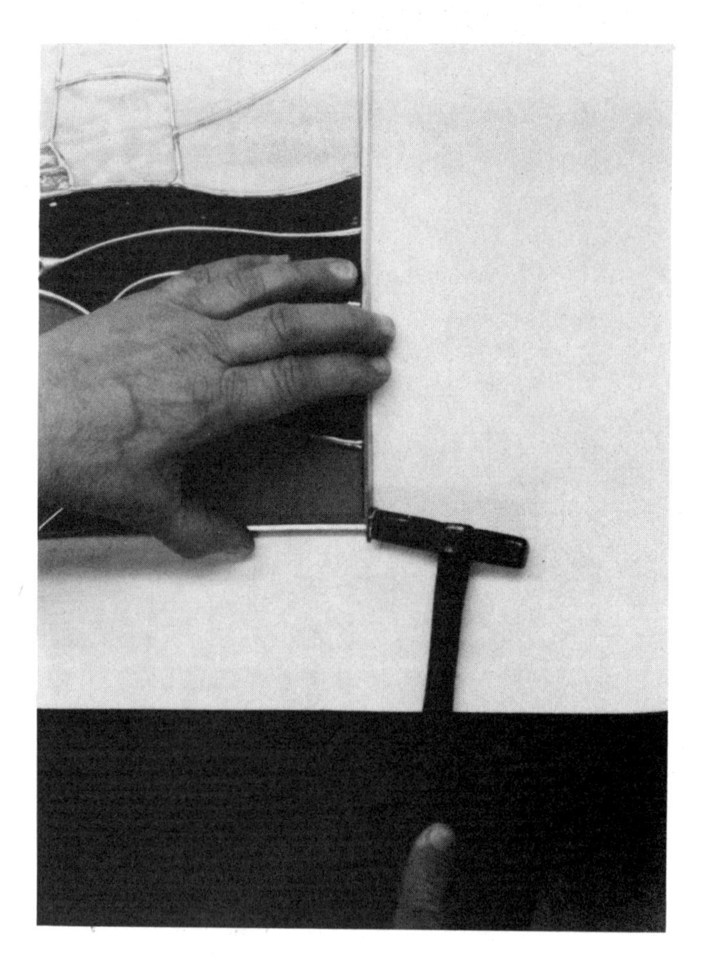

Illustration 6-20

We've reserved the sky-edge came for last because you will have to glue this on since there are no foiled seams to which to anchor it with solder. The gluing technique is the same as outlined in Chapter 2, pp. 35–36, with these slight enhancements:

1. Lay the came strip groove up.
2. After you dab the glue in the grooves, immediately place the lead came on the top edge, tapping with your rubber-tipped hammer from the top to ensure a tight fit. (*See* Illustration 6-23.)
3. Press tightly and hold for a minute or two until the glue sets.
4. Solder the corners.

Thoroughly clean your finished panel again, (*See* Illustration 6-24), patina or darken it if you wish, and clean and polish it again (refer to Finishing Techniques section in Chapter 2 on pp. 45–50, and Chapter 3 on pp. 83–84).

Should you decide to enclose your panel within a wood frame, you're all set. (*See* Illustration 6-25.) Just make sure that your frame has at least a ½'' border or molding to securely hold the panel in place. By attaching a chain to your wood frame, you now have

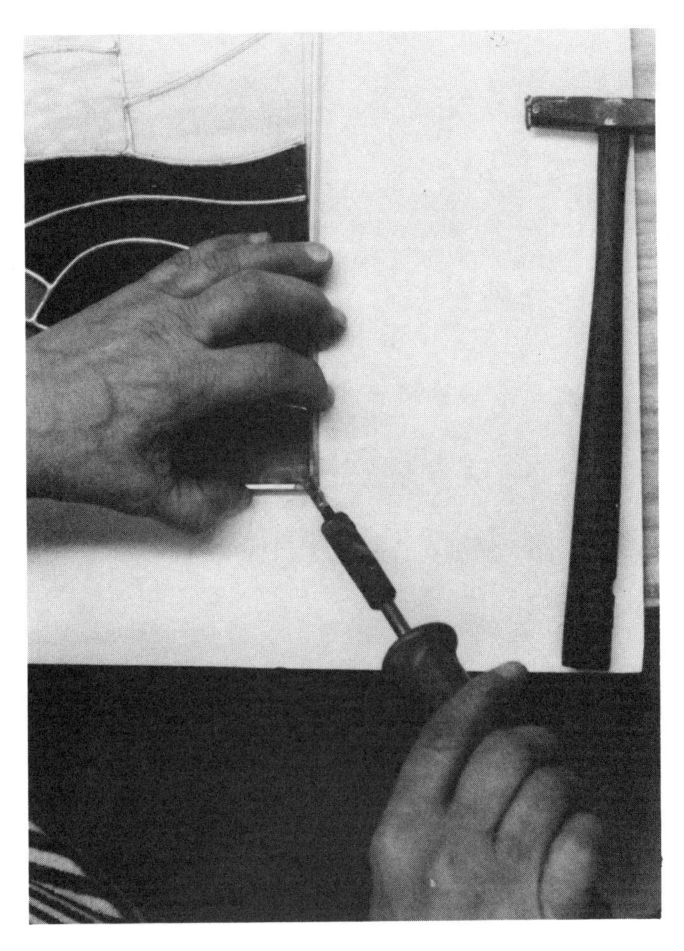

Illustration 6-21

a glass painting that's mobile enough to hang in any window by merely screwing in an eye hook at the top of the frame.

Rather than constructing a wood frame, you may wish to hang your panel by a decorative chain or wire soldered right to the panel itself. You'll have to attach the chain or wire to the lead by hooks:

1. Make two hooks about ¾'' long, shaped like an E with the center line missing.
2. With the hook extending beyond the sides of the panel and at points equidistant from the top (about ½''), solder them to both sides of your panel.
3. If you're going to use *wire*:
   a. Cut a piece about 6'' longer than the distance between the hooks.
   b. Attach one end to one hook and twist three or four times.
   c. Making sure that the slack wire does not go above the top of the panel, attach the other end, twist, and remove excess wire.
4. If you're going to use a *decorative chain*:
   a. Cut a strip that will allow you to hang the panel on a hook. The chain should go *above* the top of the panel (any height you want).
   b. Attach it to one hook by *soldering it* to the hook.
   c. Solder the other end to the opposite hook.

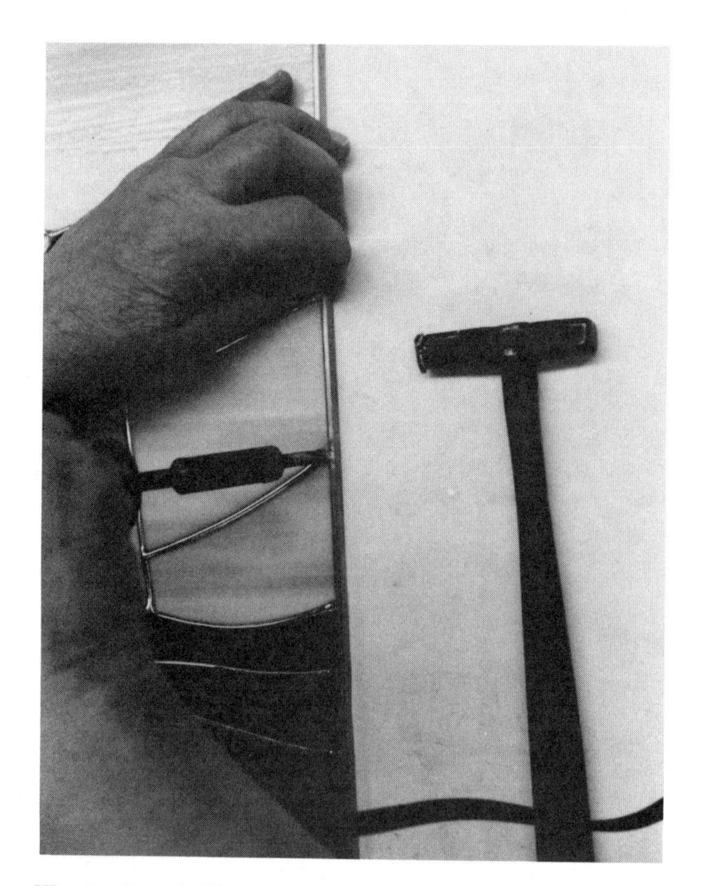

Illustration 6-22

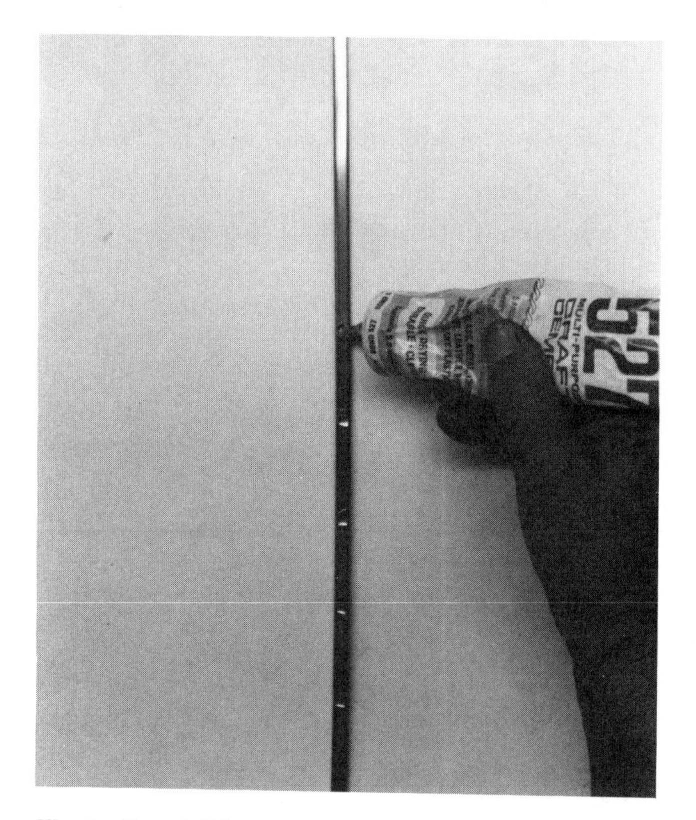

Illustration 6-23

Illustration 6-24

Illustration 6-25

Summing Up

This chapter completes your basic stained glass instruction. We've presented the fundamentals which will allow you to move on to larger and more challenging projects. The methods in themselves are not difficult or unlearnable; it is in the disciplined application of these methods, a faithful adherence to their underlying philosophy, and constant practice that will determine the quality of your individual technique. Methods can be learned within a relatively short time; technique requires a nurtured development and commitment throughout a lifetime.

We hope that we've given you a good introduction to the art of Stained Glass. Our second book, *Challenging Projects in Stained Glass*, will expose you to other areas of stained glass activity when you feel you're ready. With our help and your desire, stained glass will provide you with many hours of enjoyment, satisfaction, and beauty that will linger long after the work is accomplished.

Appendix

A NOTE ON STAINED GLASS SUPPLIERS

Any kind of "comprehensive" list of stained glass suppliers would probably be incomplete, inaccurate, and exclusionary by the time you buy and read this book.

If you've bought this book from a stained glass supplier, you shouldn't have a problem purchasing everything you need to accomplish all our tasks and projects. If you acquired our book at a local bookstore, and you really don't know where to go, you can do one of the following:

1. Check the Yellow Pages of your local telephone directories under "Glass—Leaded" or "Glass—Stained." They should provide enough leads. (You can also visit a public library and peruse the Yellow Pages of a large city directory and call or write for their catalogues.)
2. You can write or call local, regional, or state art councils or associations for a list of their members. Some of them may deal in stained glass supplies.
3. Or, you can send a self-addressed, stamped, legal-sized envelope and $2 to us—Mt. Tom Studio, 58 Strong Street, Easthampton, MA 01027; and we'll send out our regional and country-wide list of suppliers and mail order houses that will satisfy your stained glass requirements.

Glossary

anneal Hardening of glass (after heating or scoring) which renders the glass less brittle.

blocking The framing of cut pieces with push pins or molding that "blocks" the pieces from moving which guarantees pattern adherence and facilitates soldering.

flashed edge A razor-thin, "extra" edge that remains on a piece of glass after a score and needs to be filed away before caming or foiling.

grain Usually present in the opal glasses; streaks of color (usually white) flowing in one general direction which resembles the grain in wood but is textureless.

grozing The gradual filing away with pliers of glass at the edges of uneven or incorrectly scored glass.

relief cuts A series of scores emanating outward from an original score which "relieves" the curved score for an easier separation of the glass.

score (cut) The grinding (or cutting) out of a groove in a piece of glass which creates a weakness in the surface along which a fracture travels.

teasing The delicately slow and careful method of coaxing apart two pieces of glass from a complex or angled score.

Index